What others are saying about

FUTURE IMPACT

Connecting Child, Church, and Mission

Future Impact shows you how to reach, equip, and empower children to maximize their transformational impact and mobilize them for continuing impact throughout the rest of their lives. This is the way to re-energize your church ministry.

—**Luis Bush**, International Facilitator, Transform World Connections

Massive amounts of material are available on Christian education in general, but Dan Brewster's book deals with the topic of ministry to children in its totality. *Future Impact* should be a text in every seminary, college, and Bible institute; no pastor or youth leader should be without it. Congratulations, Dan, on providing a work that has been needed for decades.

—**Manfred W. Kohl**, Th.D., Ambassador, Overseas Council

The church needs to work to bless the children by strengthening their families and being the prophetic voice to those who have little or no concern for the future that is right before their eyes. *Future Impact* will help us all focus on the precious little ones.

—**Dr. Darrow Miller**, Founder, Director of the Disciple Nations Alliance

At a time when the church seemingly continues to pay scant attention to children's ministry, *Future Impact* succeeds in refocusing our attention on the critical issues. Dan takes his readers through a journey which will impress on them the urgency of the church playing its rightful role in this vital ministry.

—**Reuben Van Rensburg**, Principal: South Africa Theological Seminary

When Jesus placed a child in the midst of His disciples (Matthew 18:3) He shone light on the nature of the kingdom of heaven, as well as the way of the cross. Without that light, the church misses a vital clue to its nature and calling. *Future Impact* is a valuable contribution to the process of understanding and applying this clue.

—**Dr. Keith J. White**, Chair of the Child Theology Movement

If you want to be a significant player on the world landscape for missions in the decades to come, then weave *Future Impact* into your personal and church strategies for evangelism and church growth.

—**Dr. Mark P. Gonzales**, pastor, author, broadcaster

Future Impact is an excellent resource that can be used in different cultural contexts, adapted for different levels of training, while still communicating the depth of God's heart for children. This book is a must-read for all children advocates.

—**Rosalind Lim-Tan**, Director, Holistic Child Development Institute, Penang, Malaysia

Dan Brewster has spent his entire life helping the church help children. His experience and insights are gained first-hand amongst practitioners operating in Africa, Latin America, and Asia. His passion for children's well-being flows from a consistent and tenacious walk with Jesus Christ. His work is timely, apt, and highly relevant. Study it.

—**Patrick McDonald,** Founder and CEO of VIVA

Future Impact is a gift to all of us who care about God's mission on earth and God's kingdom. May your local church respond to Future Impact's call to shape children into world-changers for the gospel.

—**William C. Prevette**, Ph.D., Research Director, Oxford Centre for Mission Studies

As intended by Dan, this book has informed, inspired, and influenced me. It informs me of the strategic role of children in furthering God's kingdom. It inspires me to look at children from God's perspective and care for them. It influenced me to help in developing workers, advocates, and leaders for the holistic development of children. *Future Impact* is a must-read for those who want to make a difference in the lives of needy children around the world.

—**Dr. Theresa R. Lua**, Dean, Asia Graduate School of Theology

Future Impact by Dan Brewster is an excellent book for those working with needy and other children. It gives direction for those desiring to work with needy children and provides the resources to reach them with the gospel, discipleship, and church programs. *Future Impact* is probably the best book in print with practical and godly advice concerning all aspects of ministry to children.

—**Doug Nichols**, Founder & International Director Emeritus,
Action International

For 20 centuries, the vast majority of Christian theologians, educators, and missiologists have failed to perceive the ontological value and strategic importance God has endowed to persons 18 years and below. As the Global Holistic Child Development movement gathers momentum, it will be increasingly evident that God has used and is using this book to help bring about a 21st century reformation to radically change the thoughts and actions of readers regarding the church, mission, and the next generation.

—**Rev. Anthony Oliver**, Ph.D., Vice President Academic Affairs,
Caribbean Graduate School of Theology, Kingston, Jamaica

To me this book is an absolute "must" for every pastor, theological student, director or leader in children's ministry around the world. It has a huge potential for bringing deep changes in your heart and will certainly make a huge difference in your life if you allow the Spirit of God to work in you, just like Dan did years ago.

—**Anne-Christine Bataillard**, International President, Hi Kidz
International, Lausanne, Switzerland

FUTURE IMPACT

Connecting Child, Church, and Mission

FUTURE IMPACT

Connecting Child, Church, and Mission

Dan Brewster

Releasing children from poverty

Compassion
in Jesus' name

ISBN 978-0-9841169-1-1
Printed in Canada
10 9 8 7 6 5 4 3 2 1

CONTENTS

About Future Impact...xiii

SECTION ONE: THE CHILD IN BIBLICAL PERSPECTIVE................................1

1: Why Children?...5

2: What the Bible Says About Children 21

3: The Ministry of Child Development..45

4: A Spiritual Understanding of Poverty 75

SECTION TWO: THE CHILD *AND* THE CHURCH..101

5: The Role of the Church..105

6: Why Care for Children Is the Particular
Responsibility of the Church...131

SECTION THREE: THE CHILD *IN* THE CHURCH..147

7: Faith Development in Children 151

8: Characteristics of Child-Friendly Churches...169

9: Child Protection in Church Environments 189

SECTION FOUR: THE CHILD AND MISSION..201

10: Mission: What the Church Is Called to Do..205

11: Practical Issues in Mission and Children 227

SECTION FIVE: AVENUES FOR ADVOCACY..247

12: Non-Confrontational Advocacy..251

13: The United Nations Convention on the Rights of the Child..........265

14: Networking on Behalf of Children 283

Conclusion...291

About Compassion International 295

Appendices...297

Notes 305

References 325

Index...335

ACKNOWLEDGEMENTS

Writing a book is always a much larger task than one anticipates. *How hard can it be*, I thought, *to connect all the presentations from the* Child, Church, and Mission *course I teach at Malaysia Baptist Seminary, with some verbiage and a few illustrations?* Surely, simply a matter of stringing a few sentences together. Many drafts and a fair bit of frustration later, I now know better.

This work benefits from the encouragement and work of many others. My first thanks goes to my colleagues in Compassion International with whom it has been my pleasure to work and serve for over 25 years. Foremost among them is my friend and mentor in the Asia Area Office of Compassion International, Dr. Bambang Budijanto. Dr. Bambang first envisioned the Program in Holistic Child Development, which has now become part of the curriculum at Malaysia Baptist Theological Seminary, and for which I developed the ideas and notes, which became the course called *Child, Church, and Mission*. Dr. Bambang then encouraged me to translate the concepts and lessons from the course into book form for wider use. I thank him for the inspiration and encouragement, as well as for his very valuable appraisals and critiques of the work in process.

My thanks also go to the faculty and staff at Malaysia Baptist Seminary. The visionary president, Dr. John Ong, has led and nurtured a seminary that reaches out to all of Asia and recognizes the strategic importance of children as both objects of mission and as key agents for furthering God's kingdom in

FUTURE IMPACT

our generation. Under Dr. Ong's leadership, the particular hard work and always friendly encouragement from the Academic Dean, Dr. Sunny Tan, and his wife, Dr. Rosalind Tan, Director of the Holistic Child Development Institute in Penang, have been exceptionally helpful. They have provided both vision and leadership for the program in Holistic Child Development and have administered a complex cross-cultural program, which is, I believe, the finest such graduate-level program in existence. It has been a pleasure to teach and now to write in that stimulating environment.

During the course of many rewrites, I received valuable editorial assistance from Ms. Siew Ling Lim, who also provided lots of insights using her sharp Asian eyes. Mrs. Carmen (Menchit) Wong, the delightful Filipino international director of Compassion's Advocacy Initiative, also provided very helpful cultural and organizational insights. My thanks, too, to Megan Rieger, Steve Wamberg, and the rest of the very pleasant and able team at The Elevation Group, for their editorial assistance and shepherding this project to completion.

Finally, I thank my extraordinarily encouraging and supportive wife, Alice, who cares for me in ways and to an extent that some would feel is excessive or overindulgent. The sense of well-being and predictability she provides, (and her tolerance for my long hours in front of my computer), helped immeasurably to see this task through to completion.

Dan Brewster
Penang, Malaysia

ABOUT FUTURE IMPACT

The material in this book was originally prepared for the course called "Child, Church, and Mission" taught in the Master of Arts Program in Holistic Child Development at Malaysia Baptist Theological Seminary in Penang, Malaysia. It was designed to help students develop their understanding of the meaning and nature of the relationships between child, church, and mission. From a biblical perspective, it provides an overview of the child, poverty, and holistic child development, and thoughts on the relationships between holistic child development and the ministries of the church.

This material may be used as a course of study in seminaries or Bible colleges. We hope this material will also serve as a resource for training other groups and in other venues— such as training for children's ministry workers, workers with at-risk children (specialized groups), and training conducted by Christian child development networks.

For more information about the course, please contact:

Dr. Rosalind Lim-Tan
Director: MBTS HCD Institute
40 A-D, Mk. 17 Batu Ferringhi,
Penang 11100, Malaysia
Email: rosalindlyw@gmail.com
Tel. /Fax: 604-881-2462

Dr. Dan Brewster
Compassion International
Email: dan.brewster@yahoo.com
Tel./Fax: 604-890-1440

THE CHILD IN BIBLICAL PERSPECTIVE

OVERVIEW

There are nearly two billion children in the world today—one third of the world's population. And all of these children could be said to be at risk. Very many, of course, are at risk because of poverty—in danger of suffering, exploitation, neglect, and death. Indeed, according to the UNICEF *Child Info 2008*, 8.8 million children died before their fifth birthday—an average of more than 24,000 per *day*—from diseases that could easily have been prevented or treated.[1]

At the same time, millions of children are at risk due to prosperity. The post-modern mind-set and modern materialism leave hundreds of millions of children with "everything to live with, but nothing to live for." We will examine the issues, obstacles, and challenges facing children both in poverty and in prosperity in chapter one.

However, neither the needs of children nor their potential and promise are new issues. In fact, the Bible has much to say about children—far more than most people realize. In the second chapter, we will look at the child in biblical perspective. We will find that the Bible is not silent, and what we learn of God's heart for children must surely characterize our view of children as well.

God's expectation is that all children will develop as

holistically as Jesus did as recorded in Luke 2:52: "in wisdom, in stature, and in favor with God and man." But many children do not have this opportunity for development in this four-fold way. How should Christians promote the holistic development of children? In chapter three, we will look at some biblical perspectives on development and give attention to what it is and to what it is not. We will also review the important matter of self-reliance as a component of development and facilitate an important approach to *doing* development.

A main emphasis in this book is the child in poverty. Chapter four looks at the issue of poverty, again from a biblical point of view. The key idea is that poverty is not simply a matter of a lack of resources or of deficits. Rather, poverty is fundamentally a *spiritual* problem. God and Satan have very different agendas for children. God's intention is that all His children thrive—that they have life with abundance. The thief—Satan—is a liar and he wants to steal, kill, and destroy that abundant life. People caught up in the lies of Satan will not have the abundant life that God wants them to have. What people believe and act upon has important implications for both their spiritual and physical well-being. Beliefs have consequences. We will look at these issues generally but with special attention to the child and development.

Just as Jesus did for His disciples so long ago, we place the child in the midst of our discussion and watch for "upside down" perspectives.

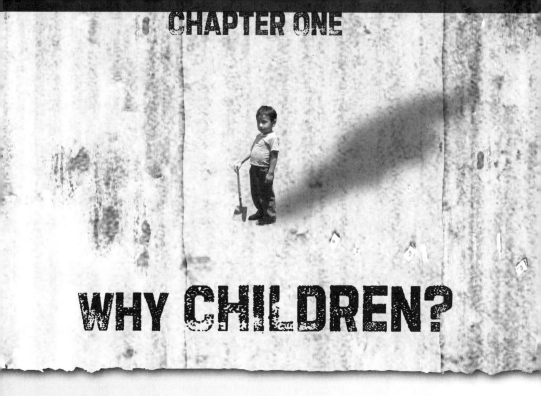

CHAPTER ONE

WHY CHILDREN?

We will tell the next generation the praiseworthy deeds of the LORD, his power, and the wonders he has done. He decreed statutes for Jacob and established the law in Israel, which he commanded our forefathers to teach their children, so the next generation would know them, even the children yet to be born, and they in turn would tell their children. Then they would put their trust in God and would not forget his deeds but would keep his commands.
Psalm 78:3-7

Never before in history have we had so many children among us, and never before have so many of them been at such great social risk. Children ages 15 and younger comprise one-third of our world's six billion people. In many developing countries, children make up nearly half the population. An additional 26 percent[1] are young

people ages 15 to 29. Another one billion children may be born in the next decade, many into extreme poverty.

One of our best spokespersons for children, VIVA Network founder Patrick McDonald, highlights the importance of children and the particular responsibility of the Church to care for them.[2]

> Children are a priority for the King and His kingdom: They are many, they are strategic, they suffer and God's unambiguous mandate in their favor shouts for urgent action right across the pages of Scripture. They are both key to the great commission and an essential expression of the great commandment. The Christian response to children today stands in many ways at a crossroads. Most children at the turn of the century are "children at risk," or children that need more than mere words to demonstrate the love of God. They are hungry children, homeless children, hurting children. Faced with the urgent need to nurture and protect these children lots of Christians respond compassionately, even sacrificially, but most struggle to engage effectively and consistently. The increasing need for professional standards in care pose a defining challenge for the church.

MILLIONS OF CHILDREN SUFFER FROM POVERTY...

An overriding reason for the Church to focus on children is that, more than any other segment of humanity, children suffer. In a sense, they pay for the sins of adults. Every year tens of millions of children are victims of exploitation, violence, and abuse. Today more than 37 percent of children around the world live in absolute poverty—a total of 674 million children.[3] Many, many more live in conditions of severe deprivation, facing lack of income; hunger and malnutrition; ill health; limited or lack of access to education and other basic services; homelessness and inadequate housing; unsafe environments; social discrimination and exclusion.

Yet the news about children is not all bad. According to UNICEF's *State of the World's Children 2009*[4] only about 24,000 under age 5 children are dying each day around the world—down from nearly 40,000 a decade ago. Between the early 1990s and 2000, the average under-5 mortality rate declined by 11 percent, and child deaths from diarrhea, the foremost killer of children at the beginning of the 1990s, declined by half—saving an estimated one million lives.

The staggering truth, however, is that more than a billion children (56 percent) around the world are living in severe deprivation! The risks and ravages facing children are many and complex. Some are as obvious as children simply not getting enough to eat. Perhaps 30 percent of the children under the age of 5 around the world suffer from severe or moderate malnutrition. And even in the richest countries, many children are raised in families who live below the poverty line. In spite of the existence of vaccines and other measures that protect children in the industrialized world against diseases, millions of children still die each year from diseases that could have been prevented. Despite a near-universal consensus on the life-affirming importance of education, 72 million primary aged children in the developing world have no access to school, with 57 percent being girls.[5] A half million mothers die every year while giving birth, leaving babies at extreme risk. A woman living in West or central Africa has a 1 in 17 lifetime risk of maternal death.[6]

Moreover, in the last decade perhaps two million children have been killed and more than six million children have been injured or disabled in armed conflicts. Tens of thousands of children have been maimed by landmines and thousands have suffered in conflicts fueled by the greed for land and gems and oil.[7]

Much is said today about the new "flat" earth and the rise of the global marketplace. The effects of increasing globalization are not all bad, but they tend to have their most negative effects on the poor. Food supplies, for example, may suffer as land use and trading focuses more on national economies and less on reasonable diets for marginalized people. In urban areas around the world, poverty tends to drive an increase in street children. Child labor puts children at great risk of injury, abuse, illiteracy, and many other perils, not to mention the loss of childhood itself. Child trafficking and sexual exploitation put children in a dark domain that makes them difficult to locate, much less liberate. Armed conflict often perversely targets at-risk children and their families.

These and many other issues add up to massive misery and suffering amongst children. And every statistic, of course, represents a real hurting child whom God loves and for whom Jesus died.

...AND MILLIONS OF CHILDREN SUFFER FROM PROSPERITY

On the other hand, for many children in America and in developed countries around the world, the future looks bright. Their education is secure. Their health is usually sound. Doctors are rarely more than a phone call away. Technology promises to bring them to greater achievements than we could ever dream. But the truth is, of course, that even these very affluent and "privileged" children are at extremely great risk.

Many are coddled and spoiled. They are often without a sense of meaning, responsibility, or purpose in their lives. They are well-fed (in many cases overfed), secure, have expensive clothing and every possible gadget and plaything. For many, no demands are made on them beyond "Don't do drugs" and "Show up for classes." They know that they will be given anything they want—especially if they whine enough.

Overexposure to adult experiences threatens the childhood and well-being for many of these children and young people. Their innocence is stolen. Their lives are marked with the ambiguities of postmodern philosophies. They may be highly connected in a borderless digital world but ironically highly disconnected in the real world—from parents, neighbors, friends, community, and, worst of all, themselves.

Millions of children in prosperous homes and highly developed countries are suffering from neglect, lack of parental care, nurture, and protection. Too many children lash out in violence, mimicking or influenced by what they learn from television and Hollywood. Too many teenagers hate themselves. Too many children are confused and discouraged by the disheartening premises of postmodernism:

- Life is absurd and has no meaning.
- There is no truth.
- You are the only one who cares about yourself; therefore
- Don't trust anything or anyone.

Many children are raised in environments of hatred, injustice, mistrust, and confusion. Many are caught up in complex adult problems, including divorce and sexuality. Inwardly they cry for adults to help them find their true selves and purpose in life. Outwardly, they act out their frustrations in tragic and self-destructive ways.

It is ironic that parents may spend the least time with their children in cultures with the most leisure time. Countries with the easiest access to family counseling and services often have the highest divorce rates. Materialism draws attention away from making better families toward making bigger paychecks. These are just a few issues that demonstrate a trend of cultural values shifting away from the family.

Families really are in trouble, and children pay the price. When 1,500 school children were asked, "What do you think

makes a happy family?" they did not list money, cars, nice homes, or television. Their most common answer: "Doing things together."[8]

Are we listening?

A GLOBALIZED MEDIA WORLD

Perhaps the greatest challenge faced by children today—and by those seeking to reach them—is the unprecedented globalized media world. In many countries today, children begin to have unsupervised access to a 24-hour global media from a very young age. "Electronic communication is now one of the earliest formative influences in the life of the young child."[9]

The influence and impact of the Internet is pervasive, all encompassing and omnipresent. This is especially true for teens and 'tweens and increasingly true of ever younger children. Tom Hayes, in his fascinating book *Jump Point: How Network Culture is Revolutionizing Business*, describes the "bubble generation," people between the ages of 13 and 25:

> The Bubble Generation has grown up with the Internet and can't remember a world without it. Theirs is a world of social media, third screens, peer-to-peer platforms, bit torrents, wikis, blogs, vlogs, podcasts, RSS, SMS, IMS, texting, GPS, video sharing, and photo swapping. Their culture, mores, tastes, and wants have been defined by their use

of this technology. They have never taken a photo-
graph they couldn't see instantly, or watched TV
without a menu, or used a pay phone. Instead, they
are comfortable finding anything on the Internet,
they communicate via instant messaging, and they
happily shop online and use collaborative tools
that help them to keep in touch with friends and
family as well as to work better and more produc-
tively with their colleagues.[10]

Hayes is writing to the business community. But what he
has to say about the interests and attention and networking
communities of the next generation applies just as readily to
those of us seeking to touch their hearts as well as their minds.
Using the lens of a concerned parent, pastor, or caregiver
seeking to guide and protect them, read the following descrip-
tions of the reality of the lifestyle and worldview of children
and young people today:

Today's audiences are accustomed to having
their attention overwhelmed; they want to be overwhelmed with experience. They are comfortable
with a multiplicity of concurrent stimuli; at home
and work they multitask easily between e-mails,
virtual meetings, and Webcasts; and their social
lives are a blur of texting, game playing, videos,
and hours of unfettered kvetching with friends, all
to the beat of their iPods.[11]

No one has the right to impose personal beliefs on anyone, and anyone claiming to have a corner on the truth market will be ridiculed out of court. Mottled hair, tattoos, piercings, and a liberal exposure to ethnic cultures and foods are representative of the diversity with which this generation has grown up. Progeny of the civil rights and gender-equity movements, these children of boomer parents reject prejudice and are incredibly accepting of other people—their looks, experiences, and personal preferences.... They are nonjudgmental about their friends' personal lives and don't see what all the fuss is about concerning some of the hot-button issues of the day, such as abortion.

In fairness, it should also be noted that this generation is also highly passive compared to its predecessors (a product of years of sitting in front of a computer screen), less cognizant of its place in history or the surrounding society, and increasingly less capable of extended commitment to anything—from social causes to relationships to institutions to attention itself. The Bubble Generation is quick, clever, almost superhumanly facile with technology . . . and often terrifyingly shallow. [12]

It may seem a bit of a stretch to apply the opportunities and threats of globalized media to impoverished as well as affluent children. Yet the reach of media has no borders or boundaries. Children in the slums of the Mathare Valley in Nairobi may live in appalling squalor, but many still have access to cell phones and cable television.

CHILDREN ARE STRATEGIC BECAUSE "THE CLAY" IS STILL SOFT

Whether suffering from poverty or prosperity, childhood is the most formative and therefore the most strategic stage of life. The saying is true: "To shape an adult, reach a child." Children need our attention more urgently than any other group of people, for childhood is quickly over.

Most parents intrinsically know that childhood years are formative. Our brains are 90 percent formed before we reach the age of 3,[13] and most of our adult personality is formed by the time we reach 6 years of age. There is substantial truth in the saying attributed to the Jesuits: "Give me a child 'til he is 7, and I'll show you the man." The Bible simply states in Proverbs 22:6, "Train a child in the way he should go, and when he is old he will not turn from it."

Compassion International president Dr. Wess Stafford reminds us,

> Every major movement in history has grasped
> the need to target the next generation in order

to advance its agenda and secure its legacy into the future. Political movements (like Nazism and Communism) trained legions of children with the goal of carrying their agenda beyond the lifetimes of their founders. World religions have done the same with the systematic indoctrination of their young—even the Taliban places great emphasis on recruiting children. Nebuchadnezzar, in his conquest of Israel, poured his efforts into shaping the future by seeking to influence children like Daniel, Shadrach, Meshach, and Abednego. It seems that, historically, the Christian evangelical movement is one of the few that has allowed children to remain a second-rate mandate—the Great Omission in the Great Commission.[14]

To ignore children as if they don't exist is at best a strategic mistake, and at worst an invitation for the evil around us to ruin them.

TRAILING CLOUDS OF GLORY

Reflecting on the nature of children and childhood and their reality today, Dr. Vinay Samuel, long the director of the Oxford Centre for Mission Studies, makes a fascinating observation. He says, "Children are born with transcendence. While they are born into risk, children recognize transcendence. Yet if they are not immediately invited into the kingdom . . . if they do not experience and enjoy the realities of kingdom, they will lose that sense of transcendence."[15]

The idea of transcendence resonates with me. I believe it points to a sense or sensitivity that children may inherently have of their being created in God's own image and to the touch of God in their lives. Pay close attention to young children and notice their openness to nature, to feelings, and to others, along with a simple yet profound sense of awe and wonder. Notice the sense of the present and the uncomplicated view of life, as they find it easy to trust and accept the things of God. Is this pointing to some "mystery" of the Divine with which all children are born? Does it hint of something vastly significant, more precious even than their presence and yet terrifyingly fragile, which we so carelessly and flippantly mishandle?

My friend Keith White suggests that the real quality Jesus saw in the child He placed in the midst of the arguing disciples was more than just the humility, but was in fact *transcendence.* It wasn't just that the child was humble, though apparently he was. What really sets a child apart and what Jesus would have admired in this boy (and in children in general) is perhaps more than just humility. Perhaps it was the child's transcendence. The quality Jesus liked was not just that children don't argue about who is the greatest, *but that to argue in this way would not even occur to them.*

There is something compelling about the confident statement that children inherently have transcendence. At the same time, a child's transcendence is fragile and vulnerable

and may be lost forever if not given its proper respect. Vinay continues:

> Jesus [said], "Come children into the community of the kingdom, with the king, this is the space where you belong. There you will experience transcendence, you will not lose your sense of transcendence." Children in the West need transcendence desperately. Children need that sense that there is a reality beyond just the television. They need transcendence that is real.

As long as they are well-fed, healthy, and comfortable, it doesn't really matter if they are rich or poor (until peer pressure sets in!). Children transcend cultural differences. Until they are taught to notice, children don't normally make the kinds of distinctions of beauty and ugliness that some adults do. Children can and do transcend poverty.

Surely, that transcendence is something borne of the fact that each child is a person created in the image of God with all the dignity and inherent worth that this implies. Surely, Jesus was fully aware of transcendence in children. Katherine Copsey, in her fine essay "What Is a Child?" asks,[16]

> What, then, are the qualities, which naturally tumble out of children, which Jesus encourages us to learn from when He urges us to 'become like a child'? In other words, what characterizes a child's spirituality—those qualities which a child carries

within by virtue of having been made in God's image?

She answers her question with this summary:

Openness:

- To nature—children exhibit a sense of awe and wonder
- To feelings—children tend to be direct, in touch with their feelings
- To others—children naturally tend to have an open, welcoming nature

Ability to be Present:

- Children tend to live in the "here and now" and think in concrete terms.
- Children have a gift for perception—what we really mean, how we feel.
- Children tend to accept things at face value, taking as much as is needed for a given time.

Uncomplicated:

- Children can find belief easy and uncomplicated; they do not need to analyze.
- Children can find trust easy if they are brought up within a trustworthy environment.
- Children have simple, basic emotional and physical needs.

Nothing can destroy the fact of that "createdness" in God's likeness, but there are many ways in which the sense of transcendence can be lost. Copsey says, "We may simply be unaware of it, we may fail to recognize it and therefore fail to nurture it. We may rubbish it, crush it, clutter it; we may allow it to be lost under the weight of a materialistic, consumerist culture."[17] This happens, she says, if[18]:

- We give children the message that feelings are wrong.
- We offer them environments that have no beauty, which are soul-less, and fail to help them discover a sense of awe and wonder in what lies around them.
- We destroy their sense of trust, openness, and their perception through various forms of abuse and insincerity.
- We fail to meet their basic emotional and physical needs.
- We make belief too cognitive, too complicated, failing to recognize the value of affective learning.
- We kill their imagination and their sense of fantasy.

Whether suffering from poverty or prosperity, children around the world need and deserve the loving attention of caring Christians. As we will see in the next chapter, the Bible has much to say about children—far more than we have noticed in the past. Children are there, in so many of the narratives and teachings in the Bible. They are receptive and responsive. God speaks to them and through them. They are His instruments and agents; they participate in and provoke worship, reverence, and faith.

Yes, we Christians have done a fair amount to teach the children we find in our Sunday school classrooms. Too often, however, Christians have concluded that caring for those outside—especially the impoverished, the noisy, the dirty, and the desperate—must be someone else's responsibility.

The title of a book by Wess Stafford, president of Compassion International, declares that children are *Too Small to Ignore*. That is the premise of this book as well. The church can no longer pass off the responsibility to others. Caring for even impoverished children is the *particular* responsibility of Christians and of the Church.

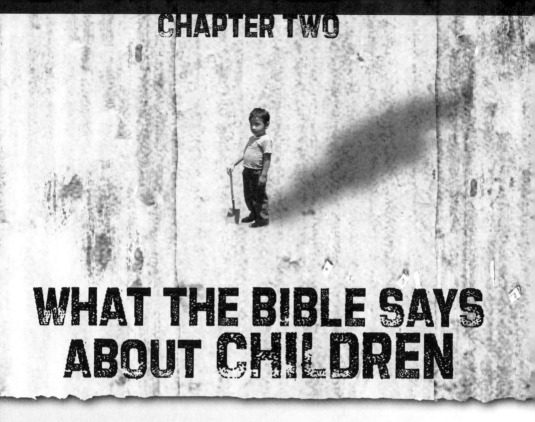

CHAPTER TWO

WHAT THE BIBLE SAYS ABOUT CHILDREN

But if anyone causes one of these little ones who believe in me to sin, it would be better for him to have a large millstone hung around his neck and to be drowned in the depths of the sea.
Matthew 18:6

What does the Bible tell us about God's heart for children?[1]

Some people who should know better have said that the Bible has little to say about children and childhood. But a closer examination of Scripture—one with the child in focus—reveals that children are very prominent in the Bible. Children play a significant role in the unfolding of the message of the Bible. God loves and protects children. The Bible demonstrates that children are extremely perceptive in understanding the things of God. God often used them as His messengers and models—especially, it seems, when adults may have been too corrupt and deaf to listen or respond.

The Bible also clearly teaches that we need to be serious about children, because God surely is! Perhaps nothing upset Jesus more than "hindering" the children. In Matthew 18:5-6, Jesus says that anyone who causes one of these little ones to sin should have a millstone hung around his neck and be drowned in the depths of the sea. The original Greek reveals that the millstone referred to is a *very large stone* and the person is to be thrown into the *deepest part* of the ocean. Clearly, Jesus had no patience or sympathy whatsoever with anyone who would do such a thing.

In this chapter we will take a broad look at what the Bible says about children. It will be just an overview—there are more than 1,700 references in the Bible to children and childhood, to God's concern for those neglected or exploited, to the roles and responsibilities of parents, and to the special ways in which children are integral parts of His unfolding plan. So rest assured, there's plenty to consider.

CHILDREN AND CHILDHOOD IN THE BIBLE

Whatever the realities of a child's life, God regards children as precious.[2] The Scriptures are rich with principles that illustrate this point.

First and foremost, children are a sign of God's blessing.[3] They are an essential part of the covenant community. In fact, children's attitudes and teachableness illustrate the relationship God wants with adults.[4] Jesus uses children as examples of the humble dependence that the kingdom of God requires of adults.[5]

As such, their families and communities are to treasure and teach them in the ways and Word of God.[6] God is on the side of the vulnerable and considers children worthy of protection.[7] When children are neglected, abused, or victimized, God grieves. Jesus strongly advocates for their protection.[8]

Children seem to have an innate sense of how best to serve God. Children are worshippers. They are designed to praise God.[9] Praise is not something they learn when they are older—it is their nature and purpose now. Children praise Jesus even when adults reject Him.[10] Further, in the Bible children prove to be choice agents of God's mission. Children are not only the ones who follow, but also the ones whom God sends to lead.[11] Children are key figures in the biblical narrative: Isaac, Moses, Samuel, David, Naaman's wife's maid. God Himself chose to enter this world as a baby, not as king, rabbi, or high priest.

God loves children unconditionally. Jesus blessed the children brought to Him, without conditions or demands.[12] Jesus makes children a focus in His ministry. He heals children[13] and welcomes them.[14] He uses children as examples of humility.[15] Simply put, Jesus values children.[16]

The fact that theologians and the Church have for so long overlooked these biblical realities may have had serious consequences in our overall understanding of Scripture and of children. Dr. Keith White[17] asks,

What if we have misheard or neglected God's revealed teaching about children and childhood? What of the likely effects of such a process on the history and current life and shape of the church? What if by default we have not been salt and light in God's world? What if our vision of the kingdom of heaven is a pale reflection of what Jesus revealed?

The studies in this book, and many other initiatives to see more clearly *the child in the midst,* are beginning to address some of these oversights and defects in our understandings.

CHILDREN ARE CREATED WITH DIGNITY

A look at what the Bible says about children reveals first that children, like all of humanity, are created in God's own image. This very fact endows them with dignity and inherent value. This is true of all children regardless of tribe, language, nationality, age, gender, ability, behavior, caste, or any other human characteristic. It is true even for unborn children, as is clear from Psalm 139:13-16:

> For you created my inmost being; you knit me together in my mother's womb. . . . I am fearfully and wonderfully made. . . . My frame was not hidden from you when I was made in the secret place. When I was woven together in the depths of the earth, your eyes saw my unformed body.

All the days ordained for me were written in your book before one of them came to be.

The Lord gave His own life and shed His blood for the dignity and salvation of every child. God also preserved and restored the dignity of children by using them to do His work, by taking time to bless them, heal them, and even raise them from the dead.

God showed His respect for children by making them a priority, even when the disciples had no time for them. He valued them by giving them an understanding of His kingdom.[18] As noted earlier, Jesus valued children by accepting their worship and by protecting them—warning those who might do them harm.[19]

OFTEN NEGLECTED AND EXPLOITED

Throughout Scripture we see many examples of the neglect or exploitation of children. Many of the same things that shock and appall us today were problems in biblical times as well.

Then as now, children in some cultures were subject to seizure for debts. Job 24:9 states, "The fatherless child is snatched from the breast; the infant of the poor is seized for a debt." We find another example in 2 Kings 4:1: "The wife of a man from the company of the prophets cried out to Elisha, 'Your servant my husband is dead, and you know that he revered the Lord. But now his creditor is coming to take my two boys as his slaves.'"

Children are usually the first victims of hunger and nakedness. Job 24:7, 10 reflects on the state of children in need: "Lacking clothes, they spend the night naked; they have nothing to cover themselves in the cold. . . . Lacking clothes, they go about naked; they carry the sheaves, but still go hungry."

The Bible offers examples of child exploitation that sound like today's headlines. The book of Joel even mentions child trafficking and prostitution! "'They cast lots for my people and traded boys for prostitutes; they sold girls for wine that they might drink. . . . I will sell your sons and daughters to the people of Judah, and they will sell them to the Sabeans, a nation far away.' The LORD has spoken" (Joel 3:8).

Biblical prophets roundly condemned parental abuse, especially that which led to child sacrifice. Consider this example (one of several in the Old Testament): "They built high places for Baal in the Valley of Ben Hinnom to sacrifice their sons and daughters to Molech, though I never commanded, nor did it enter my mind, that they should do such a detestable thing and so make Judah sin" (Jeremiah 32:35). This horrific practice against children is documented again in Psalm 106:37-38: "They sacrificed their sons and their daughters to demons. They shed innocent blood, the blood of their sons and daughters, whom they sacrificed to the idols of Canaan, and the land was desecrated by their blood." Jeremiah again speaks, "This is what the LORD says: 'A voice is heard in Ramah, mourning and great weeping, Rachel weeping for her children and refusing to be comforted, because her children are no more'" (Jeremiah 31:15). So burned into the memories of the Jews was that experience that this same lament is recalled at the time of the birth of Jesus, when Herod slaughtered the innocents in Bethlehem in an attempt to eliminate the infant Jesus.

Though these things happen to children, God is not silent. Throughout Scripture, we see the unmistakable and pervasive evidence of God's love and care for children. Over 30 passages in the Old Testament attest to God being the defender of the fatherless. One of my favorites is Deuteronomy 10:18, reminding us that God "defends the cause of the fatherless and the widow, and loves the alien, giving him food and clothing."[20]

Numerous other passages demonstrate God's concern for hurting children and commanding that His people share His concern. Genesis 21:17 records the concern and care God shows toward the exiled Hagar and Ishmael, Isaac's rival and half-brother. God heard Ishmael's crying. Lamentations 2:19 also passionately instructs God's people in exile, "Arise, cry out in the night, as the watches of the night begin; pour out your heart like water in the presence of the LORD. Lift up your hands to him for the lives of your children, who faint from hunger at the head of every street."

We know, too, that God commands His people to instruct and train children. For example, consider Deuteronomy 6:6-8:

> These commandments that I give you today are to be upon your hearts. Impress them on your children. Talk about them when you sit at home and when you walk along the road, when you lie down and when you get up. Tie them as symbols on your hands and bind them on your foreheads.

The theme continues in Proverbs, where parents are commanded to train a child in righteousness and wisdom.[21] The book offers strong support of discipline—including *loving* corporal punishment—as a key tool in successful parenting.[22]

In the New Testament, too, Jesus' concern for children is always evident. Jesus said that whoever welcomes a child welcomes Him. When the disciples were arguing about who would be the greatest in the kingdom, Jesus placed a *child in the midst* of them. He said that if people were not willing to become like that child, they wouldn't even get into the kingdom—let alone have any place of prominence!

I love the word picture I see in Matthew 18:10: "See that you do not look down on one of these little ones. For I tell you that their angels in heaven always see the face of my Father in heaven." To me, this verse suggests that the children's angels (they have angels looking after them!) have special access to the Father, which perhaps even other angels don't have. It also seems to indicate that, whatever God may be doing at the moment, if one of these angels sees a child in trouble that angel will let God know about it right away!

CHILDREN CAN UNDERSTAND THE THINGS OF GOD

It is not only God's love and care for children that is notable in the Bible. We also see that God has a very high regard for their ability to understand the faith and to participate in His redemption activities.

From the start of God's covenant with His chosen people, God expected that the children would be included so that they too would learn to love and fear the Lord. We see for example in Deuteronomy 31:12: "Assemble the people—men, women and children, and the aliens living in your towns—so they can listen and learn to fear the LORD your God and follow carefully all the words of this law."

When Joshua became the leader of Israel, he too saw to it that the children were included in the reading of the Law:

> Afterward, Joshua read all the words of the law—the blessings and the curses—just as it is written in the Book of the Law. There was not a word of all that Moses had commanded that Joshua did not read to the whole assembly of Israel, *including the women and children*, and the aliens who lived among them (Joshua 8:34-35, emphasis added).

Children were included everywhere in the drama and ritual of worship in the Old Testament. Exodus 12 records that the ritual of the Passover begins when the children ask what it means. In Leviticus, we see the children participating in the dialogue about the meaning of the Passover. Children's questions also provoke the remembered ritual of the 12 stones taken from the bed of the river Jordan.[23]

Much later in the Old Testament chronology, Nehemiah showed the same confidence in the ability of children to understand and participate in the faith development of the community. "And on that day they offered great sacrifices, rejoicing because God had given them great joy. *The women and children also rejoiced.* The sound of rejoicing in Jerusalem could be heard far away" (Nehemiah 12:43, emphasis added).

When the Law was read out, children were part of the crowd, echoing the occasion of the renewal of the covenant in Joshua 8:35.[24] They were present again in the celebrations on the completion of the wall.[25]

In the New Testament, Jesus also shows a very high regard for the ability of children to understand the faith. He Himself is shown "confounding" the religious elders as a 12-year-old boy. Jesus rebuked the teachers for questioning the children's worship and their recognition of Jesus.[26] Once in the midst of some harsh teaching about repentance and judgment, Jesus stopped, seemingly awestruck that somehow in God's scheme of things in some sense these truths were hidden from the "wise" and "learned" but known to little children, "I praise you, Father, LORD of heaven and earth, because you have hidden these things from the wise and learned, and revealed them to little children."[27] (Have you ever wondered precisely what it is that little children understand that we adults cannot? Is it something inherent in their spirit that cannot be articulated? Or perhaps simply an ability to trust and respond that is often so difficult for adults?)

The early church leader Timothy is another example of a young child who knew the Scriptures.[28] Throughout the Bible, youth are encouraged to influence their communities by maintaining personal purity, by obeying God's Word,[29] by being exemplary in their speech, love, and faith, [30] and by pursuing godly virtues.[31]

GOD USES CHILDREN FOR SPECIAL TASKS

Wess Stafford, president of Compassion International, likes to say that often when God had something REALLY important to do—something that He couldn't entrust to adults—He used children instead.

Think of how different the history of Israel would be, for example, if Moses' sister Miriam—just a child herself—had not rescued Moses from the Nile! As we read in Exodus 2, Pharaoh had decreed death to all the boys under the age of 2. Against all odds, Moses' mother hid him in a basket among the reeds at the edge of the Nile. And who should come along but Pharaoh's daughter herself!

Picture little Miriam coming up to admire the little baby with Pharaoh's daughter. "Isn't he a sweet little thing?" she asks timidly.

"Oh yes," she agrees. "He is just precious!"

"Would you like me to get someone to help you raise this little boy as your own?"

"That is so thoughtful of you! Yes, that would be a wonderful idea. Would you do that?"

"Right away," says the resourceful little Miriam as she dashes off to get the child's own mother to raise Moses in the household of Pharaoh!

Or think of the stern message God had for Eli, the highest spiritual leader in the land. First Samuel 3 tells us that God confidently entrusted that difficult message to a very young Samuel. Verse 7 tells us that Samuel did not yet know the Lord: "The word of the LORD had not yet been revealed to him." So

Eli was the only was the only spiritual voice that Samuel knew. Yet God gave him a very disturbing message to deliver. Wess Stafford puts it this way:[32]

> God didn't say, "Oh well, it's just little Samuel. I'll start him off with a simple, pleasant message." No, God saw this child as capable and worthy of doing a major intervention in the life of a powerful man. He didn't shade the assignment at all. And in fact, Scripture says the next morning that young "Samuel told [Eli] everything, hiding nothing from him" (verse 18). He let fly with the full message God had given him in the night.
>
> I ask you, would you entrust such a message to a child? Of course not—but God did. Obviously He feels differently about children we do.

Or finally consider a young captive servant girl, who knowing how God was using Elisha, urged the powerful Syrian general Naaman to go to the prophet for healing. As recounted in 2 Kings 5, the young girl who might have been bitter and resentful, instead was caring and wistful: "If only my master would see the prophet who is in Samaria! He would cure him of his leprosy."[33] She had a heart full of compassion.

Only as we read Scripture *with the child in the midst* can we see how even this extremely brief mention of a little servant girl is an enlightening lesson on how God uses the children for His purposes. Esther Menn notes that this narrative presents a sustained and ironic contrast between what appears "big" and important, and what appears "small" and insignificant.[34] We do not know her name, her exact age, what happened to her parents and siblings when she was captured, or how long she served Naaman's wife. ". . . the child is introduced simply as 'little,' as if that is the one thing that matters, her smallness in the midst of everything mighty, powerful, and gross."[35]

Naaman and his wife listened to this young slave girl and sought permission from the king to carry out her idea. The King of Aram elevated the little girl's suggestion into something of an international crisis when he tried to turn it into an economic and political transaction, but he wisely encouraged Naaman to take the journey to Israel.

The little girl's knowledge and faith combined with her familiarity with the work of God through Elisha enabled her to significantly impact her nation and generation. She was still very young. She lived in a foreign land with low social status and limited freedom. Yet the faith and confidence of this young girl made an impact that led toward holistic transformation in the lives of Naaman and his family. It is clear from the text that she might have even helped create reconciliation and peace between two hostile nations.

The result was the acknowledgement by this great Aram commander that the God of Israel is the only God in the whole world. "Now I know that there is no God in all the world except in Israel."[36] This "now I know" confession formed the core of the Israelites' confession of faith.[37] Even today, our missionary enterprise activity is all about getting the peoples of the earth to make the same "Now I know!" declaration as Naaman.

OLD TESTAMENT THEMES REGARDING CHILDREN

The above shows that children are neither hidden nor insignificant throughout the Bible. But on a broader canvas, Dr. White notes several overriding themes into which these references are set, beginning in the Old Testament and continued and further developed in the New Testament.[38]

First, consider the Father/child and mother/child relationship God has with His people. One portrayal of that relationship (subsequently developed in the New Testament), is God as a Father. Dr. White writes:

> In Deuteronomy 8 God disciplines those whom He has chosen as a father. In Psalm 27 a child may be abandoned by father and mother, but not by God, the heavenly Father. God's compassion is like that of a father to a child (Psalm 103). The Wisdom literature is written largely as from a father to a son (e.g. Psalm 34; Proverbs 1-7). . . The mother/child relationship is significantly used as an embodiment of the bond between God and us. There is a beautiful description of the weaned child in Psalm 131 representing a stilled and quietened soul. Isaiah closes with a tender description of childbirth that concludes: 'As a mother comforts her child, so will I comfort you' (Isaiah 66:13).[39]

Second, children are ordained and designed to praise God

and His glory. We see this best in Psalm 8:2: "From the lips of children and infants you have ordained praise because of your enemies to silence the foe and the avenger." Too often the first part of this verse has been dismissed as polite but quaint. In doing so, we may fail to see the significance of this verse. Children and infants are not just consumers or future adults; rather, they are specifically ordained and designed to praise God and His glory. That this is their true nature and purpose is reinforced throughout Scripture. This is how God sees them, and how we ourselves must view children.

Amazingly, we also see that in some way even the cries of infants have a role in silencing Satan. We are not told how the cries of a child have such an effect, but this stunning insight should warrant close attention by scholars and theologians. That, after all, is one ultimate aim of our life in Christ.

Third, "a little child will lead them." In some way, children illustrate the coming kingdom. In Isaiah 11, the Messianic kingdom is vividly portrayed: "The wolf will live with the lamb *... and a little child will lead them.*" The coming kingdom will be a safe environment in which children can play, unlike the urban, war-torn, consumer/market-dominated jungle of today. The future kingdom has children at its heart.

Fourth, God's salvation is not through kings and warriors, but unexpectedly through a child. Moreover, in many places in the Old Testament, the child is also *a sign* of the coming kingdom. Isaiah talks of God's righteous anger against sin and hypocrisy in 7:14. This situation seems unimaginably bleak and hopeless, and yet God gives a sign: "The virgin will be with child and will give birth to a son, and will call him Immanuel."

Isaiah 9:6 offers the beloved proclamation, "For to us a child is born, to us a son is given, and the government will be on his shoulders." The focus of God's promise of salvation is not a warrior king, a wise rabbi, or a high priest, but a child.[40]

NEW TESTAMENT THEMES REGARDING CHILDREN

In the New Testament we see the further development of these same themes. There are, of course, many incidents involving children in the life of Jesus: the daughter of the Canaanite woman,[41] the boy with a demon,[42] the official's son at Capernaum,[43] Jairus' daughter,[44] and others. "In all, we see that Jesus has a heart for children and they are drawn to Him. His preferred method of teaching by story and sign is, as in the [Old Testament] worship and ritual, equally accessible to children and adults. The most pervasive description of God's love is, as Jesus taught us, 'Our Father.'"[45]

Jesus often took advantage of the special faith of children in order to influence adults. In the touching account of Jairus' daughter, Jesus used the occasion to strengthen the faith of her parents. He encouraged Jairus not to be afraid, but to believe. He took both Jairus and his wife with Him to raise up their little girl. Jesus also included Peter, James, and John in order to teach them how to minister to the family.[46]

Jesus was a role model to the disciples in the way He placed His hands on the children and prayed for them and touched them.[47]

More broadly again, Dr. White[48] draws our attention to some overarching themes surrounding children in the New Testament.

The incarnation. At the outset of the New Testament, Matthew quotes Isaiah 7:14 about the virgin and child. Luke 2:12 tells of a sign for the shepherds that replicates the prophecy of Isaiah: "You will find a baby wrapped in cloths and lying in a manger." Simeon prophesies that the child is "to be a sign" in Luke 2:33. Keith White remarks,

> The word *child* is repeated in both Gospels again and again. What is the significance? God has chosen to enter the world *as a baby*. Perhaps we are so accustomed to Christmas that we do not realize how radical this is. The fullness of the creator God in a tiny child? Is it possible? If so what does it mean?
>
> From God's point of view there is no problem, but it shakes our preconceptions. A baby is small, weak, dependent and vulnerable, lacks education and training and language. "Yes," says God, "and you must learn to find me in these things, in little ones. You must learn, to move from the palaces and encounters with the learned and the powerful, to the manger and the child."[49]

The kingdom of heaven. The kingdom of God was the central theme of the ministry of Jesus and is perhaps the most powerful theological perspective supporting holistic child development. Just as it permeated all of Jesus' ministry and gave it coherence and clarity, so the kingdom of God provides coherence and clarity to holistic ministry to children.

The teaching of the kingdom is essential to understand the role of the Church in caring for the needy. The surprising teaching about the kingdom of God is that it is so "upside down," so unexpected. The last will be first, the lowly will be exalted, and the meek will inherit the earth. Describing the *Upside Down Kingdom of God* Donald Kraybill observes,

> Again and again in parables, sermons, and acts, Jesus startles us. Things are not like they are supposed to be. Good Guys turn out to be Bad Guys. Those we expect to receive rewards get spankings. Those who think they are headed for heaven wind up in hell. Things are reversed. Paradox, irony, and surprise permeate the teachings of Jesus. They flip our expectations upside down. The least are the greatest. The immoral receive forgiveness and blessing. Adults become like children. The religious miss the heavenly banquet....[50]

Jesus' disciples could not think of a kingdom in any way other than in terms of the exercise of authority and power. They accepted that Jesus was the king, but kings have chief ministers and advisors and were very curious to know which of them were to occupy these positions. Jesus shocked them by placing a child in their midst, giving the child a hug and saying, "I tell you the truth, unless you change and become like little children you will never enter the kingdom of heaven" (Matthew 18:3). What an upside down way to think of significance, importance, and influence!

Jesus used some "upside down" teachings about the kingdom, which show children as an important part of mission in the New Testament. For example, Jesus blesses the children brought to Him and teaches that the kingdom *belongs* to them. Then He tells adults that unless they become like children they won't even get into the kingdom, much less be the greatest in it. Further, He is angry when the disciples keep the children from coming to Him.

All this should come as no surprise. Jesus also used the picture of a child to teach Nicodemus a basic theological truth on entering the kingdom of heaven: "You must be born again!" Jesus used childbirth as an illustration of the only way to God's kingdom.[51]

There are moments in the Gospel accounts when you hope an adult finds the faith of a child, and fast. In the healing of the boy with an evil spirit recounted in the middle of Mark 9, Jesus challenged *the father* to trust in the impossible and declare his faith in a powerful God. Indeed, in the Gospels (e.g. Luke 1:26-32, Isaiah 7:14, 9:6) we find the child is a sign that points humankind to salvation. Keith White puts it plainly: "God has chosen to enter the world, to reveal Himself as a baby and as a child."[52]

Children help us understand the remarkable truths of the kingdom, for both they and the kingdom are "already" and also "not yet." The kingdom is already at hand, and each time we give that cup of cold water, we manifest the presence of the kingdom. The kingdom is also "not yet," for there are many who do not yet believe and there is still much evil in the world. Similarly, children are fully present and inherently valuable now, regardless of what their future might hold. But they are certainly not all they will be. "Childhood and the kingdom illuminate each other."[53]

The third New Testament theme is the common, but enigmatic truth that "You must be born again" (John 3:3). The truth is well-known and often cited, but we have allowed it to become detached from children and childhood. "Jesus is teaching exactly the same truth: you've got to let go of all your adult, culturally-laden preconceptions and be ready as it were to start all over again . . . in Christ, just as a baby is starting life for the first time."[54]

GOD'S EXPECTATIONS OF ADULTS REGARDING CHILDREN

Finally, in this overview of what the Bible says about children, we look briefly at God's expectation regarding the adults in children's lives, relating to their care for, protection of, and training and nurturing the children.

Parents are to train and teach their children. Proverbs 6:20 encourages children to "keep their father's commands and not to forsake their mother's teaching." Proverbs 22:6 talks about the responsibility of parents to create a desire for spiritual things in children from a young age: "Train a child in the way he should go, and when he is old, he will not turn from it." Deuteronomy 6:7 exhorts adults to teach their children to love and obey the law at every possible opportunity, "talking about them when you sit at home and when you walk along the road."

Adults are to love, respect, and welcome children. Jesus modeled for us concern for children though His own approach. He insisted that His disciples receive the children and not hinder them coming to Him:

> Then little children were brought to Jesus for him to place his hands on them and pray for them. But the disciples rebuked those who brought them. Jesus said, "Let the little children come to me, and do not hinder them, for the kingdom of heaven belongs to such as these" (Matthew 19:13-14).

Parents are the primary caregivers for children. The fact that God Himself trusted His own Son to humankind as a vulnerable child is indicative of the primary place of parents. God required that His Son be nurtured by a frail but able family and community. Jesus' experience as a child provides a model of trust and responsibility for us to follow.

In the early church, parents were encouraged to "bring children up in the discipline and instruction of the Lord."[55] Fathers are encouraged not to "exasperate" their children, "in case they lose heart."[56] These teachings are both in the context of children themselves being encouraged to obey their parents, yet they also challenged the assumption that parental role carried with it unlimited authority over the children of the family.

In the Old Testament, children were entirely subject to the authority of the head of the household and counted legally as his property. However, God expected adults to give careful attention to their care and training. From an early age, adults were to include children in the rituals of the faith. As the well-known passage from Deuteronomy 6 and elsewhere illustrate, parents were to focus on their responsibility for children more than their rights to them.[57]

Following in this light, Jesus' parables emphasize that the love of a father will be sacrificial. Two such examples come from Luke in the parable of the tenants[58] and the prodigal son.[59] Jesus' mother illustrates the sacrificial love of a mother. In Luke 11, Jesus also teaches that parents will naturally want to give their children good things. Paul notes how parents will encourage, comfort, and urge their children.[60]

The community is also important in the nurturing of children. While the Bible shows that parents have the primary responsibility to care for and nurture children, the role of the community is also crucial. In the Old Testament, part of the covenant of the community of God's people involved the cohesion of the relationship between children and parents.[61] According to Malachi 4:6, unless the hearts of children are turned to their fathers (and vice versa) the land would be cursed. It doesn't take much imagination, if one walks the slums of any of the major cities of the world as I have, to see that the land has been stricken with a curse. That is not the way that God intends His people—His children—to live.

In his letter to Timothy, Paul describes the living church as "God's household" where there is a caring community of believers who are role models in the way they manage their own family households. Children who are fatherless/orphans in the early church are seen to need special attention[62] because they are outside the "normal" household family unit. This is an extension of God's particular defense of the fatherless expressed throughout the Old Testament.

It is clear that children are neither absent from nor insignificant in the Bible. In countless ways they are both objects of God's love and care and agents for the outworking of His dealing with humankind. They are signs of His kingdom and illustrative of the qualities He values most.

Moreover, God's whole redemptive plan is both illustrated and embodied not in the corridors of power, but in the light and life of a child. Despite the faith community's habit of keeping children in the margins, the biblical record shows indeed that "a little child will lead them."

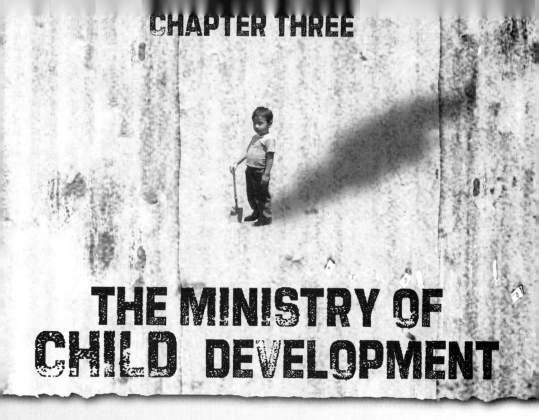

CHAPTER THREE

THE MINISTRY OF CHILD DEVELOPMENT

Two things I ask of you, O Lord; do not refuse me before I die:
Keep falsehood and lies far from me; give me neither poverty nor
riches, but give me only my daily bread. Otherwise, I may have
too much and disown you and say, "Who is the Lord?" Or I may
become poor and steal, and so dishonor the name of my God.
Proverbs 30:7-9

One of the first things we notice when we look closely at God's Word is how deeply God cares for the poor. Both the Old and the New Testaments are filled with examples of God's love for the poor, His hatred of the injustices that often cause poverty, and His concern that the poor be aided.

Jesus said the poor would always be with us. But He didn't leave it at that. Yes, they will always be with us, but what are we going to do about it? Jesus showed us His concern by what He **did** for the poor. There is much we can learn about our responsibility to the hurting people of the world as we search the Scriptures.

Deuteronomy 26 shows that it was God's concern for the oppressed people that led Him to bring the Israelites out of Egypt. Later, it was the Israelites' own mistreatment of the poor that led to their destruction. In the Book of Amos, we see that the Israelites trampled the poor. They got rich at the expense of the poor and took advantage of them by bribing the judges.[1] Even the Israelite women—the "cows" of Bashan—oppressed the poor and crushed the needy.[2]

God, who loves the poor, got fed up with their hypocrisy, their religious feasts, their assemblies, their burnt offerings, and the noise of their songs. "Cut the nonsense!" He shouts. Standing in the heart of a religious sham, the prophet cries out the familiar words recorded for us in Amos 5:24: "Let justice roll down like a river and righteousness like a never failing stream."

GOD'S HEART FOR THE POOR AND OPPRESSED

God has always been concerned about the poor and the oppressed. From the earliest history of the people of Israel, God was concerned about their suffering in slavery under the Egyptians. Indeed, it was for this very reason that God stepped in to rescue them from that bondage:

But the Egyptians mistreated us and made us suffer, putting us to hard labor. Then we cried out to the LORD, the God of our fathers, and the LORD heard our voice and saw our misery, toil and oppression. So the LORD brought us out of Egypt with a mighty hand and an outstretched arm, with great terror and with miraculous signs and wonders. He brought us to this place and gave us this land, a land flowing with milk and honey (Deuteronomy 26:6-9).

Proverbs 14:31 further shows that God actually identifies with the poor and their suffering. We read, "He who oppresses the poor shows contempt for their Maker, but whoever is kind to the needy honors God."

Care for the poor is central to God's nature. These truths from Psalm 146:6-9 speak for themselves:

The Maker of heaven and earth, the sea, and everything in them—the LORD, who remains faithful forever. He upholds the cause of the oppressed and gives food to the hungry. The LORD sets prisoners free, the LORD gives sight to the blind, the LORD lifts up those who are bowed down, the LORD loves the righteous. The LORD watches over the alien and sustains the fatherless and the widow, but he frustrates the ways of the wicked.

God loves the poor, but there is nothing inherently wrong with wealth. God wants His people to prosper. He wants all people (including children) to have "abundant life" as Jesus says in John 10:10. Material blessing is often a promised blessing for those who obey His commands. Several of the Ten Commandments end with the phrase "so that it may go well with you," and so that we might prosper.

> Honor your father and your mother, as the LORD your God has commanded you, *so that you may live long and that it may go well with you* in the land the LORD your God is giving you (Deuteronomy 5:16, emphasis added).
>
> Oh, that their hearts would be inclined to fear me and keep all my commands always, *so that it might go well with them and their children forever*! (Deuteronomy 5:29, emphasis added).
>
> The LORD commanded us to obey all these decrees and to fear the LORD our God, *so that we might always prosper and be kept alive* (Deuteronomy 6:24, emphasis added).

Clearly, wealth is neither bad nor evil in and of itself. But our attitude toward wealth and riches should be one of moderation, reflecting Proverbs 30:7-9:

> Two things I ask of you, O LORD; do not refuse me before I die: Keep falsehood and lies far from me; give me neither poverty nor riches, but give

me only my daily bread. Otherwise, I may have too much and disown you and say, "Who is the LORD?" Or I may become poor and steal, and so dishonor the name of my God.

THREE PROBLEMS WITH WEALTH

While there is nothing wrong with wealth and possessions in and of themselves, they are inherently dangerous. The Bible clearly shows that it is extremely difficult for a wealthy person to get into the kingdom of God. That in itself should make us pause. Wealth may not be evil, but there is something very scary about it. In fact, Scripture reveals at least three scenarios in which God is indeed against the rich or when riches were a serious stumbling block.

The first problem stems from **the rich acquiring wealth by oppressing the poor.** James 5 and Jeremiah 22:13-17 are among many Bible passages that clearly speak on this:

"Woe to him who builds his palace by unrighteousness, his upper rooms by injustice, making his countrymen work for nothing, not paying them for their labor. . . . Did not your father have food and drink? He did what was right and just, so all went well with him. He defended the cause of the poor and needy, and so all went well. Is that not what it means to know me?" declares the LORD. "But your eyes and your heart are set only on dishonest gain, on shedding innocent blood and on oppression and extortion" (Jeremiah 22:13-17).

Our own wealth and possessions may be a lot more dependent on oppressing the poor than we imagine. Just our insistence on getting the lowest and best prices we can get for food, clothing, or other goods imported from overseas may mean that the growers or factory workers are forced to accept extremely low wages and to live in poverty. Thoughtful Christians will want to understand such dynamics and interactions.

A second problem is that almost inevitable one of the wealthy **setting their hearts on their wealth,** as we read about in the story of the rich young ruler:

> When Jesus heard this, he said to him, "You still lack one thing. Sell everything you have and give to the poor, and you will have treasure in heaven. Then come, follow me." When he heard this, he became very sad, because he was a man of great wealth. Jesus looked at him and said, "How hard it is for the rich to enter the kingdom of God! Indeed, it is easier for a camel to go through the eye of a needle than for a rich man to enter the kingdom of God" (Luke 18:22-25).

The third problem with wealth is created when **the rich are not willing to share** from their abundance. The Luke 16 account of Lazarus the beggar speaks of eternal separation from God for the rich who ignore the poor just outside the door. This echoes several Old Testament passages, such as God's call to action in Isaiah 58:6-7:

> Is not this the kind of fasting I have chosen: to loose the chains of injustice and untie the cords of the yoke, to set the oppressed free and break every yoke? Is it not to share your food with the hungry and to provide the poor wanderer with shelter— when you see the naked, to clothe him, and not to turn away from your own flesh and blood?

It's this simple: God rewards those who care for the poor. But our tendency to hoard and accumulate is contrary to God's expectation. He blesses us and even promises prosperity to those who are generous and willing to share with others. "And if anyone gives even a cup of cold water to one of these little ones because he is my disciple," Jesus says, "I tell you the truth, he will certainly not lose his reward" (Matthew 10:42). Proverbs 11:24-25 spells out the practical results of generosity, saying, "One man gives freely, yet gains even more; another withholds unduly, but comes to poverty. A generous man will prosper; he who refreshes others will himself be refreshed."

Remember, too, that actions speak louder than words. In Matthew 25:41-45, there is the stunning suggestion that right practice is more important even than right doctrine! Note carefully the shocking basis on which the Son of Man will separate people at the final judgment—the sheep from the goats.

Then he will say to those on his left, "Depart from me, you who are cursed, into the eternal fire prepared for the devil and his angels. For I was hungry and you gave me nothing to eat, I was thirsty and you gave me nothing to drink, I was a stranger and you did not invite me in, I needed clothes and you did not clothe me, I was sick and in prison and you did not look after me."

They also will answer, "Lord, when did we see you hungry or thirsty or a stranger or needing clothes or sick or in prison, and did not help you?"

He will reply, "I tell you the truth, whatever you did not do for one of the least of these, you did not do for me."

John, too, warns us to love not only with words, but also with actions. "If anyone has material possessions and sees his brother in need but has no pity on him, how can the love of God be in him? Dear children, let us not love with words or tongue but with actions and in truth" (1 John 3:17-18).

James 2:14-18 has a similar message:

What good is it, my brothers, if a man claims to have faith but has no deeds? Can such faith save him? Suppose a brother or sister is without clothes and daily food. If one of you says to him,

"Go, I wish you well; keep warm and well fed," but does nothing about his physical needs, what good is it? In the same way, faith by itself, if it is not accompanied by action, is dead. But someone will say, "You have faith; I have deeds." Show me your faith without deeds, and I will show you my faith by what I do.

What was true then is still true today. Certainly there is more to the task of caring for the poor than mere words. Yet responding to the poor with material goods alone will not fulfill the biblical mandates for human development, either. We must embrace a more encompassing model.

HOLISTIC CHRISTIAN CHILD DEVELOPMENT

Since this book is about holistic child development, it is good at this point to clarify what we mean by this term. We start with the word *holistic*. We have said that holism has to do with wholeness. In our context, we are talking about the truth of persons made in the image of God being spiritual as well as physical beings. Biblical holism sees all aspects of the person as equally significant, and refuses to dichotomize the spiritual from the physical or other aspects of the person.

When we speak, then, of *biblical* (or *Christian*) holistic child development we are emphasizing that the attention given to any component of the person needs to be done from a biblical perspective. We seek to understand God's view of personhood.

A fully biblical (Old and New Testament) perspective of the person will provide a fully Christian perspective. By definition, a biblical or Christian view of development will include spiritual nurture as well as attention to physical, social, psychological, and other aspects of the person. *Christian*, then, refers primarily to the biblical roots of our understanding. It also refers to our motivations and intended outcomes, whereas *holistic* refers to the scope of our development interests.

The biblical concept of holism embodies the ideas of completeness, perfection, oneness, integration, soundness, integrity, harmony, regained health, restored relations with God, peace with ourselves and our fellow human beings, and respect for the environment.[3] Dr. John Wong helpfully suggests that the concept of *shalom* (peace) in the Old Testament is congruent with the concept of Christian Holism.[4]

> "*Shalom*," he writes, "which occurs some 250 times in the Old Testament, has a basic meaning of completeness, soundness, welfare, peace, contentment, peace with God, making whole, making good, restoring what was lost or stolen (Joel 2:25, Exo. 21:37). The word embodies the meaning of material prosperity in comprehensive meaning of rest, freedom from care, safety, trustfulness, and ease; communal well-being in contrast to war; and a state of law and order leading to prosperity. It denotes bodily health; contentedness on living and at death. It also has the sense of salvation (Isa. 43:7, Jer. 29:11; 14:13). It has a social and political reference beyond the personal dimension. It is

associated with righteousness, concrete ideas of law and judgment."

Dr. Wong suggests that the starting point for Christian holism in the New Testament is Jesus' affirming the overarching, most important commandment, "Love the LORD your God with all your heart [*kardias*] and with all your soul [*psyches*] and with all your mind [*dianoias*] and with all your strength [*ischus*]. The second is this: "Love your neighbor as yourself. There is no commandment greater than these" (Mark 12:30-31; Matthew 22:37-40; Luke 10:27).[5]

The overlapping aspects of a child, Dr. Wong writes, are represented here by the **heart**—the seat of physical, spiritual, and mental life, encompassing the whole inner life of thinking, understanding, spiritual enlightenment, volition, will, moral decisions, emotions, love, desires, wishes, feelings; and by the **soul**—the center of life in its many and varied aspects, in all the expressions of what makes a human human; and by the **mind**—the reasoning, thinking, intellectual, cognitive creative, purposive, imaginative, conceptual and psychological domains; and by the **strength**—the physical, corporeal, tangible, sexual, biological, bodily dimension of a person.[6]

Luke 2:52 is a key verse that provides a model for the kind of development we are talking about. This verse simply says, "Jesus grew in wisdom and stature and in favor with God and men." These four components—wisdom, stature, favor with God, and favor with man—neatly encompass all aspects of the whole person. They also provide a useful model around which to create meaningful holistic development programs. Our objective in Christian holistic development is that all those with whom we work, especially the children, have the opportunity to grow and develop in wisdom, in stature and in favor with God and man.

One other point: We are reminded by Keith White not to view the spiritual (or other components) as just one piece of a puzzle or a mosaic with lots of pieces. Doing so encourages looking at the various components in isolation. A more helpful view is to think of a fabric—where the spiritual and all the other components are woven together inseparable and where every part contributes to an indivisible whole.[7]

I like the way the aspiration toward, and benefits of, biblical wholeness—everything coming together for good—is reflected in Eugene Peterson's version of Philippians 4:6-7:

> Don't fret or worry. Instead of worrying, pray. Let petitions and praises shape your worries into prayers, letting God know your concerns. Before you know it, *a sense of God's wholeness, everything coming together for good*, will come and settle you down. It's wonderful what happens when Christ displaces worry at the center of your life (emphasis added).

It is one thing to speak of biblical wholeness in theory. It is far more rewarding to see it embodied. Biblical wholeness is embodied in Mukamwiza Jeannette, a young Rwandan woman. Jeannette lost both her parents and all but one sibling during the war and genocide of 1994. Jeannette was 7 at the time.

Jeannette and her surviving brother were taken in by a kind person from Kigali, Rwanda's capital city. Shortly after, their newfound guardian registered the children in a Compassion child development center. Through this Christian holistic development initiative, the children were provided an education, clothing, medical treatment, and meals as needed. Just as important, they were nurtured spiritually through encounters with both the Bible and a caring staff.

Every component of that well-rounded development program was necessary. A year into the program, Jeannette began having flashbacks. Horrible memories of her parents' and loved ones' murders haunted Jeannette night and day. Robbed of sleep and peace, Jeannette began having seizures. Jeannette's support network helped in every way they could, including appointments with psychiatrists to supplement her regular regimen in the development program.

For Jeannette, moving forward meant a visit with one staff person who explained the comfort and freedom to be found in a relationship with Jesus Christ. Once Jeannette took that step, she learned how to deal with her illness through prayer. The symptoms diminished, and then vanished. Today, Jeannette is a healed and healthy young woman in her early 20s. She looks back with thanksgiving for the care given to her whole person—physically, emotionally, socially, and spiritually.

For Jeannette, God's wholeness—everything coming together for the good—is reaching its full measure.

WHAT DO WE MEAN BY *DEVELOPMENT?*

Development is not a biblical term, but the idea is certainly present in terms that express the ideas of growth and revelation. (Some evangelicals prefer the term *transformation* to development. They believe that *development* is too wedded to a secular agenda to convey the radical change that is needed in order to bring blessing to a world of need).[8] God created human beings with full potential for growth. He created us to handle the resources of the earth in cooperation with others in a way that would reveal His wisdom and glory as our Maker.[9]

People involved in the work of development know that it is hard to define; it's also often misunderstood. Experienced development workers know that they don't always have answers to relevant questions. (We may suspect that we don't have many at all.) Development is not simply a linear process in moving a child from A to B. Nor is it just a matter of mixing in all the ingredients in proper measure to ensure that the child turns out right. Some would like development to be bounded like that.[10]

Part of the difficulty is that development workers, particularly those from the West, prefer predictability. We don't like surprises. Especially in our development efforts, we like to see something concrete accomplished. We like to see our efforts produce dependable, predictable, visible results—like accountants or builders get, for example.

Too often development workers and organizations take a "bounded" view of development. With such a view, they are ones who define development. Child development will be what they say it is. They will assume that they will recognize it if and when they see it. They will set up specific criteria and "minimum standards," which will enable them to measure development and evaluate progress.

Those with a bounded view of development will seek to retain almost all control.

Unfortunately, they may ignore the processes that characterize development. If child development is bounded, then children are either developed or undeveloped, right? When the undeveloped children meet our standards—and not before—they will be "developed." In this view, the steps along the way and the processes of change may be seen as necessary struggles but without value.

With such a view, the goal of the development workers will be to see children reach our standards. We may not realize that even if all standards or goals are achieved, the result may be a failure. For example, if we have created dependence (as in the U.S. welfare system) or if the goals were misguided in the first place, we have failed. Likewise, we will not be aware that it is possible to miss the standards/goals entirely and still achieve success.

The result may be evil as well as good. Affluence can bring greed, selfishness, and materialism. The Bible points out that the rich become prisoners of their wealth. The oppressed may readily and quickly become the oppressors when given the opportunity. Disruption of the family may come with relatively small increments of wealth. ("Development" in the west has been coincident with rising crime rates, oppression, and many other social problems.) Good theory doesn't always work in practice.

Development is characterized by growth, change, and learning. It is a process of *becoming*. Development should be a process by which people become whole. And so we are back to holism.

Holistic child development is also a *ministry*. For our purposes here, we are talking specifically about the work that Christians do on behalf of the needy, and in our case, what they do on behalf of children. We call it not simply good works, but a *ministry* of *Christian holistic* child development. This ministry is the work of the Church and God's people to enable needy children and families to overcome their poverty and neediness and to become all that God has intended them to be.

It is helpful to contrast the *ministry* of development—that is the work of God's people on behalf of the poor and oppressed—with the kind of secular development work done by many non-Christians and organizations that are not specifically Christian in motivation or objective. Many organizations do what they call *holistic* development, or *integrated development* or some other term, emphasizing that they are concerned with the "whole" person. In such cases, the "whole person" usually refers to the physical, emotional, psychological, and other aspects of the individual. All of these aspects of the person are important, and indeed, the activities and interventions made on behalf of the *whole person* following these strategies may be more or less the same whether done by Christians or non-Christians. However, the motivations and intended outcomes of these programs may be quite different from those in programs done by Christians.

Most important, secular development by definition leaves out the crucial consideration of the essential spiritual needs of the individual. They can't include it because they know nothing about it or even deny its existence. Christians know that true development is impossible without attention to spiritual needs.[11]

It should be clear from the above that development is not about providing money or material goods or any other kind of "stuff." That is exactly the problem with many well-intentioned but shortsighted secular approaches to development. As we will see, "welfare" is a disastrous manifestation of this truncated approach to helping.

Below are a few things that may characterize Christian holistic development with respect to children. Some of these ideas will be developed in later chapters. (This is not a complete list, but a good foundation upon which to build.) Christian holistic development is characterized by:

1. Helping children grow like Jesus did—in "wisdom and stature and in favor with God and man" (Luke 2:52).
2. Helping children and families know the truth of their worth and potential because they are made in the image of God.
3. Enabling children to become what God wants them to be.
4. Awakening children to their self-potential—that they can and must make a difference in their own lives.
5. Helping children understand their role as stewards and their relationship to creation.
6. Providing children and families with

opportunities—not just things—and a mind-set to grasp those opportunities.

7. Creating an understanding of their *dominion over creation* and their opportunities and responsibilities to use God's resources for their benefit.

8. Promoting self-reliance. (See below)

9. Directing toward wholeness and completeness.

10. Ensuring that goals, motivation, and methods are biblical and seek to bring people into a right relationship with creation and their Creator.

WHAT CHRISTIAN HOLISTIC DEVELOPMENT IS *NOT*

It is also useful to state clearly what Christian holistic development is *not*. Holistic development is certainly not **welfare.** Many societies have created extensive "welfare" programs to care for the needy and less fortunate among them. Welfare programs usually make no distinctions between the *deserving* and *undeserving* poor. Assistance is provided simply based on a person's income or status, regardless of why that person has become needy, what destructive behaviors he or she may have engaged in, or what his or her real needs, abilities, and potential are. Continued giving, especially of money, aggravates the problem rather than solving it.

Holistic development is also most certainly not just a matter of having more money. Money is useful, but it is not the answer to the problems of poverty and underdevelopment. The continued problem of poverty in the United States, in spite of *massive* amounts of money distributed to the poor in various welfare programs, is a good example of the ineffectiveness of welfare. In the 1960s, U.S. President Lyndon B. Johnson declared "war on poverty." Since that time, the U.S. has spent nearly seven *trillion* dollars on programs to alleviate poverty in the U.S. Seven *trillion* dollars is a lot of money—even in Washington! Has it solved the problem of poverty in America? Of course not. There are more poor people and people caught in a poverty trap than ever before. Why? Because poverty, as we will see, is not a matter of money. In fact, the roots of poverty are not material at all. At its most basic level, poverty is a spiritual problem.

Christian holistic development is also certainly not **westernization**. As we will see, the secularism of the West is one of the "hollow and deceptive philosophies" as warned against in Colossians 2:8. Secularism leads to death and destruction, perhaps not immediately or directly, but ultimately and inevitably. A great deal of "development work" is done by secular people from affluent Western countries. Sometimes these well-intentioned practitioners import their Western values, attitudes, economic theories, and secular worldview. They also mistake their Western cultural values for universal development principles. Such values are often quite inappropriate for needy people in a non-Western context.

Indeed, holistic development is not **something done for children and families** at all, but rather *with* them. The well-known development poem by James Yen[12] says it well:

Go to the people.
Learn from them.
Work with them.
Plan with them.
Teach by showing; learn by doing.
Not a showcase, but a pattern.
Not odds and ends, but a system.
Not relief, but release.
Start with what they know,
and build upon what they have.

Finally, holistic development is also not **paternalism or patronism.** The first is giving without dialogue on the perspectives, capacities, and felt needs of those we would assist. **Paternalism** is an attitude based on the belief that the more powerful and better-off can help those who are needier but without changing the hierarchical status between the two. Paternalism assumes that the "father figure" is wiser and has the right answers and the right methods, without consideration for the wishes and the giftedness and the contribution of those who are being helped.

Patronism is similar. It also assumes a fatherly figure who wants to help, is generous, "knows what is best," and gives anything and everything without assessing suitability, alternatives, or consequences. Usually such giving has a self-serving component, ensuring that the recipient understands the dependent relationship and will give suitable recognition to the giver.

A KEY RESULT OF DEVELOPMENT: SELF-RELIANCE

One aspect of development—whether child, community, health, economic, or spiritual—is to bring the person to a position of self-reliance or self-sufficiency. This result means that the ones once in need now look to their own knowledge, strength, funds, or other resources to meet their own needs. Self-reliance is a fundamental concept. It is talked about a good deal but needs closer examination to understand and to achieve.

Self-reliance, of course, combines two words—*self* and *reliance. Self* is the identity or character of the person, one's personality, or one's own welfare or interest. *Reliance* is to rely on, to trust, to depend upon, or to have confidence in. When we speak of self-reliance, we mean the trust or confidence that one has within himself or herself. Development activities that do not bring people to a greater trust, dependence, or confidence within themselves are not authentic development.

Note, however, that self-reliance is not a mindless independence that refuses outside assistance in whatever form simply because it is from the outside. A defiant refusal to learn from one's parents, peers, or neighbors, for whatever reason, will stifle imagination and lead to stagnation.

Self-reliance is also not the selfish independence of the Westerner whose individual drive makes him ever more greedy and ruthless. The model of the West is, "You can do it! Look at me. I did it!" Or to put it in the words of an old popular song,

"I Did It My Way." These egotistical tendencies tend to lead to a breakdown of the extended family ties and of the willingness to work with others.

The secular socialist or communal economic models are no better. The premise in these systems is that, given the right circumstances and resources, people will tend toward creating supportive, harmonious societies. Unfortunately, the premise is false because human values are flawed. Without Christian values, people tend to think only selfishly of themselves.

Finally, self-reliance is not a substitute for faith. As Christians, we believe that all good things come from God. We have only what He gives us and what He wants us to have, whether it be money, talents, or other resources. The more we mature as Christians, the more we learn to lean on His wisdom and to depend on Him for what He will provide. The paradox of self-reliance for the Christian is that it means more and more dependence, not on our own resources, but on the infinite resources of Christ.

What characteristics distinguish the person or child who is becoming self-reliant from the one who is becoming dependent? The following stand out:

1. The self-reliant person is aware of her own resources and of their value. She knows she is made in the image of God and has inherent worth. She knows that her gifts, talents, money, time, land, muscles, good will, cultural insights, etc. are worth much in enabling her to cope with and solve her own problems.

2. She is aware that she can make a difference in her own life through her own efforts. She knows that things do not always have to be the same as they have always been. She recognizes that change can be a rewarding process and does not fear it.

3. A self-reliant person has a feel for the value of her own contribution. She knows where she fits in, and she knows her worth. And she knows that all these are valuable.

4. A self-reliant person does not depend on someone else to meet her basic needs. While she is not a person who relies solely on herself, she is not dependent on outside money, ideas, motivation, know-how, technology, food or materials to satisfy her needs and aspirations.

5. The self-reliant person is self-confident, but not cocky or arrogant, knowing from experience that she can do worthwhile things and overcome problems. Henry Ford is credited with saying, "Think you can, think you can't—either way you will be right." The self-reliant person thinks she can—and usually she is right.

6. A self-reliant person is a problem solver. She recognizes that everyone has problems and that problems can be opportunities for learning, growth, and achievement.

7. A self-reliant person has alternatives and makes choices.

PROMOTING SELF-RELIANCE

In considering self-reliance, there are useful insights to be gained from our efforts to promote self-esteem and self-confidence in our own children. We do not make our own children independent and self-reliant, for example, by giving them everything they want. We know that some things are not useful to them, some things are dangerous, and some things are detrimental.

On the other hand, we do not make our children self-reliant by withholding support. We help them with things they need. We give them security and a warm, loving environment. We encourage, we teach, and we give room for experimentation and room for failure. We do not give indiscriminately but as needed and as appropriate. We ensure that the children make their own contribution—that they do their chores, participate in family activities, come to meals on time, and cooperate with the goals and the aspirations of the family.

We don't ignore or minimize the contributions of the children's own parents, relatives, and communities in the nurture and development of their children.

Self-reliance is a delicate balance. While it refers to a condition of independence, in another sense it most assuredly is not independence that is sought. Rather, the ideal is a vulnerable "interdependence" on resources and goodwill—not just from within the person or group, but from appropriate resources wherever they may be found.

How can we provide input to children to encourage healthy self-reliance? What kinds of assistance can we provide so that they can concentrate on their studies and have the security that they need, while at the same time not create an unhealthy dependence on the funds that we provide? Here are a few ideas:

1. Don't do for people—children, parents, teachers or others—what they can do for themselves.
2. When planning interventions, look for a contribution both in cash and in kind from the beneficiaries. Often people tend to undervalue their own time, labor, or other intangible inputs.
3. Put the focus on learning. Learning is the one thing that children can acquire that they will be able to take with them and use in future situations. Learning will serve them not just for today, but for the future.
4. Start where the children are and with what they have available in and of themselves, including their own interests and priorities.
5. Encourage! Positively reinforce the small steps that children and their parents take to meet their own needs and solve their own problems.
6. Take a little at a time. Go at the pace of the child or group of which he is a part. Small successes are crucial to gain the confidence to take the next steps.
7. Know when to phase out. Recognize the indicators that let us know when we have provided enough of one kind of input for the children and move

on to something else. (If a project doesn't phase out, it will probably fizzle out!)

8. Understand how people define "success" in their own context. What results and outcomes of child assistance activities will they perceive as successful or worthwhile?

9. Give the people the same luxury we give ourselves—the right to fail. We learn to depend upon ourselves not only through our success experiences, but also in overcoming our shortcomings and our failures.

10. Don't make promises that cannot be kept. Don't start things that cannot be sustained.

Self-reliance is a process, not a point in time. Long-term programs give the opportunity for interaction between the children and the people responsible for their development over a long period. But long-term assistance can create either a healthy self-reliance or a helpless dependence on our funds and other inputs. We have a big responsibility to ensure that the assistance is beneficial, rather than destructive in the end.

FACILITATING GOOD DEVELOPMENT

Let's briefly note some of the key components of good development work. A full treatment of the work of development is beyond the scope of this book. However, here are some of the essentials of good development work and development workers. In every case, we will see Jesus as an example and model.

Raising awareness. Effective development workers (often called facilitators) never *impose* change. They recognize that fundamental change comes from both *within* people and that any kind of manipulation implies lack of respect. Rather, change can be *facilitated* by respectful awareness-raising. (Some people have called this process *conscientization.*) It implies starting where people are, appreciating what they already know and understand, and building on those things in appropriate ways. It is oriented toward helping children and their families discover their own abilities and resources. Facilitation combines listening, questioning, provoking, and challenging people (children and families) to reflect on their situation and discover internal or local resources to address that situation.

Jesus was a master facilitator. He took every opportunity to get people to think about what they were experiencing. His methods in building spiritual awareness are the methods of good facilitators in holistic development. Jesus asked leading questions,[13] used contextual illustrations,[14] and responded aptly to their leading questions.[15]

Increasing knowledge, skills, and attitudes. Effective facilitators communicate more, though, than just raising awareness. In particular they build self-esteem, self-confidence in children, and the motivation and creativity that spring from new hope. Complementing this, they promote an increased sense of responsibility especially in such areas as stewardship of talents, resources, and opportunities, care for the environment and commitment to diligence and quality in work ethics. They also seek to enhance the overall development of children in terms of knowledge, skills, and attitudes.

Here again, we learn from Jesus. He exposed the disciples to situations that taught them a range of basic truths. He affirmed the dignity of all people, especially the poor or marginalized[16] and, as He taught what is recorded in Matthew 20, "not to be served but to serve." As seen in Matthew 10, Jesus gave His disciples opportunities to gain practical experience and learn related guidelines. He taught appropriate information, often allowing it to arise from the immediate context.[17]

Building relationships. Relationship building is primary. Without it, anything else the development facilitator may strive to do will be impossible. Relationship building involves building trust, two-way communication, understanding, and mutual respect.

John 4 is an example of Jesus doing relationship building. The Samaritan woman at the village well presented a significant challenge to Jesus' relationship-building skills. The barriers of gender, race, culture, historical tensions, education, social status, and fatigue all added to the fact that these two were simply strangers. Yet Jesus broke through using a remarkably simple approach of affirmation, respect, provocative state-ments, and gentle probing questions. We can learn more about Jesus' relationship building from His dealings with Nicodemus, Zacchaeus, the rich young ruler, the father of a demonized boy, sick and poor people, Mary and Martha, and many others.

Modeling—setting an example. Modeling is essential for any development worker but especially so for those who work with children. Childcare workers make as much of an impact through their lives as in their words. This is true both in the teaching/showing/doing of learning activities as well as in providing a spiritual example.

Modeling was Jesus' approach throughout His ministry. He clearly communicated messages by His own actions and attitudes, as well as by the service itself.[18] He expected the disciples (and others) to take notice.[19] Sometimes His actions were deliberately provocative, as in His demonstration of His attitude to children[20] and the use of these incidents to teach about the kingdom. Jesus also taught that following Him would result in a life of light, because He is the light.[21]

Resource linking. A final aspect of facilitating development is helping to link people to needed resources. The resources may include local materials, government goods and services, low-cost supplies, advice, expertise and counseling, information, pastoral care, and spiritual resources.

Even in this area, Jesus left us with examples. When He sent the disciples out for ministry, He linked a resource—the disciples—with the needs of the people of the towns and at the same time the people of the towns had to use their resources to supply the disciples' needs.

THE DIRECTION OF DEVELOPMENT

The direction of development is always toward wholeness. It is not enough to improve only one dimension of a person's life and leave other dimensions inadequate. To treat parasitic infection is noble. But if a treated child is left in an unsanitary environment with contaminated water, the intervention is incomplete. If a family's economic situation is improved but a debilitating health problem is not solved, the intervention is incomplete. If a person receives an education but social structures prevent him from getting a job, the intervention is incomplete. If a person is introduced to faith in Christ and enjoys spiritual freedom but is left in poverty and oppression, the intervention is incomplete. The scope of development is toward completeness and holism.

Holistic development releases people to exercise responsibility for themselves. The bonds and restraints of poverty, ignorance, and oppression are broken, and people are free to take charge of their own lives. Holistic development leads children and families to options. They can make choices. A range of opportunities opens up to them. All of this is therapy to the mind and soul. They feel better about themselves. Confidence and self-esteem rise. Defeatism dies. And hope blossoms.

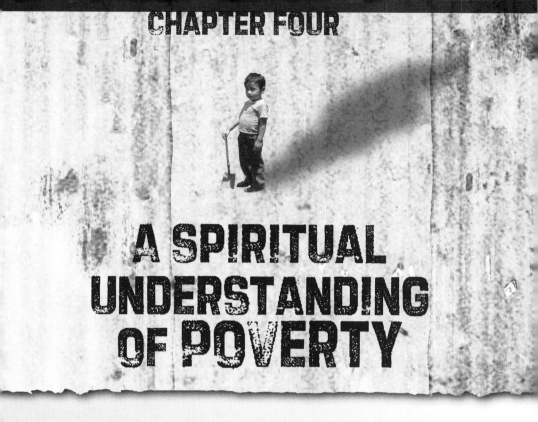

CHAPTER FOUR

A SPIRITUAL UNDERSTANDING OF POVERTY

The thief comes only to steal and kill and destroy; I have
come that they may have life, and have it to the full.
John 10:10

Child poverty cannot be defined solely in terms of
the hunger, malnutrition, trafficking, exploitation,
or even by the child's parents' financial or economic
situation. These things give us only a part of the
picture. The same is true for poverty. What makes a
person poor is not simply a lack of material things.
Poverty is a complex issue with profound spiritual
roots. In search for the solution, it is important to
address the nature of the problem. So what exactly
is poverty? And what are some of the causes of
poverty, especially among children?

WHAT IS POVERTY?

Poverty has been defined in many ways. Most common are varieties of explanations of ineffective economic or distribution systems, ignorance, warfare, or ethnic conflicts, and other evils, all of which contribute to much suffering and the misery of the poor. Very briefly, some of the more common theoretical understandings of poverty follow.

Poverty as deficits. The poor lack things such as food, shelter, land, and clean water. Sometimes they lack ideas, skills, or knowledge. Christian development workers will often suggest a lack of understanding about God and the gospel is another important kind of deficit.

This view is the flipside of the "development as 'stuff'" approach. Of course, it is true that the poor have many deficits and shortages. Often an appropriate response *is* helping children and families gain access to the things they need. However, viewing poverty as primarily a matter of deficits suggests that the work of development should be viewed as a matter of providing what is lacking. Taken to an extreme, this view of poverty can lead to development workers being viewed as a kind of "Santa Claus," bringing good things and providing what the poor lack.[1]

Poverty as a "web of entanglements." Robert Chambers from the Institute of Development Studies at the University of Sussex in England uses the phrase "web of entanglements," which, he says, create a poverty trap for the poor. The web of entanglements includes material poverty, physical weakness, isolation, vulnerability, and powerlessness. To this list Bryant Myers again adds spiritual poverty, for each of these has a spiritual dimension.[2] Each element in the web is interrelated to, and reinforcing of, the others. A problem in one area means problems in every other area, resulting in a downward cycle of greater and greater poverty. This web of entanglements view is a helpful approach to understanding poverty.

Lack of options. Others suggest that poverty is essentially a lack of choices or options. The lives of the poor are dictated for them. They rarely take part in the choices that shape their environment and future. Governments and those with power often make decisions on behalf of the poor. Since the poor do not own land or businesses, they are not seen to contribute in significant ways to the development of a country. Consequently, they are overlooked in the decision-making processes.

Needy children of this world are denied opportunities that could contribute to their complete development. Many do not have access to schooling, medical care, or adequate nutrition. Children who grow up without options turn into adults without options.

Without sufficient education, needy children will discover that well-paid and reputable jobs are out of their reach. Business owners know their desperation and offer unskilled and low-paid jobs in frequently appalling conditions. In many cases, the desperation of a family is so bad that even the children are forced to work or even be sold.

The debilitating message of poverty is, "You have no options and there is nothing you can do to change your situation." This sense of powerlessness chips away at self-esteem in the poor. Too often, they abandon hope. A spirit of fatalism sets in—and another generation becomes victims.

This view, too, provides helpful insights into the complexities of poverty.

Poverty as a lack of wholeness.[3] This view sees poverty as a lack of wholeness, not just a lack of money or other necessities. It is based on the simple observation that we have stressed, about the "wholeness" of every human, and the many elements of life that contribute to that wholeness.

Poverty as a lack of wholeness can be represented like a wheel that is inadequate for the load it is supposed to carry. It may be either totally broken or just out of balance. Either condition renders the wheel inoperable. (Have you ever tried to ride a bicycle with a broken or bent rim? Then you have an idea of what life out of balance is like.)

The poverty wheel shown here has six spokes: spiritual, physical, economic, social/political, mental/emotional and environmental. (It could have several more, representing other

aspects of the whole person.) Each of these sections must be adequate in relation to others in order for the wheel to be balanced and run smoothly.

In some places, children grow up in conditions where virtually every spoke of their "wheel" is inadequate. That is extreme poverty. In other places, children have the appearance of being better off but, in fact, are equally poor because of a serious inadequacy in one or more section of their "wheel." They are not whole or complete. They will grow up to be less functional than they might have been as adults had they developed more holistically during their childhood.

Notice that a spoke in the wheel that is *too long* will also prevent the wheel from turning smoothly. Suppose the economic spoke is exaggerated; a person has so much wealth that he loses all focus on other aspects of life. As a result, he becomes socially or environmentally unfit, also suffering from a form of poverty.

THE CAUSES OF POVERTY: ALL THE USUAL SUSPECTS?

The ideas we hold about poverty invariably connect to our core beliefs about the causes of poverty. There are, of course, many factors that may contribute to poverty. Calamity, war, and injustice are very common—and real—causes of poverty.

For many years, development strategists pointed to what they viewed as a looming problem of **overpopulation:** the inability of the world's resources to keep up with the food and employment needs of growing masses of people. Frightening scenarios were painted of exploding populations and shrinking food supplies leading to mass starvation and food scarcity violence. While population trends are now decidedly trending toward too few new births rather than too many, it is surprising that many people still trot out overpopulation as a significant cause for poverty in the world.

Walking the crowded, filthy slums of any major city in the world will certainly lead one to agree that too many people in one place can be a significant cause of massive poverty. Without a doubt, *overcrowding* (not overpopulation) in the major cities of the world, especially in the developing nations, overwhelms the capabilities of these cities. Overcrowding causes shortages in water, sanitation, and power systems; unfairness in political and justice systems; inadequacies in the provision of education, jobs, and other services.

There is no denying that the problems caused by local overcrowding are immense. Plenty of alarmists believe that population growth is *the* most pressing problem facing the world today. But overcrowding is, in fact, more often *a result* of poverty—not a major *cause*. And the truth is, as we all now know, that global population is beginning to level off. A much bigger problem for the future of many countries will not be overpopulation, but not having enough people!

To maintain the same population, a nation needs to have 2.1 children per woman. (It would be 2.0 except for infant and other mortality before some reach childbearing age.) This is called the Total Fertility Rate (TFR). Ben Wattenberg, in his book *Fewer*, notes that TFRs have dropped dramatically not only in more developed countries, but also in less developed countries.

For example, Wattenberg notes that due to the One Child Policy, China has a TFR of around 1.8. There are a number of outcomes that spring from China's TFR. My daughter and her husband are missionaries in China and recently made me aware of some of the outcomes not noted elsewhere. It was simple logic. She began by noting that none of the One Child Policy children will have any brothers and sisters. (I knew that!) But, she added, neither will those children have any aunts or uncles. They will have no cousins. They will have no nieces or nephews. In short, *the whole of the extended family will be destroyed.* This is indeed happening not just in China where One Child is an official policy, but also in the many other nations and societies where there is a *de facto* one-child policy. This is not to mention the other terrible costs, including widespread female infanticide, a hugely distorted gender ratio, and horrors such as mass sterilization and forced abortions.

Surprisingly, Wattenberg predicts that if, as seems likely, TFR rates continue to fall throughout the world (there are now more than 100 nations whose TFR is below 2.1),[4] it is quite possible that total world population will peak at slightly fewer than eight billion people in the middle of the century and then drop to 5.5 billion by the end of the century[5]—fewer people than are on our planet today! Clearly, overpopulation is *not* a major cause of poverty in the world now, and it will apparently be less of a problem in the future.

Another commonly cited cause of poverty is **ineffective economic systems or poor distribution.** Some development theorists argue for wealth creating strategies for the rich and powerful, and the benefits then "trickle down" to the poor. Others maintain that the leveling effect of eliminated class structures in the communist systems was supposed to do away with economic inequalities and bring prosperity (or at least adequacy) to all.

Somehow, though, both systems tend to lead to a concentration of wealth and power in the hands of a few. The poor get left out. These inherently unequal and unjust economic systems can contribute significantly to poverty.

Corruption and exploitation, in any of their many forms, also contribute substantially to the poverty and misery of many people. There is always a very high correlation between high levels of corruption and poverty. Undeniably corruption, which inevitably includes or leads to exploitation of the powerless and a long-term wounding of a whole society, is a significant cause of poverty.

"Structural" causes of poverty focus on perceived societal barriers to an adequate lifestyle. These can include oppressive class structures; the lack of access to (and the unfairness of) judicial systems for the poor; and the manipulation, corruption, and ruthlessness of landowners, merchants, money lenders, monopolistic industrial producers, "foreigners," and other entities in positions of power. Such analyses are the basis of much radical political thinking and theological reflection. Historically, they led to, for example, the rise of Marxism and communism. More recently, they gave rise to various kinds of liberation theologies and much effort on the part of many activist NGOs.

These structural and systemic issues have a profound adverse effect on the poor. However, a weakness of this structural view of poverty pointed out by Jayakumar Christian,[6] former director of World Vision in India, is the tendency for this view to place all the blame on the "outside" other. This tendency focuses on the outside, without a commensurate critique of internal factors. Christian notes that this can cause the poor to take on a "victim posture."[7] This victim posture— "My problems are someone else's fault"—often leads to a kind of *pauperism*, a mind-set of poverty, and a failure or even refusal to do anything to help oneself or deal personally with one's problems or challenges. It is this level at which I would like to give most attention here. Personal responsibility for one's problems is an essential premise in overcoming them.

Moreover, from a biblical standpoint, it is very important to understand that these are all rooted in sin and the fallenness of mankind—in other words, they have spiritual roots.

A SPIRITUAL VIEW OF POVERTY

Dealing with poverty demands a perspective that goes beyond mere economic matters straight to issues of the heart. All of the above factors are significant in causing and perpetuating poverty. All of the above reflections on the causes of poverty—corruption, exploitation, overpopulation, deficits, entanglements, and the like—contain elements of the truth. All of the above warrant attention from the careful development worker.

However, as Christians, we must be aware that these and other "causes" are, in fact, primarily the *results* rather than *causes* of poverty. As we study the Bible, we will begin to understand that poverty is not just a lack of material wealth or other shortages. Poverty is not only corruption or calamity or disempowering entanglements. We should not make the mistake of thinking that the problems of poverty and underdevelopment have only material roots.

The perspective that I want to explore here is the fact that, at its most basic level, the problem of poverty is most fundamentally a **spiritual** problem. A biblical view of poverty understands its rootedness in sin, which Genesis 3 tells us entered the world through Adam. Sin has resulted in brokenness in our relationships with each other, with ourselves, with the natural world, and fundamentally with God. The consequences of such broken relationships are far-flung and widespread. Unjust social and economic conditions, scarcity of natural resources, some natural disasters, and exploitative, self-destructive or irresponsible behaviors are just the beginning.

This is not to say that the poverty of individuals is necessarily rooted in their personal sin. For sure "all have sinned," and a person's sin and unrighteousness very often does result in poor choices, dissipation, and impoverishment. But we are not saying that the poor are poor because they are personally sinful. Instead, the fallenness of mankind and the effects of sin have resulted in a world where exploitation, corruption, and many other factors both internal and external now work together to produce the ugliness and misery of poverty.

Thankfully, this understanding of the root of poverty is also what gives hope. The brokenness that once came into the world does not have to continue. Romans 5:10-12 states that God has sent His Son, Jesus, to bring life and reconciliation. The very life and ministry of Christ shows how He intended men and women to overcome the depth and breadth of the poverty that afflicts so many.[8]

This is why the work of holistic development—the kind of development that addresses the problem of the whole person, including the physical and the spiritual needs—must be the work of Christians. It is Christians who, through the Bible, have the answer to the problem of sin, and thus the necessary and essential means of addressing it.

WORLDVIEW—A KEY TO UNDERSTANDING POVERTY

Worldview is an essential key to understanding how holistic development takes root in people's hearts and minds. Some have said that worldview is like a pair of colored glasses or lenses that "color" or influence how a person understands the world around him. Dr. Charles Kraft of Fuller Seminary defines worldview as "all the assumptions, values, and commitments/allegiances underlying a people's perception of reality."[9] Similarly, Darrow Miller puts it this way: "A worldview is a set of assumptions held consciously or unconsciously in faith about the basic makeup of the world and how the world works."[10]

Worldview, then, is the mental map that all people have that helps them make sense of an often confusing and unpredictable world. Consider the basic human questions: "Why do bad things happen to good people?" "Is there a right and wrong?" "What is truth, and does it even exist?" "Is there a God?" "Why do bad people prosper?" All people in the world, at all times, have puzzled about these seeming injustices. (See, for example, the cry of Habakkuk, or that of Job in 24:1-12). For some, these seemingly unfathomable "wrongs" in the world are enough for them to conclude that there is no God. "How could a loving God," we often hear them ask, "allow such suffering and injustice in the world?"

A person's (or a society's) worldview helps people come to grips with such imponderables. Indeed, as Darrow Miller points out, an individual's worldview can affect his or her destiny—can tend to lead to hopefulness and sufficiency, or to despair and deprivation:

> All people ask basically the same questions. The answers they give, however, are radically different, depending on their worldviews. The way people and societies answer these questions determines the types of cultures and societies they create. Some answers to these questions lead to poverty and barbarism; others to development and civilization.[11]

Miller identifies three basic broad categories of worldviews that encompass in broad strokes the worldviews of most of the people in the world. An exploration of the premises—and consequences—of these worldviews provide profound insight into the nature of poverty, as well as the most promising road map out of that poverty. These three *macro* worldviews are: [12]

1. **Secularism.** Secularism is the worldview of modern western societies. Secularists deny the existence of God and anything spiritual. They believe that "life is the result of the interactions of matter and energy, time, and chance." For secularists, matter, (or the material world) is the ultimate reality. Secularists do not believe in any universal truths or absolute morals.

2. **Animism.** A second major worldview is animism in all its various forms, such as Hinduism, Buddhism, "New Ageism" and many other variations. "Spirits animate everything, and everything moves toward oneness of spirit. The material world is 'bad' or unimportant. The real world is unseen, truth is hidden and irrational, all is mystery . . . filled with evil . . . [and] amoral."

3. **Theism.** Miller writes that theism "sees ultimate reality as personal and relational. God exists. He created a universe of physical and spiritual dimensions, seen and unseen worlds. Truth, as revealed by God, is objective and can be known by man. God's character establishes absolute morals. Theism holds to one personal-infinite God, the great 'I AM' of Scripture."[13]

All Bible-believing Christians should hold to some form of this worldview.

WORLDVIEWS HAVE CONSEQUENCES

As we reflect on poverty, the very important thing to note here is that *believing and living out the basic assumptions of each of these worldviews leads to more or less predictable consequences.* Both of the two nonbiblical worldviews *do* lead to moral ambiguity, to fatalism, to spiritual poverty and very often, ultimately to material poverty as well. On the other hand, a biblical worldview will contribute to wise stewardship of the resources that God provides, and very often an accumulation of material blessings as well. It will lead to an understanding of the sufficiency of the resources God has provided, and His intention that we steward and make use of them for our benefit. It will lead to an understanding of God's intention for His people to take effective action on their own behalf, not being slaves to fate and subject to the whims of chance or circumstances. Most often, at the very least, a biblical world-view will lead to an "adequacy" of material resources and to a sense of well-being. This is the experience of the "abundant life" that Jesus desires for all people.

Of course, neither animism nor secularism will necessarily lead *immediately* or *automatically* to material poverty, hope-lessness, and despair. The "live for the present" aspects of both of these worldviews may, in fact, lead to material wealth through greed, avarice, and a focus on accumulation. Many "bad" people are very well off. However, as we have said, these worldviews will ultimately and inevitably lead to death and destruction.

Likewise, people with a theistic (biblical) worldview will not always be materially wealthy or self-sufficient. Such people may, because of their biblical worldview, tend to be very generous and keenly focused more on spiritual resources than on material wealth. They may happily have only enough to get by. Or, due to persecution or harassment, they may be deprived of their possessions and live lives of scarcity and poverty. They may still be wronged, mistreated, or persecuted, and subjugated by exploitation, corruption and unfairness.

However, believing *and consistently acting on* the assumptions and understanding of the theistic (or biblical) worldview will, *inevitably*, lead to biblical wholeness, spiritual well-being in spite of circumstances, material adequacy, and resourcefulness in using one's own talents and available resources. Given opportunity, energy, and inspiration, they will take advantage of open doors and resources for their own good and that of others. How do we know this? As we have seen, there is ample practical evidence as well as many biblical promises to this effect.

JESUS COMES TO GIVE ABUNDANT LIFE

This abundant life is, in fact, what Jesus desires for all children and families regardless of race, background, nationality, or any other feature. We might say that this was Jesus' mission in coming to earth. Let us look closely at this important passage.

The declaration from Jesus, "I am come that they might have life and that they may have it more abundantly" (KJV), is set in the context of a shepherd's care for his sheep. The good shepherd, Jesus says, will care for the sheep, protect and provide for them. The sheep hear His voice, and know that they are free from danger. The sheep will "come in and go out, and find pasture" (John 10:9b).

The picture here is one of security and peacefulness. It is a picture of the sheep being what they are designed to be. The analogy of the Good Shepherd is, of course, a picture of Jesus' desire for His followers. His intention is that everyone will live in the same peace and security and, as it says in Psalm 23, "goodness and mercy" (KJV) will follow all the days of their lives. This is the wholeness in every aspect of the person about which we have written and which God desires for all His children.

Let us be careful, however, not to suggest that *abundant life* refers primarily to material wealth. It certainly does not refer to excesses of accumulation and acquisition. We are not preaching here some kind of "prosperity gospel." Abundant life does not mean "abundant stuff"—lots of material possessions and worldly goods. That is not what abundant life is all about.

What it *is* about is a life of wholeness and adequacy as described above. It is a life where one's own talents, giftedness, and creativity are developed and enjoyed. It is an environment where people (including children) are productive, have adequate education, and have enough resources to be healthy and well-nourished. They know that God's creation is there to meet all our needs and will learn to "take dominion" over the resources and aspects of their physical world. They have the motivation and inspiration to use their abilities and resources for their and others' benefit and well-being. They enjoy close and satisfying family relationships, joy (even in the midst of difficult circumstances), hope and peace and contentment with whatever God has provided.

The most important thing we can give poor children and families then, is not money, material assistance, or any other kind of stuff. Rather, it is an understanding of biblical truth and how to apply it in their own lives. Jesus said He is the way, the truth, and the *life* (John 14:6). They will know the truth, and the truth will make them free (John 8:32). That is God's intention for all His children, young and old alike.

THE THIEF COMES TO STEAL

In contrast to God's plan, there is also a thief out there who has exactly the opposite intentions for the sheep. That is why at the beginning of John 10:10, Jesus says, "The thief comes only to steal and kill and destroy." Who is this thief? Obviously, it is Satan. Satan does not want children or their families to have that abundant life. Satan is a liar. In fact, lying is his native tongue (see John 8:44)! And Satan will lie and do anything else he can to kill, steal, and destroy.

The apostle Paul talks about people exchanging the truth of God for a lie.[14] Ignoring God and believing Satan's lies leads to a downward spiral of poverty, death, and destruction. For so many hurting children around the world, Satan has stolen that abundant life. They are surrounded by ugliness, mistrust, corruption, exploitation, suffering, and misery. Satan wants children and families to believe his lies and to be enslaved, regardless of what opportunities and resources may be available.

The question is, are we going to believe the truths of the Bible or the lies of Satan? Having a biblical worldview—believing and following the truths of the Bible—leads to freedom, wholeness, and abundant life. But believing and following the lies underlying both the animistic and secular worldviews will ultimately lead to misery, death, and destruction.

In Colossians 2:8 Paul warns, "See to it that no one takes you captive through *hollow and deceptive philosophy*, which depends on human tradition and the basic principles of this world rather than on Christ." As we will see, nonbiblical worldviews are characterized by "hollow and deceptive philosophies." They are built on the human and worldly traditions. They are not based on truth. Rather, they are rooted in the lies of Satan.

BIBLICAL RESPONSES TO HOLLOW AND DECEPTIVE PHILOSOPHIES

So we ask the question, what are some of the fundamental "hollow and deceptive philosophies," or the lies of Satan that tend toward entrapment and enslavement in poverty? Here are some examples: [15]

1. One fundamental and extremely debilitating lie of Satan is the suggestion that **"There is no absolute or**

universal truth." Both **animism** and **secularism** say that there is no objective truth. Animists also argue that there is no truth, or that truth is unknowable. Secularism does no better. Western secularists say, "Believe anything you want." What is truth for you may not be truth for me. There is no objective right and wrong. Both Western secularism and Eastern animism say that the universe is amoral, irrational, and without compassion.

What the Bible says: You will know the truth and the truth will set you free. It is the truth—not money, not welfare, not handouts, not programs or schemes—that sets children and families free. When we look at Scriptures, we see how important truth is. God wants all people (including children) to know the truth.[16] The biblical mind-set understands that the universe is rational, understandable, and orderly. We can know truth because God has revealed it by His works and by His words.[17] In John 8:32 Jesus said that when people know the truth, "the truth will set them free."

2. **Some children are born better than others.** For the animists, some people are born with higher status (worth) than others. Some will be given respect and dignity while others will be despised and discriminated against. The caste system in Hinduism is one of the worst examples. Millions of people in the lower rungs of the caste system are condemned to lifelong poverty. Tribalism, ethnic prejudice,

racism, and other "isms," often leading to warfare, discrimination and abuse, are symptoms of this lie.

What the Bible says: We are all created in the image of God. This remarkable truth is found in Genesis 1:27, which states, "So God created man in his own image, in the image of God he created him; male and female he created them." This truth is also *unique to biblical theism.* The Psalms tell us, "For you created my inmost being: you knit me together in my mother's womb. I praise you because I am fearfully and wonderfully made" (Psalm 139:13-14).

This truth affirms the worth and dignity of every human being, including every child. This inherent worth and dignity provides the foundation for ministry to all people without distinction. Moreover, it provides the basis for a self-worth that says "I *do* matter. I *do* have gifts, talents, abilities. I *can* put my gifts and abilities and intellect and energy to good use to defend my rights and better my life."

I was once visiting a project in Cebu in the Southern Philippines. A few others and I were told that a 9-year-old boy was going to sing for us. I have heard 9-year-olds sing before and so did not expect a spectacular performance. However, this little guy had a marvelously mature voice, and we were amazed at his poise and confidence as he picked up the microphone and sang. This young lad could SING! It was the finest singing I have ever heard from a person that young. However, what really caused our jaws to drop was the awesome truth of the song he chose. He belted out lyrics to the effect that, yes, he was just a small, poor little boy who probably didn't look like much. Yet he knew he was special because he mattered to God! Knowing they matter is a first step for children and families toward finding their way out of poverty.

3. **Nature has dominion over mankind.** Both the animists and the secularists believe that mankind is ultimately at the mercy of the stars or of nature. The universe is a "closed system," so I must grab and hold whatever I can. This lie leads to jealousy, hoarding, and selfishness rather than resourcefulness. Neither the animist nor the secularist sees the truth of man having dominion over creation and with a God-given responsibility for stewardship and nurture.

   What the Bible says: We are created to have dominion. In Psalm 8:6 the Psalmist marvels at the fact that God made man ". . . a little lower than the heavenly beings and crowned him with glory and honor. You made him ruler over the works of your hands; you put everything under his feet." Genesis 1:28 affirms that God has given to mankind "dominion" or control over all of creation.

   God has given to mankind both the resources and the responsibility to enjoy, care for, and use the abundance he has provided. Moreover, abundance is to be created and stewarded. Mankind has the ability to grow, expand, invent, and create things that are beautiful and useful, and the responsibility to care for and conserve these resources. This understanding restores productivity and care for creation, stewardship, and management of resources.

4. Life is insignificant or has no meaning. Many animists believe man's existence is an endless cycle of birth and reincarnations. Survival is the goal. History is something that happens to you. On the other hand, Western secularists believe that this life is all there is or ever will be. They are not "going anywhere." This life is all there is. For both the animist and the secularist, the result is the same. Their existence has no larger meaning or purpose. For both, survival becomes the only goal of life. For the poor, pessimism, rather than hope, rules both in this life and their expectations of what is to come.

What the Bible says: God wants children to have a future and a hope. Not only are all people created in God's own image, but they are also created with purpose and meaning. Their lives and collective histories are going somewhere. They are created with unique personalities and designed for harmonious relationships with God, with others, and with all of the rest of creation. God uses individuals to work out His plans and purposes, and each one has a significant role and purpose.

Seeing life as an endless cycle of rebirths and reincarnations can have devastating consequences. Hougn (not her real name) is an 8-year-old Cambodian girl. She was raped by a man well known to her mother. However, her mother did not want anything done to the perpetrator. She said he would get his punishment in the next life. Worse still, she believed that what happened to her daughter was just her "karma"—retribution for some of the bad from one of her previous lives. What could be more devastating for her development, self-esteem, or hope?

The truth is that life should be purposeful and hopeful. Children and families can take control of their lives, instead of being mastered by unseen and incomprehensible forces or by a harsh and unbending environment, and purposefully making their lives better. Poor children can hope for a better future. That is the work of holistic child development.

EXPERIENCING GOD'S TRUTHS CAN SET PEOPLE FREE

So what are we saying about why people are poor and hungry? "Except for catastrophic events such as war, drought, or flood, physical poverty doesn't 'just happen.' [To a large extent, it may be] the logical result of the way people look at themselves and the world. . . . Physical poverty is rooted in a culture of poverty, a set of ideas . . . held corporately that produce certain behaviors, which in turn yield poverty."[18]

How can children and families break the chains of Satan's lies? Most basically, they can do it through a change in world-view and by learning about and following biblical truths.

The theistic/biblical worldview says that we don't have to be deceived by hollow and deceptive philosophies—philosophies that

- Deny objective truth and result in ambiguity and confusion;
- Deny that we have control over either our environment and our fate, and worse, say we must not seek to alter our condition, for fear of adversely affecting a future life;
- Condemn some to discrimination and lack of opportunity solely due to caste or race;
- Have no vision or hope of a future, resulting in fatalism, passivity, and pessimism.

Children and families no longer have to be enslaved by Satan's lies. In John 8:32 Jesus says, "You will know the truth, and the truth will set you free." Paul reminds us in Colossians 2:15 that God has "disarmed the powers and authorities and made a public spectacle of them triumphing over them by the cross." The bottom line of this discussion is this: Fundamentally, poverty is not a matter of a lack of resources or a result of man-made problems, but is, in fact, a *spiritual* problem.

God's intent has always been that His people, including children, be whole and complete in all aspects of life. This involves helping children and families understand biblical truths. Is material and physical assistance still necessary? Of course. The poor are whole persons and still have needs that must be met. We are commanded to provide help with nutritious food, education, health care, and other interventions. But don't make the mistake of thinking that it is the money or material aid that is the most important. *It is as that assistance is converted into learning opportunities and an understanding of the biblical truths—a change in worldview—that the children will be able to become what God wants them to be.*

Will we still need to confront the "structures of evil"—the corruption, exploitation, and injustice? Of course. But if the children and families we work with come to believe and follow biblical truths, they will more readily discover true freedom, release, wholeness, a future, and a hope.

One other thing: Since the root problem is spiritual rather than material, a holistic approach to the problems of poverty requires spiritual as well as physical responses. It is the Church—not governments, secular NGOs, the UN, or other secular bodies—that has an adequate response to the real causes of poverty. Therefore, effective holistic child development must be done from a Christian standpoint. **Indeed, holistic child development is the *particular* challenge and opportunity for Christians and the Church.**

Our non-Christian friends do very good development work, from which we may learn a great deal. Much of our work may be very similar to that of non-Christians. However, it is *Christians* who can respond most completely and effectively to the problem of poverty.

We will look at this reality more in the following section.

THE CHILD AND THE CHURCH

OVERVIEW

This is the first of two sections on the child and the Church. There is a subtle difference in the two. The first is titled "The Child *and* the Church." The second is "The Child *in* the Church." The first focuses on the Church's biblical responsibility to care holistically for children both inside *and* outside the Church. We will look at some biblical and theological foundations for the Church's mandate to care for, redeem, and reconcile *all* children and families, and indeed all of creation. It is this mandate that provides the basis for the role of the Church in doing holistic ministries, including holistic child development.

In "The Child *and* the Church," we will also review the old (but still with us) debate on evangelism vs. social action. Then we will discuss two important *structures* that are uniquely suited to carrying out the various ministries and functions of the Church as a whole. Finally, in chapter six, we will examine some important passages of Scripture that demonstrate why care for needy children is the *particular* responsibility of the Church.

The section "The Child *in* the Church" deals with improving the ministry of the Church to the children already in the Church—faith development and making the church programs, facilities, and staff more child-friendly. That follows in section three.

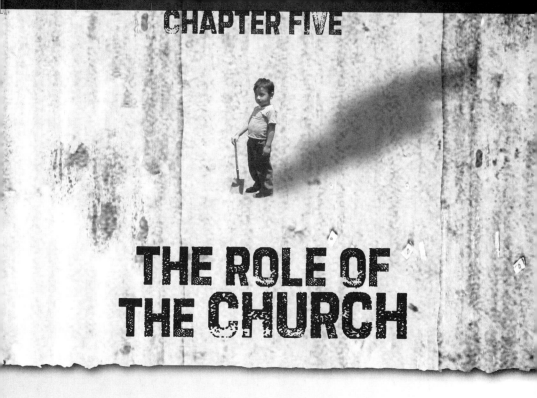

CHAPTER FIVE

THE ROLE OF THE CHURCH

For God did not send his Son into the world to condemn
the world, but to save the world through him.
John 3:17

The Bible tells us that God's intention is to love
and redeem all of His creation. This is the central
message of the entire Bible. Holistic child development is a theological response to the truth of a good
but fallen creation, and of a God wanting to redeem
not just individuals, but whole cultures and societies. God has used many people and instruments
to further this intention—from creation itself, to
the covenants He made with Adam, Noah, Abraham,
Abraham's descendents, the nation of Israel, and
ultimately through the sacrifice of His Son on the
cross to redeem the whole world (the *cosmos*).

As we will see, God has also entrusted the Church as His sole agent on earth with the responsibility to bless and redeem all of creation. How we carry out His intention defines our commitment and creativity alike.

THE WHOLE PERSON—AND THE WHOLE OF CREATION

We have seen that holistic child development deals with the whole child—the physical, spiritual, and other aspects of the person. But our commitment to the whole child must also encompass the whole of God's creation and His designs for the world and the regulation of human life.

Creation is good and worth redeeming. From the Genesis narratives on creation, we understand that God created *all* things. Hence, *all* of His creation has value. God called it "good."[1] The essential goodness of creation is important. The early heresy of gnosticism, which is still with us today, denied the goodness of creation. Gnosticism said that salvation should shun the creation, and all material and physical things, and (like some mystics today) a gnostic should seek to distance oneself from the material world. Yet Albert Wolters reminds us,

> God does not make junk, and we dishonor the
> Creator if we take a negative view of the work of
> His hands when He Himself takes such a positive
> view. In fact, so positive a view did He take of what

He had created that He refused to scrap it when mankind spoiled it, but determined instead, at the cost of His Son's life, to make it new and good again. God does not make junk, and He does not junk what He has made.[2]

The point is that it is not only *people* who are to be redeemed and led to fullness in Christ, but also *all* of God's creation.

Humankind (including children) have a special place in creation. As we have seen, God imparts special worth and dignity to humans by creating us in His own image. Moreover, God has empowered us to be co-creators with Him and to participate in His redemptive relationship with the rest of creation.[3] As implemented by the Church, the work of holistic child development participates in empowering children to fulfill their divinely ordered role of creating cultures.

REDEMPTION, RECONCILIATION, AND CHILD DEVELOPMENT

The Bible tells us in Genesis 1:26-28 that the first man failed in his responsibility to "fill, subdue, and rule the earth on God's behalf." Adam chose his own self-interest and with his disobe-dience—the fall—his relationship with God and the right relationship of all creation with God was broken. Even down to this present day, our lives, families, societies, and even the environment suffer the consequences of this rebellion.

God's response to the fall was His plan to redeem and

reconcile all of that fallen creation back to Himself. God wants to redeem not just individuals but whole cultures and societies. Both the words *redemption* and *reconciliation* imply going back to an original state. Reconciliation is concerned with the relationships that people and all elements of the creation have with each other. God's redemptive relationship with the creation, through the church, is designed to restore creation's order. Reconciliation implies that creation is so good that God intends to purge it of its infirmities and bring it to perfection.

Albert Wolters puts it this way:

> [T]heologians have sometimes spoken of salvation as re-creation—not to imply that God scraps His earlier creation and in Jesus Christ makes a new one, but rather to suggest that He hangs on to His fallen original creation and *salvages* it. He refuses to abandon the work of His hands—in fact He sacrifices His own Son to save His original project. Humankind, which has botched its original mandate and the whole creation aloing with it, is given another chance in Christ. . . . The original good creation is to be restored.[4]

This active work of redemption culminates in the New Testament with the coming of Jesus and His death on the cross.

Every evangelical Christian is familiar with John 3:16. It is central to our understanding of the salvation available to all who believe. Fewer evangelicals, however, are as familiar with (or as comfortable with) the next verse, John 3:17, nor its implications for holistic ministry: "For God did not send his Son into the world to condemn the world, but to save the world through him."

The Greek word used for *world* in both verses is *cosmos*. It refers to the *whole of creation*, all the human social structures and relationships, as well as individuals. It is the global matrix of human cultures that serve as the arena in which people live their lives. The construction and redemption of the cosmos highlights the need for Christians to hold salvation and redemption together. Modern evangelicals are susceptible to reading John 3:16 and ignoring John 3:17 because we limit the atonement to personal salvation. Our emphasis on personal salvation influences us to ignore the redemption of the cosmos.

Paul's towering passage in the first chapter of Colossians (verses 15-20) affirms that salvation, reconciliation, and redemption are intended not just to save souls, but rather apply to all of Creation:

> He is the image of the invisible God, the first-born over all creation. For by him all things were created: things in heaven and on earth, visible and invisible, whether thrones or powers or rulers or authorities; all things were created by him and for him. He is before all things, and in him all things hold together. And he is the head of the body, the church; he is the beginning and the firstborn from among the dead, so that in everything he might have the supremacy. For God was pleased to have

all his fullness dwell in him, and through him to
reconcile to himself all things, whether things on
earth or things in heaven, by making peace through
his blood, shed on the cross.

"Seven times, this passage reminds us that God's agenda is
as big as *all creation!* Paul was making a point! Jesus' blood
was shed for the restoration of *all things.* Why? *All things*
were broken in the fall. God loves His creation and He wants
all things reconciled to Himself."[5]

Holistic development, including holistic *child* development, is a way we Christians participate both in God's work of
redeeming and reconciling all things to Himself.

THE MYSTERY OF THE ROLE OF THE CHURCH[6]

From the New Testament onward, God's chosen instrument
for His redemptive work has been His Church. In Ephesians
1:9-10, the apostle Paul calls this a mystery and a mystery it
is—that God would entrust the reconciling to Himself all of
Creation to us, His people, His body, the Church, is mysterious
to us as well.

And he made known to us the mystery of his
will according to his good pleasure, which he
purposed in Christ, to be put into effect when the

times will have reached their fulfillment—to bring all things in heaven and on earth together under one head, even Christ.

Ephesians 1:22-23 continues, And God placed all things under his feet and appointed him to be head over everything for the church, which is his body, the fullness of him who fills everything in every way.

Paul then explains in Ephesians 3:8-11 that he was given the grace to reveal to us the mystery of this role of the church:

Although I am less than the least of all God's people, this grace was given me: to preach to the Gentiles the unsearchable riches of Christ, and to make plain to everyone the administration of this mystery, which for ages past was kept hidden in God, who created all things. His intent was that now, through the church, the manifold wisdom of God should be made known to the rulers and authorities in the heavenly realms, according to his eternal purpose which he accomplished in Christ Jesus our Lord.

For whatever reason, (it's a mystery!) God chose the Church to be His instrument in redeeming all of His creation back to Himself. The church is the *only* plan He has to redeem His creation.

Dr. Bambang Budijanto, Asia Vice-President for Compassion International, notes,

> The Ecclesia [the Church] has only one mission—that is to make disciples. In the Great Commission Jesus did not command the Ecclesia to "engage in making disciples and also to care for the poor"; or to "make disciples and to care for the creation"; or to "make disciples and to engage in the public square." This is because making disciples includes all of those aspects. . . .[7]
>
> The dynamic community of Ecclesia of Jesus Christ powerfully operates in advancing the kingdom of God every single day—seven days a week (Acts 2:46-47). Unfortunately this non-stop transformation has, in many parts of the world, been reconfigured into a single event on Sunday. Ecclesia as primarily a weekly "event" on Sunday strips the new meaning Jesus invested in the term when He designated it for His kingdom community.[8]

There is much that implies that, in reality, true holistic development can *only* be done by Christians or the Church. It is *only* Christians who have the understanding of the nature of sin, of God's intention for His people and His creation, and of the power of the gospel to bring substantial holistic healing to the whole person.

The *already* aspects of the dawning kingdom began to transform societies throughout the ancient world, often at the cost of much persecution and individual sacrifice. God's new way of doing things[9] was a totally new paradigm for people in Jesus' day, just as it is in ours. Christianity as manifested in the Church introduced surprising new ideas and understandings of relationships and behaviors that were unheard of in other religions and societies. The Church provided a compelling new vision of humanity, transforming individuals and changing societies.

Rodney Stark[10] identifies some revolutionary aspects of God's way of doing things that were so different than what was commonly understood or practiced that they astounded the Roman world.

1. **The idea of a loving God.** Always before the gods had their own agenda and spent their time fighting each other and competing for allegiance and dominance. Those *gods* had little interest in the people who worshipped them.

2. **The loving Christian God expected that His followers—the Church—would also be loving.** Up to then, people did not generally love anybody except their own families or those whom it was politically or economically advantageous to love. "Pity was a defect of character unworthy of the wise and excusable only in those who have not yet grown up."[11] This new God even said, "I want you [the Church] to love those who are poor and hurting. I want you to love, especially, those who are in a humble position in the world."[12]

3. **It was also shocking that this new God said that there should be no rank or status differences among believers.** This was different! The rich and poor, humble, and powerful were all equal in His sight. The church manifested a whole new vision of human relationships!

4. **God is a merciful God who requires mercy.** Rome was well-known for its casual cruelty. "Since mercy involves providing unearned help or relief, it was [viewed as] contrary to justice."[13] They could not understand why anyone would care for the poor, but that was a central belief of Christianity and practices in the newly established church.

Later the gospel helped to transform Europe from barbarism to leadership in civil societies. Throughout the centuries, the church has always been at the forefront of doing good works and showing love for mankind. As powerful and pervasive as the ideas of the New Way were, however, and as radical as it was for the church to respond to the needs of the whole person, it was in fact not uncommon for the church to fall short in doing good.

Even as the church grew and the New Way spread, the *not yet* reality of the kingdom often compromised the willingness and effectiveness of the church in holistic ministry. In fact, the question arose on some fronts as to whether the church should be involved in doing good works at all. Indeed, the role of the church in doing social action has been questioned in recent years, and evangelicals especially have often been negligent in following through on this biblical responsibility. One reason for this is an understanding among some that the kingdom of God was not for the present but for the future, that is, after Christ's return.

The struggle for relief and development ministries in general, and for holistic child development in particular, is in understanding the relationship between social action and evangelistic ministries. To that long-standing issue we now turn our attention.

EVANGELISM OR SOCIAL ACTION: THE GREAT DEBATE

The Church *should* make a profound difference in the lives of all people, including the poor. The work of Christians among the poor is, in fact, extensive. The Church is the largest movement working on behalf of children at risk today in terms of children reached, ministries established and workers on the ground. Much of this work is little known. The scale of the Church's work in the field of children at risk is often a surprise to people, even to those within the Church.

Viewed in another way, however, we can also see that the Church often has not had the impact that it should. Indeed, often the Church is ignorant of, or chooses to ignore, its responsibility—and unique ability—to care meaningfully for hurting children and families. The actual historical performance of the Church carrying out its role in the redemption of *all* of God's creation has not always been exemplary.

The evangelical segment of the Church has, at times, particularly failed in its responsibility to care for the needy. A theological movement called "higher criticism" came out of the seminaries of Europe in the 1850s which eventually produced something known as the "social gospel." Bob Moffitt explains:

> The focus was shifting from an emphasis on the future, spiritual kingdom of God to a present, earthly, physical kingdom—an improved society that would be achieved here and now through social action and enlightened government programs, by human effort and good works. Believing this, the liberal wing of the church began to focus heavily on social issues. In short, the social gospel said that the kingdom of God would come to earth as a result of good works. It was no longer necessary for individuals to be personally converted to Christ."[14]

More recently, an important debate arose between the various "streams"—liberal or mainline, evangelical, charismatic—regarding the legitimate functions of the Church. In some ways, this was a debate between the mainline churches—those mostly affiliated with the World Council of Churches (WCC)—and the evangelical churches—those more affiliated with the World Evangelical Fellowship (WEF, now World Evangelical Alliance, WEA). At a WCC conference in Uppsala,

Sweden in 1966, "the emphasis shifted from God speaking to the world through the church to God speaking to the church through what He was doing in the world."[15]

Betray the two billion? This position was consolidated in Bangkok WCC meetings in 1973 where it was argued that "salvation today was to be determined by what we perceive God to be doing in the world today, whether within the church or not. . . . [E]vangelism received very little attention and no mention was made of the unreached."[16] Among the various programs set up to implement this new understanding of mission was the Program to Combat Racism, which included financial grants to guerilla groups in what was then Rhodesia (now Zimbabwe).

"Most evangelicals reacted strongly against these changes in the understanding of mission. Even before the Uppsala Assembly, Donald McGavran had written an article asking 'Will Uppsala betray the two billion?'"[17]

It was partly in reaction to this direction by the WCC churches that many evangelicals moved to a greater emphasis on evangelism. Many evangelicals were dismayed at what they understood to be a total betrayal of evangelism and mission to the unreached. So many, while understanding biblically the responsibilities implied in the Great Commandment, "threw the baby out with the bath water," and abandoned caring ministries altogether.

THE SOCIAL GOSPEL

It is easy to see why evangelical Christians would distance themselves from this kind of a *social gospel*. In fact, in reaction to this emphasis, many evangelicals began to reject *good works* as a legitimate function of the Church. Conservatives began to focus primarily on evangelism and spiritual conversion, rather than the whole of God's concern.

A second factor causing many evangelicals to turn away from holistic ministries was the argument that the world would inevitably get worse and worse until Jesus returns, regardless of what anyone did about it. One evangelist, Dwight L. Moody, put it this way: "The world is like a sinking ship, and God has put me in a lifeboat and given me a life preserver and said, 'Moody, go out and save all you can. Don't worry about the ship. It's sinking anyway.'"[18]

Clearly, the poor are still with us. Just as clearly, sometimes the Church has not valued children. More ominous, all too often the Church has been unaware of, or even denied that, holistic care for the needs of children falls within its sphere of responsibility. This "great omission" is to some extent rooted in historical misunderstandings and theological differences about the fundamental role of the Church.

Whatever the reason, or reasons, historically, the Church has not done nearly all she could or should do to show Christ's love through acts of kindness. In fact, one person has said, "Evangelicals have retreated from the kingdom of God to soul saving."[19] This is despite the fact that the conditions of poverty and injustice have worsened. "Despite all the theorizing and the actions that have flowed from it, we have to face up to the fact that the problem of poverty is as great as it ever was. . . . The rich have gotten richer and the poor have gotten poorer. . . . The poor are still with us in greater numbers than ever."[20]

In his book *Living the Faith Community*, John H. Westerhoff III reflects on the role of the church.

> There is surfacing once again a tendency for the church to become an institution, which specializes in religion. . . . If the church is essentially a social institution, it may choose to place its sole attention on the religious domain. But if the church is to be a community of faith, a base community more like a family than an institution, then it must be concerned about every aspect of human life and seek to integrate the religious, social, political, and economic on behalf of justice and fullness of human life for all people.[21]

We have to keep grappling with this choice for the sake of the children. What role will we, the Church, take on as we go forward in history?

THE RELATIONSHIP BETWEEN EVANGELISM AND SOCIAL ACTION

As is obvious from earlier sections of this book, I believe that both evangelism and social action are essential aspects of the role of the Church. Indeed, doing both is another way of doing the holistic development that this book is all about. However, since this debate has not gone away, it may be useful to explore the various possibilities and positions that have been taken concerning the relationship between evangelism and the so-called social action.

The late Tokumboh Adeyemo, former general secretary of the Africa Association of Evangelicals, offered eight possible options as to the relationship between social action and evangelism.[22] These options include:

1. **Social action is a distraction from evangelism.** Evangelism is the exclusive mission of the church; social action ministries might be necessary for Christians to engage in, but they do so only to meet the "felt needs" of the people whom they are serving.

2. **Social action is a betrayal of evangelism.** This position carries *social action as a distraction* to an extreme. It demands that Christians protect themselves from the betrayal of social action ministries and focus their efforts exclusively on saving souls.

3. **Social action is a means to evangelism.** Christians engage in social actions ministries to create opportunities for evangelism. Social action ministries, though, do not have a place in Christian missions.

4. Social action is a manifestation of evangelism. Christians engage in social action ministries as a demonstration of God's love. Social action is a tangible expression of the gospel.

5. Social action is a consequence of evangelism. Christians engage in social action ministries because social action ministries empower Christians to live abundant lives.

6. Social action is a partner in evangelism, albeit unequal partners. Social action and evangelistic ministries are distinct expressions of the gospel of Jesus Christ, and they are in partnership with each other.

7. Social action and evangelism are equal partners of Christian ministries. Social action and evangelistic ministries complement each other like two wings of a bird. One wing is not more important than the other; they need each other to fully function.

8. Social action is part of evangelism. This position argues that social action ministries have a central place in Christian mission because the gospel of Jesus is concerned with redeeming every aspect of human life.

THE GREAT COMMANDMENT AND THE GREAT COMMISSION ARE BOTH VALID

It is obvious that the position taken in this book is that it is and always has been God's intention to use the Church to transform society, and to do it in holistic ways. Is evangelism important? Of course, it is. Is social action important? Yes, it is also very important. The Great Commandment and the Great Commission are both valid. The Lausanne Covenant (1974) said, "The two are like 'two blades of a pair of scissors, or the two wings of a bird." This partnership is clearly seen in the public ministry of Jesus, who not only preached the gospel but fed the hungry and healed the sick."[23]

What would happen to a child like Joshua if a needlessly artificial division between the gospel and practical help continued? Joshua is one of many children served by a church-based child development center in Ghana. For Joshua—like his peers—one mosquito bite can trigger a malaria relapse that can keep him out of the development program for days, sometimes weeks, at a time. Isn't it obvious that taking action against mosquito bites is a valuable strategy to keep children coming to the center on a regular basis? So Joshua's church became one of many in Ghana who took part in a campaign to distribute treated mosquito netting to the children and families they serve. Families spend less time seeking medical care for sick children. Churches and centers report markedly increased attendance at their child-focused programs.

For these churches, there is no dichotomy between teaching the gospel to children, holding weekly worship services for families, hosting a school on their grounds, and ensuring that every family possible receives the netting that can protect them from the ravages of malaria. It is all part of holistic Christian child development.

The Manila Manifesto, drafted during the second Lausanne Congress on World Evangelization declared that God's intention was for the "Whole Church to take the Whole Gospel, to the Whole World." This declaration was a specific response to the fact that different parts of the Church tend to emphasize different parts of the gospel. As we have seen, the reality was that *parts* of the Church took *parts* of gospel to *parts* of the world.

Evangelicals might hope that their mainline counterparts would have a greater concern for evangelism. Evangelicals on the other hand must also take more seriously the demands of the Great Commandment, lest we preach only half the gospel and dishonor God's compassion for those who suffer physically. In fact, each has played its role. Meg Crossman reminded us, "The liberal church show[ed] us the need: the evangelical church show[ed] us the plan; and the charismatic/pentecostal church remind[ed] us that God is in it!"[24]

It is my contention that development ministries are theological responses:

- To the truth of a good but fallen creation.
- Of a God wanting to redeem not just individuals but whole cultures and societies.
- Of a God who wants to reconcile a fallen world to Himself.
- To the towering passages of Scripture (such as Isaiah 65, Colossians 1:15-20, Luke 4:16-18) about

God's love and His redemptive purposes for humankind.

Indeed, we seek to embody the truth of Isaiah 65:17-25,

> Behold, I will create new heavens and a new earth. The former things will not be remembered, nor will they come to mind. . . . I will rejoice over Jerusalem and take delight in my people; the sound of weeping and of crying will be heard in it no more. Never again will there be in it an infant who lives but a few days, or an old man who does not live out his years; he who dies at a hundred will be thought a mere youth; he who fails to reach a hundred will be considered accursed. . . . They will not toil in vain or bear children doomed to misfortune; for they will be a people blessed by the LORD, they and their descendants with them. Before they call I will answer; while they are still speaking I will hear.

THE KEY STAKEHOLDERS IN THE MINISTRY OF THE CHURCH[25]

There are three particular groups of people who are the key stakeholders in the ministry of the Church. They are the poor,[26] the victims of injustice or the oppressed,[27] and the children.[28] From the beginning, the poor and the outcast had a prominent place in the kingdom of God. In Luke 6:20 Jesus teaches,

"Blessed are you who are poor, for yours is the kingdom of God." In a parallel passage in Matthew 5:10, He says, "Blessed are those who are persecuted because of righteousness, for theirs is the kingdom of heaven."

Jesus' own mission statement in Luke 4:18-19, taken from Isaiah 61, had a primary focus on the outcast:

> The Spirit of the Lord is on me, because he has anointed me to preach good news to the poor. He has sent me to proclaim freedom for the prisoners and recovery of sight for the blind, to release the oppressed, to proclaim the year of the Lord's favor.

Even Jesus' instructions to His disciples began with exposure to the poor and the needy. Dr. Budijanto points out,

> Instead of laying the theoretical foundations in a classroom setting, Jesus began this disciple-making process with real life experiences. He took the 12 men to meet face to face with the key stakeholders of the kingdom of God. For immediately following the calling of the 12, Luke records seven encounters (between chapters five and eight) Jesus had with the poor, the outcast, and those who did not belong to the mainstream Jewish society—the man with leprosy, the tax collector, a paralyzed man, a sinful woman, a Roman soldier[29], a demon-possessed man, and an unclean-sick woman.[30]

He continues:

> Jesus wanted to make sure that the future pillars of the Ecclesia would always remember that engagement with the poor, the weak and the outcast was at the core of the disciple-making process. Moreover, not only did Jesus provide the twelve with the opportunity to meet face to face with the key audience and stakeholders of the kingdom of God; He also demonstrated how a disciple of Christ should engage with them.[31]

Likewise, our own journey with Christ cannot be authentic without a significant engagement with the poor. Whether one is aware of it, as one takes the journey of becoming like Christ with and within a kingdom community, the transformation process will impact the poor, the weak, and the outcast.

Similarly, it is clear that children have a special place in the kingdom of God. Jesus said that only those who receive the kingdom like little children can become its citizens.[32] Astonishingly, when the disciples argued who was the greatest among them, Jesus referred to the little children.[33] Jesus set children and their humility as the measure of greatness in the kingdom of God in Matthew 19:14, where He said, "Let the little children come to me, and do not hinder them, for the kingdom of heaven belongs to such as these."

The kingdom of God belongs to little children. The way people perceive and treat children will determine their eligibility for the kingdom of God, as Jesus warned:

> And whoever welcomes a little child like this in my name welcomes me. But if anyone causes one of these little ones who believe in me to sin, it would be better for him to have a large millstone hung around his neck and to be drowned in the depths of the sea (Matthew 18:5-6).

TWO STRUCTURES, ONE FUNCTION

We have established, I believe, that the church *ought* to care for needy children. But a few words are in order about *how* the Church is to care for children.

It is, of course, quite often true that the local church has the vision to carry out the effective, long-term, innovative holistic child development but may lack the personnel, skills, facilities, or other key resources. Surely, it is not only the larger, well-established, talent-laden churches that should carry out such development. So more clarity is in order about the common *structures* of the Church.

In this, we can learn from the way the Church has traditionally done missions. Throughout church history, there have always been two kinds of church structures. One is the *gathered* church—the local congregations, nurturing and caring for people of all ages and gender. But from the beginning of the Christian era, the gathered church frequently spun off into more specialized "appendages," which carried out new outreach or the more specialized ministries of the Church.

The late missiologist Dr. Ralph Winter called these two structures *modalities* and *sodalities*.[34] A *modality* is the congregational fellowship with a settled membership. A *sodality* is an arm or extension of the church that is established to carry out more specialized outreaches or caring ministries. The modality—the church on the corner—has a well-defined role, that of welcoming and nurturing the whole of the body of Christ. She provides a settled membership, authority, overall unity, continuity, and ensures stability in the body. The sodalities enable the church to reach out and to carry out specialized ministries not possible or feasible for the gathered church.

These two structures exist at both the macro (global church) and micro (local church) levels. At the macro level, for example, the Catholic Church has been well known for spinning off sodalities—the Jesuits and Franciscans for specialized missions activities. Protestants have created mission societies, youth movements, specialized ministries such as Campus Crusade, and other well-known parachurch organizations such as Mission Aviation Fellowship (MAF) and Compassion International.

The same thing takes place at the micro level. Local churches—the modalities—may have the vision and desire for specialized ministries, such as child development programs, church-based schools, hostels, or homes for orphans or handicapped children, but lack the ability or expertise to carry them out. Churches often then establish a committee, or other special department or structure—a sodality—to actually run the child care or outreach programs. This sodality is given the mandate to acquire the necessary staff, skills, facilities, and specialized expertise to carry out the ministry.

An example of a church-based sodality is church-run residential schools or hostels. Some children have to live away from their home villages to get an education. For these children, there simply are no schools in their remote home villages. They must find suitable and safe housing while they are in school. Many micro sodalities like the church-run residential schools or hostels, then, seem like a gift from heaven to these children and their families. These micro sodalities provide a wholesome living environment, house parenting, and *lots* of holistic development possibilities for children who must live away from home in order to have any chance for an education. The local church alone, even if it existed in their home villages, could not provide this opportunity for these children.

Such Christian institutions, though not the gathered "church on the corner," are nevertheless a manifestation of the church in action. It is still the church making a difference in the lives of needy children.

The Church at all levels, whether the gathered "church on the corner" or the many manifestations of Christians sacrificing, serving and sharing *is* God's uniquely chosen instrument to complete His work of salvation and redemption. Making children and youth a significant part of their ministry and mission plans is not only responsible and compassionate, but visionary but strategic as well.

CHAPTER SIX

WHY CARE FOR CHILDREN IS THE *PARTICULAR* RESPONSIBILITY OF THE CHURCH

Elijah picked up the child and carried him down from the room into the house. He gave him to his mother and said, "Look, your son is alive!" Then the woman said to Elijah, "Now I know that you are a man of God and that the word of the LORD from your mouth is the truth."
1 Kings 17:23-24

We appreciate all that the secular world—governments, the UN, mainstream NGOs, and similar entities—does to care for the needy. Christians can and do learn a great deal from their methods and approaches. But this book is about *holistic* ministry to children and youth. And I will argue here that not only *should* churches think holistically about children, but also, in reality, it is *only* the Church that can do so, for again, of course, it is only the Church that can deal with the needs of the whole person. Moreover, there is ample support from the Bible that caring for children is the *particular* responsibility of the Church and of Christians.

We have seen from a theological standpoint that the Church has a unique responsibility to care for the needy. The Church is God's instrument in redeeming all of His creation. And we, His people, are the hands and arms of Christ.

In this chapter, we will look at several biblical passages that provide perspectives on why, in reality, it is *only* the Church that can do holistic child development. The question we pose throughout is "Why is care for children the particular responsibility of the Church?"

ONLY THE CHURCH (CHRISTIANS!) CAN RESPOND TO THE NEEDS OF THE WHOLE PERSON

Luke 2:52 says of Jesus' own development, "Jesus grew in wisdom and stature and in favor with God and man."

As we have seen, the short verse provides a marvelous model for any child's development. Compassion International has long used this verse as the foundation for our own holistic ministry to children. We want all of the children in our programs to have the opportunity to grow as Jesus did. All the programs we support are to have at least these four components. *Wisdom* addresses our educational (or learning) initiatives, and also the training in biblical values, discernment, judgment, and wise decision-making based on biblical principles. *Stature* relates to anything having to do with health and physical growth. *Favor with God* speaks to a child's spiritual nurture and formation. *Favor with man* refers to social development and the growing ability of a child to build relationships and interact appropriately with other people. Our expectation and prayer is that all the children with whom we work will also grow in these four areas. Indeed, these four areas provide remarkable programmatic scope for ministry.

Growing in wisdom suggests virtually anything related to providing learning opportunities for the child, whether formal or informal. Growing in wisdom is much more than just knowledge or education. Learning knowledge and facts is the easy part. Children can get knowledge and facts in the classroom or on the streets or from MTV. Knowledge alone won't help children be able to discern what is true, right, and lasting.

Bill Gothard[1] says that wisdom is "seeing life from God's point of view." I like that. One thing is for sure—children in most of the education systems around the world won't learn to see life from God's point of view. Rather, they will see it from the point of view of the secular world, from the media, or from their peers. Maybe this is why Peter tells us to add goodness to our faith, and *then* knowledge.[2] Without goodness first, we don't really know what to do with knowledge.

I believe holistic child development programs need to provide much more significant and profound opportunities for children to grow in wisdom. Then, as we have seen time and again, they will usually enjoy well-rounded success in their life decisions as adolescents and adults.

One such example from Compassion's history is Roberto Christobal, a sponsored child who grew up in Bocaue, a remote barrio in the Philippines. Roberto's family encouraged him to highly value education. When he connected with Compassion sponsorship, Roberto chose to make the most of the opportunity. He excelled as a student and qualified for university training. Although it was a challenge to secure the funds for college, Roberto became self-supporting as he began college. Upon graduation, he became a secondary school teacher and continued his education through graduate school. Roberto made a series of choices to pursue and complete his education, eventually becoming not only a successful educator, but also a Compassion project director. What a transition from a sponsored child to an expert educator!

Growing in stature can mean anything directly related to improving a child's health, proper nourishment, disease prevention, and ability to care for self-health, and children's needs for clean air and water, clothing, shelter, food, and/or sanitation. Jesus was apparently strong and healthy. He had adequate nutrition and was sturdy and vigorous. He had the stamina for walking long distances. He was no doubt muscular from years of swinging a hammer and pulling a saw. He was not always "meek and mild." Apparently, he had a whip and he knew how to use it.

Growing in favor with God can involve virtually anything related to spiritual nurture and growth: prayer, worship, children's need for God, salvation, as well as such concepts as beauty and goodness. A right relationship with God implies a right relationship with all of His creation. Clearly no secular interventions can address these issues from a biblical standpoint. It is only Christians who have the spiritual truths and resources to help children grow like Jesus did in this respect.

Growing in favor with man has to do with our relationships with other human beings, including our needs for friendship, sharing, and laughter, and the learning opportunities that increase a child's sense of security, self-worth, understanding of giftedness, and creativity.

It is interesting to reflect on *how* Jesus grew in these four areas. Robert Moffitt points out that His environment was not affluent, His family did not have running water and electricity, and He probably didn't have the best secular education.[3] Jesus was also growing up in a rather hostile political climate. Does this sound like some of the environments children grow up in today? Jesus' healthy wholeness—physical, mental, social, and spiritual—was not dependent on wealth or material possessions. Rather, it was based on a right relationship with God, with his environment and his human contacts—in other words, a biblical worldview.

The hope and intention of holistic child development is that all children can grow like Jesus did. Why is working toward such development the *particular* responsibility of the Church? Because it is only the Church—we Christians—who have the understanding and biblical worldview that will make that a possibility.

BECAUSE GOD HEARS THE CHILDREN CRYING[4]

A second perspective on why the Church has a particular responsibility is because we Christians have "the mind of Christ." Part of that mind of Christ is the understanding of God's heart for children and our understanding that He expects us to have the same heart. He hears the children crying and expects us to hear, and respond to, their crying as well. Our love and concern for suffering children is a reflection of God's love and concern for those children.

In Genesis 21:17, we learn that God heard the boy, (Ishmael) crying. And God not only hears, but also acts—he does something about it. Let's have a look at that passage and see what we learn about our obligations. Genesis 21:17 tells us, "God heard the boy [Ishmael] crying, and the angel of God called to Hagar from heaven and said to her, 'What is the matter, Hagar? Do not be afraid; God has heard the boy crying as he lies there.'"

Abraham is one of the biblical heroes of the faith, yet he did not always use faith or good judgment. The story of the birth of Ishmael to his wife's maid Hagar is an example of a poor decision in Abraham's life. Yet God redeemed even this poor decision. Genesis 21 is instructive about how God hears the children crying and gives us instructions about caring for needy children.

Hagar and Ishmael are out in the wilderness after Abraham has sent them away. Before long, whatever food and water they carried along is finished. They have no further resources. Understandably, Hagar cannot bear to see Ishmael die, so she puts him in the shade of a bush and goes off some distance. She knows that she and her son are doomed. But God had other plans!

God heard the boy crying. The angel of God called to Hagar from heaven and said to her, "What is the matter, Hagar? Do not be afraid; God has heard the boy crying. Lift the boy up and take him by the hand." Then God opened Hagar's eyes, and she saw a well of water. Mother and son survived, and even thrived. The Scriptures record that God was with Ishmael as he grew up.[5]

What can we learn from this story about God's care for children? Several things come to mind.

God hears the children crying! Even today, we can be sure that God hears the children crying. He wants to respond to those cries.

But **God not only hears; He also speaks from heaven.** He sends His heavenly messengers. Yet He also sends the Church, along with its families who have the responsibility to love and care for the children today.

God asks about the problem: "What is the matter?" Just as the angel asked Hagar why her son was crying, so I believe, God is asking the Church today, "Why are the children crying?" Too often the Church leaves it to UNICEF, or to NGOs, or to governments to ask why the children are crying. The Church itself needs to find out why the children are crying. The Church needs to know about the circumstances of the poor. It must educate itself regarding the exploitation that causes poverty. It must understand that children cry because they hurt. They suffer from hunger, illness, lack of appropriate clothing or shelter, neglect, abuse, fear, illiteracy, and a lack of security. (That's just the beginning!) Children also cry for their God-given human dignity, respect, and love.

God encourages those who care for children. The angel sent by God not only asked about the problem, but also offered comfort to Hagar. The angel said to Hagar, 'Don't be afraid.' One thing the Church should understand is that caring for children—especially children in difficult circumstances—is stressful, 'fearful' work. (Caring for children in *normal* environments is hard enough!) Too often church leaders fail to understand the stresses and challenges of caring for, teaching, and nurturing children. Churches often forget to encourage and support busy mothers, Sunday school workers, day-care workers, or the social workers in church-based child development programs. Churches need to care for the caregivers! We need to tell them 'don't be afraid!'

God gives instructions on caring for the children. The angel gave instructions to Hagar as to what to do for her son: "Lift up the boy. Take him by the hand." Interestingly, these two commands seem to correspond to the ministries that today we call *relief* and *development*.

"Lift up the boy" indicates physical, emotional, and moral support. This corresponds to the relief activity of many Christian NGOs today: Do whatever is necessary so that the boy doesn't die.

"Take him by the hand" suggests walking with a child, encouraging, supporting, and discipling the child as you go. This corresponds with the long-term development work of many Christian NGOs, including Compassion—providing the longer-term training, nurture, and care necessary for children to grow and thrive.

God makes promises about children. God also made promises to Hagar about her son. Genesis 21:18 records God's promise, "I will make you into a great nation." Hagar expected that she and Ishmael would die of thirst there in the desert, God spoke of Ishmael's potential and promise. One of the challenges of the Church today is to see all children as a promise and to "make promises" about its children. Are churches today willing to make promises to its children—and then do the necessary to see that those promises become a reality?

By the way, Ishmael became a great nation that still exists and prospers today. My friend Dr. Alemu Beeftu suggests that the presence of oil under all the "Ishmaelite" lands of the Middle East may be the ongoing fulfillment of the promise God made to Hagar concerning Ishmael.

God opens our eyes to resources. When Hagar was convinced she would die of thirst, God opened her eyes to a nearby well![6] He didn't send in a water truck or a relief agency from another country, but rather met her need from resources that were close at hand. God showed Hagar possibilities she didn't know existed. Today, one of the challenges of the poor is recognizing what is available. Opening the eyes of adults is one way God responds to the cries of children.

This is one of the key lessons of this passage. Too often churches feel that they simply do not have the resources to respond to the needs of the children in their midst. But I believe that God will do for the willing, resourceful church exactly what He did for Hagar. He will open the church's eyes to resources—to precisely the resources that are needed—that the church didn't know existed. Often those resources are right under our noses!

God becomes a friend. Not only did God meet the immediate need of Hagar and Ishmael, but God was also with Ishmael for the rest of his life.[7] The presence of God brought life and hope in the desert. He is, indeed, the friend and protector of the poor. Our challenge today is to make sure that children know that God is their friend.

Make no mistake, **God hears the children crying!** He is challenging the Church to respond. He is asking about the problem. He wants the children's physical, emotional, and spiritual needs met. He will open your eyes to available resources. And He is the Friend of *all* children. Christians have a *particular* responsibility to care for children because we are the only ones who have an understanding of God's own heart for children.

BECAUSE CARING FOR CHILDREN DISPELS DISBELIEF

Another reason we Christians have a particular responsibility to care for children is because we also are interested in furthering His kingdom and giving children and youth and their families opportunity to be part of that kingdom. And, while we do not care for children only in order to reach their parents, the fact is that caring for children is a remarkably effective way to also influence parents and other adults. As a missiologist, I especially like the rich and revealing story of Elijah and the widow of Zarephath found in 1 Kings 17.

We will see why this strikes me as a missions passage later. But first, let's review this familiar story. The first thing we hear about the ministry of Elijah is in the midst of a three-year drought. Ravens are feeding him at a place called Kerith Ravine. The water there dries up, and he is sent to Zarephath far to the north. There, he asks a widow for food and drink, but she swears that she is at that moment using the last of her flour and oil. In fact, she has no idea how she will survive when that is used up.

Elijah asks her to exercise faith and first make a meal for him. She does so at God's instruction, and her faith provokes a miracle. Just as Elijah promises her, the food and oil in her home do not run out. She invites Elijah to stay in an upper room of her home. We don't know how long he stayed there—perhaps up to two years or so. What we do know is that while he was there, the widow's oil and flour did not run out.

At some point in Elijah's stay, however, the widow's son gets terribly sick. His condition worsens until finally he stops breathing. At first the woman lashes out at Elijah, expressing both her guilt and her grief as recorded in 1 Kings 17:18: "What do you have against me, man of God? Did you come to remind me of my sin and kill my son?"

Elijah too is grief stricken and cannot imagine why God has allowed the woman's son to die while he is there. "O LORD my God, have you brought tragedy also upon this widow I am staying with, by causing her son to die?"[8]

But then Elijah takes action. 1 Kings 17:21-23 reports,

> [Elijah] stretched himself out on the boy three times and cried to the LORD, "O LORD my God, let this boy's life return to him!" The LORD heard Elijah's cry, and the boy's life returned to him, and he lived. Elijah picked up the child and carried him down from the room into the house. He gave him to his mother and said, "Look, your son is alive!"

We may make a number of observations about the story so far. First, God often selects the poor to be His servants. (Think about it. Why didn't God send Elijah to live with a wealthy person?) God also asks the poor to exercise faith. In the widow's case, it takes faith for her to give her son over to the prophet. Yet this is what the Church should be saying to people today: "Give me your son. Give me your daughter." It is certainly what the world is saying. It is what the drug dealers on the corners are saying. It is what the war lords are saying. It is what MTV is saying. In like manner, the Church must say, "Give me the boy!" "Give me the girl!" "Let's work together to save and restore them!"

So Elijah takes the boy to the upper room where he was staying. (Note that the "upper room" in Scripture often alludes to a place of prayer. Elijah was a man of prayer.) Elijah stretches himself out over the boy three times. Elijah is not just an unconcerned boarder. He takes on the burden of the family as his own. He takes action and makes the woman's problem his problem. Imagine the joy and relief in the widow's heart as Elijah brings her son back down—alive! And at this point—when God restored the boy in response to the prophet's faith—we find the astonishing exclamation from the widow, "Now I know that you are a man of God and that the word of the LORD from your mouth is the truth."

Remember that the woman has seen a miracle take place in her home every day for perhaps *two or three years*! A miracle, or, if you will, a *relief and development project*, has been going on in her very home every day. But it is only when the prophet addresses a need closest to her heart—the life of her son—that she sees and understands that Elijah is truly a man of God who speaks the truth.

Many of us involved in ministries of caring for children have experienced much the same thing. Christians often have a variety of ministries to try to reach a community. But often it is only when we care for what is most precious to people, their children, that they will respond to God's truth. It is often only when we address the need closest to their hearts—their children—that they begin to realize that Christians need not be feared or chased away. Because we care for their children, many adults of all faiths have made the same awe-inspiring discovery: "*Now I know* that you really do care for us, for you care for our children!"

Here then is the understanding that warms the heart of this missiologist. The ultimate aim of Christian missions can be reduced to this objective: We aspire for our hearers to say, "*Now I know* that you are speaking the truth and that you really are a person of God!"

Why is caring for children the particular responsibility of the Church? It is because of that special role that caring for a child can have in influencing faith of adults. In many cases, children may be significant sources of and resources for Christian truths for their parents and for other adults. The main reason for caring for children is not to gain better access to their parents or other adults. But doing so is, in itself, neither illegitimate nor manipulative, and is often the door that God opens to the hearts of whole families and villages.

BECAUSE ONLY THE CHURCH CAN "REMOVE THE CURSE"

We have already noted the disturbing very *last* word in the Old Testament—in Malachi 4:6—is the word *curse*. The verse says, "He will turn the hearts of the fathers to their children, and the hearts of the children to their fathers; or else I will come and strike the land with a curse." There are obviously severe consequences for fathers failing to give attention to their responsibility to train and nurture their children. God says the failure to do so will result in the land being stricken with a curse. What is interestingly is that one of the first concerns that arises in the New Testament, in the narratives surrounding the births of John and Jesus, is the same matter—turning the hearts of the fathers to the children (Luke 1:17).

We may debate what exactly it may mean for "the land to be stricken with a curse," but as I have walked among the poor in the slums around the world, I have no hesitation to say that those places are stricken with a curse. That is not how God wants his people to live. Satan has the upper hand in such places, stealing, killing, and destroying. Nor does it take a genius to see that the hearts of the children are not turned to the fathers, nor that (perhaps because) the hearts of the fathers are not turned to the children. As we discussed in chapter four, what we see among the poor around the world is not just a material matter, but a spiritual one as well. Satan is carrying out his agenda to steal, kill, and destroy the abundant life that God desires. Note this: A curse is a spiritual matter. It is the opposite of a blessing. A curse is not removed by providing food and medicine. A curse is not removed by providing blankets and clothing. A curse is not removed by school supplies and learning opportunities.

It is only the Church and Christian believers who can turn a curse into a blessing. It is only the Church and Christian believers who can address the problem of sin—the true root cause of poverty. This is a role and a power to which our secular friends have no access.

So it is only the Church and Christian believers who can do true Christian holistic child development. The Church is God's instrument to touch the hearts of both the fathers and the children. That is why, when all is said and done, care for children the *particular* responsibility of the Church.

THE CHILD IN THE CHURCH

OVERVIEW

In this section, we will address the spiritual development of the child in the Church, the ministry of the Church to the child, and protecting the child in church environments.

First, we will explore the issues of the psychological maturity of children to make faith decisions, the longstanding question of the *age of accountability*, and if there is a unique window of spiritual receptivity between the ages of 4 to 14. Then, we address the characteristics of child-friendly churches. How can we improve the programs, facility, and the staff of the church to make them more child-friendly? We will also provide a sample covenant agreement, which churches at all levels in any country may use to identify and make commitments on behalf of children.

Finally, though it is tragic to have to bring up, we must discuss the issue of child protection and the church. Specifically, we will take up the issue of protecting children from ourselves—that is, from our own employees or volunteers who may participate with us in our programs for children *in order* to gain access to children for exploitation. We will then include the essential components of a child protection protocol for our churches and child development projects.

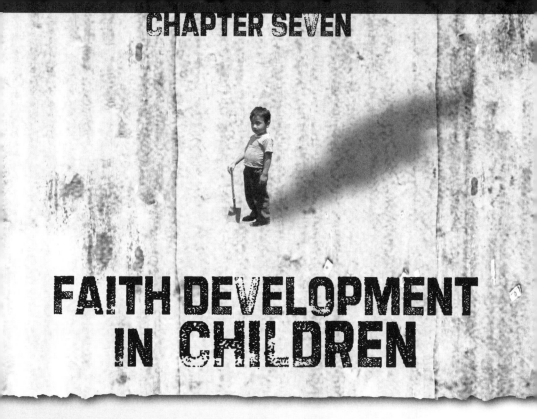

CHAPTER SEVEN

FAITH DEVELOPMENT IN CHILDREN

These commandments that I give you today are to be upon your hearts.
Impress them on your children. Talk about them when you sit at home
and when you walk along the road, when you lie down and when you get
up. Tie them as symbols on your hands and bind them on your foreheads.
Write them on the doorframes of your houses and on your gates.
Deuteronomy 6:6-9

Even in primarily Christian contexts, there are many serious theological questions surrounding the child that have important consequences to our view of holistic child development. Roy Zuck, in his excellent book, *Precious in His Sight*,[1] asks these among other probing questions:

- What is the age of accountability?
- What should young children be taught before conversion?
- Will infants who die go to heaven?
- Are children of Christian parents in a covenant relationship to God?
- Are childhood conversions genuine?
- Should children from Christian homes be confronted with the need for radical conversion, or should they be encouraged to grow up as Christians with no need for conversion?

Most of these questions are beyond the scope of this book. They hint, however, at the depths of possible theological inquiry surrounding children in the Bible. Since it is so fundamental to the spiritual nurture component of the holistic development of children, and also so important to the discussion of "The Child *in* the Church," we must consider faith development in children.

The issues raised in this chapter have primarily to do with the faith development of children *in* the Church—that is, the children who are growing up in the Church, who are primarily children of Christian parents, and who are growing up in primarily Western (and/or historically Christian) contexts. The matters surrounding evangelism to and conversion of children in primarily non-Christian contexts—that is, interfaith evangelism (or Mission) are very different. These will be discussed in chapter eleven of this book.

GOD'S INTENTION FOR CHILDREN IN CHURCHES

It is God's intention that every child in every generation come to understand how precious he or she is in His sight and to have a right relationship with Him through Jesus Christ. And God intends for His church to be a witness to children so they may know and follow His purposes in their lives. The important biblical framework developed by VIVA and others in *Understanding God's Heart for Children* puts it this way:

> Children are essential to the life and ministry of the church, bringing spiritual gifts and abilities and fulfilling definite roles. The church needs to be a place where children may dynamically connect with God and engage in meaningful participation; discipled, equipped, and empowered for life and ministry. As members of the family of God, children are to be cared for as sons and daughters and are part of the admonition to love and serve one another. God intends for churches to provide children with opportunities to know Him and fulfill their calling in the body of Christ.[2]

There has been a long-standing debate about how and when children can actually come to Christ, and if faith decisions made in childhood are legitimate or genuine. Interestingly, in a survey done some years ago by Southern Baptists, many adherents felt that ". . . it is practically impossible for a child under 12 or 13 years of age to have reached the mental, emotional or spiritual maturity which is necessary for experiencing a genuine repentance for sin and submission to Christ as Savior."[3] And yet the same people indicated that "decisions to become a Christian were made by their children before the age of twelve."[4] There seems to be a bit of a disconnect between what adults think is possible or common and what is actually happening!

Perhaps we need to ask a prior question: "Do children growing up in the Church and in Christian families need to be *converted* at all?" Not all would argue that they do. The Bible nowhere teaches infant damnation, but at the same time, children, no less than adults, are sinners in need of a Savior. When then do children become accountable or responsible for their own spiritual condition?

The term *age of accountability* refers to the time when individuals become mature enough to be morally responsible for their acts and consciously responsive to God's grace. The term is not found in the Bible. It is inferred from various Scriptures that seem to speak to the early spiritual consciousness of children and their accountability before God.[5] Quite properly, no one who argues for an age of accountability will suggest what that age is. There is no definitive biblical answer. Ultimately, it is wiser to place much more emphasis on *accountability* than on age. It is a mistake to set an arbitrary age for conversion. Likewise, it is a mistake to ignore the limitations of understanding in the very young.

In this we can no doubt learn from the approaches of the

Jews in ancient Israel. As Roy Honeycutt explains, there, the father had the primary relationship with God and the family members were included in the covenant on the basis of the father's covenant relationship:

> For many in Israel the family-centered nature of religion meant that the child not only was born into the faith but that the primary nurture he received was from the family circle, not the institution. . . . Also, religion was largely home-centered in its personal development and nurture.[6]

Honeycutt continues,

> The child would never face the possible frustration of . . . [finding] . . . that once he reached an accepted chronological age he was treated as standing outside the covenant faith. . . . He would never feel he must now do something to recapture the quality of love and joy that he had earlier known. . . . In essence, the Old Testament view of covenant theology would take seriously the presupposition that a child who is once within the saving grace of God is never abandoned.[7]

There was no need for *conversion* of children and youths in the Old Testament. By virtue of being part of a Jewish family, all children and youths were already part of the faith community.

As Honeycutt clarifies,

> [T]he only decision an individual ever faced within Israel was whether or not he would remain within the covenant, not whether he would enter the covenant, or share in the worshipping community. He, and the community with him, were already within the covenant faith. God had promised this for all ages. One's only decision was whether he would remain within the faith community.[8]

William Hendricks further observes,

> Much of our theological anxiety about very young children is a projection of our own concern for them. There is no biblical reason one should not trust the compassion and mercy of God to extend to children until they can make meaningful and depth-level decisions for themselves. In fact, the covenant of grace between God and mankind expressed in Christ, gives us every reason to presume that the young are kept by God in His compassionate concern. [9]

God's compassion for children, in fact, should drive us to better understand how faith is developed and nurtured in the children we can reach.

FAITH DEVELOPMENT IN CHILDREN

We have said that most children growing up in Christian environments make their first significant faith decisions between the ages of 4 to 14. Contrary to what some adults think, children can grasp spiritual truths easily. They can "sense the guilt of sin"[10] and understand what Jesus has done for them and what it takes to receive Jesus. Jesus Himself alluded to the special awareness and sensitivity of little children.[11] And of course, Jesus Himself is an example of a very young child with exceptional spiritual insight!

We have also noted that God apparently has a very high regard for children's ability to understand the faith. We see children participating in worship and celebration in several places in the Old Testament. The frequent biblical instruction to parents to nurture faith in their children obviously makes no sense unless children indeed have the capacity to understand and obey the commandments.

In her excellent book linking children and mission, *Daddy, Are We There Yet?*, Sylvia Foth highlights the psychological-developmental view of the capacity of children to understand the faith. She reminds us,[12]

> Brain researchers tell us that the brain, even of a newborn infant, is hardwired for trusting responses to relationships. We see this initially as kids grow a trusting bond with their mother, then with other family members. Perhaps David

understood this when he wrote, "Yet you brought me out of the womb; you made me trust in you even at my mother's breast. From birth I was cast upon you; from my mother's womb you have been my God" (Psalm 22:9-10).

This ability to trust forms the foundational capacity for children to eventually trust God, as well. Children have the capacity for early response.

Foth notes that a child's conscience develops somewhere between the ages of 3 to 6 years. Their ability to understand abstract concepts (such as God, heaven, eternity, sin, and forgiveness) grows as they move past preschool to grade school ages. Moreover, their ability to synthesize information, putting many complex ideas together to create one conclusion, develops during later school-age years.[13] Each of these maturing abilities suggests that children can and are able to "get" the matters of the faith. Foth remarks,

Of course, children can respond to the gospel without fully understanding every detail of their decision. After all, many adults have done this as well. Who of us is not still learning and understanding more about the gift of grace and salvation purchased for us through the work of Christ on the cross?[14]

Regardless of our understanding of the age of account-ability, the necessity of dramatic conversion experiences in children growing up in Christian families and in the church, or a child's particular capacities at various ages, we do need to address the matter of faith development in children. Surely, the parents and Church must be actively involved with devel-oping faith in children from an early age. Just as we know that the physical, social, emotional, and other aspects of a child's development happen over time, so we must understand that faith develops over time as well. Age specific, insightful mate-rials and instruction are essential to promote healthy growth. There is no more important role for the church than the careful, consistent, and systematic program of religious training for children and young people.

All children demonstrate a type of faith from the earliest months of life. The infant in her mother's arms shows faith not by believing or doing, but simply by trusting. We noted in chapter one Dr. Vinay Samuel's intriguing notion that children have an inherent *transcendence*—a sense or sensitivity to the divine, to "mystery" and to the touch of God in their lives. Following Katherine Copsey, we suggested that transcen-dence in children was characterized by openness to nature and others, a sense of awe and wonder, the ability to live in the now, and an uncomplicated view of life including trust and a simple acceptance of the things of God.

We also noted that, as wonderful as those things sound, they can easily be snuffed out by the harsh realities of a secu-larized society. A child's sense of openness and mystery can be, and usually is, crushed an early age, and along with it their spiritual awareness and sensitivity. In effect, says Katherine Copsey, "the image of God in the child has been scratched or spoiled."[15] She continues:

> We want to be able to use a child's spirituality as a springboard to faith, but the degree to which this spirituality has been damaged (the image scratched) will affect the child's ability to move to faith. It is very difficult for a child to understand what it is to trust Jesus, if she has lost the ability to trust. It is very difficult to marvel at the God of creation if there has been nothing in the environment to nurture that sense of awe and wonder.[16]

How important is it, then, for us to begin thinking about faith development in children at a very young age! *Attention to faith development must go hand in hand with all other aspects of development beginning soon after birth.* How will we ensure that faith grows in children right along with their physical, social, and emotional growth?

As we have seen from biblical examples, God sometimes grants a remarkably developed faith to some children. More often, however, faith grows more or less commensurate with a child's physical and psychological growth. By linking faith development to the other aspects of human development, those of us who are involved in teaching and leading others in faith can better anticipate how to reach them more effectively.

Steve Wamberg[17] points out that when the Bible uses an illustration to describe faith, it often uses an illustration that describes, or references, the process of growth. For example,

Psalm 1 describes the faithful man as being like a growing and fruitful tree. Psalm 92:12-15 describes righteous people as people who grow and flourish in faith even into old age. In Mark 4:26, Jesus described the faithful in a parable as those like the seed sown on good soil, producing a good crop. In 2 Thessalonians, Paul told the Thessalonian church that he was grateful to God because their faith was growing.

Peter told the early church that growing faith required a process much like that of a growing child: begin with milk, then take on more mature nourishment.[18] So what kind of spiritual nurture produces a healthy, growing faith?

HOW FAITH GROWS

John Westerhoff of Duke University uses an illustration of a tree to describe *how* faith grows. He uses four principles from the growth of trees to apply to the development of faith.[19]

> "First, a tree with one ring is as much a tree as a tree with four rings. A tree in its first year is a complete and whole tree, and a tree with three rings is not a better tree but only an expanded tree." A child's (or a new Christian's) faith is developmentally whole according to the child's total development. It is no less valuable a resource to God than the faith of a mature person. The goal of the faith teacher is to help each person fulfill his or her faith potential at every point.

"Second, a tree grows if the proper environment is provided, and if such an environment is lacking, the tree becomes arrested in its expansion until the proper environment exists. . . . Similarly, we expand from one style [stage of] faith to another only if the proper environment, experiences, and interactions are present . . . " Westerhoff emphasizes the need of healthy relationships with other Christians, and a healthy environment, as crucial components of faith development.

"Third, a tree acquires one ring at a time in a slow and gradual manner. We do not see that expansion, although we do see the results, and surely we are aware that you cannot skip rings. . . . The same is true of faith." Faith development cannot be rushed. It is not something you can see in a person at a glance. But over time, you can see how the process has brought growth to someone.

"Fourth, as a tree grows, it does not eliminate rings but adds each ring to the ones before, always maintaining the previous rings as it expands. It is the same with faith. . . . We do not outgrow a style [stage] of faith and its needs but expand it by adding new elements and new needs. Indeed, if the needs of an earlier style of faith cease to be met, persons have a tendency to return to that earlier style of faith."[20]

Continuing with John Westerhoff's analysis of faith development in children,[21] he says that early in life, children tend to "catch" faith—they apprehend rather than comprehend. They sense a positive environment; they hear positive things about Jesus, when they are welcomed and nurtured in places adults call church. The hugs and affirmation they get from adults are, at least in part, credited to the God the adults worship.

The absence of those hugs and affirmation will mean that children will have a difficult time developing faith at all. It should not, therefore, come as a surprise that Westerhoff encourages churches (and parents) to give even the youngest children a positive, proactive, and stimulating environment. If a church's goal is to develop faith, children cannot be shelved in sterile and passive nursery environments. They have to be engaged in development through interaction.

The impact of positive interaction with people of faith cannot be underestimated in the life of a child. Today, Juan Ramos is a successful artist in the Dominican Republic. Years ago, he was a sponsored child in a Compassion child development center. Juan makes it clear that the center provided an atmosphere of caring and affirmation that helped him understand God's love as a young elementary student. As time went on, Juan began to appreciate the sponsors who sent monthly support on his behalf. He commented, "They never mentioned the financial support that they provided for me. They always mentioned words of love and encouragement. They never made me feel that I was a burden, but that I was like a child for them, a son." Such a nurturing attitude, even from a distance, can powerfully enhance faith development in anyone.

Faith development is a process. The first faith experience of very young children is more experienced than understood. It is nurtured through affirmation, a caring environment, and the example and modeling of trust on the part of adults. Children learn that God loves them and that they are valued. A further stage of faith development takes place when children and young people begin to identify with the faith of their parents or peers. Of crucial importance at this stage is that the child senses that he/she is wanted, needed, accepted, and important in the church and faith community.[22]

As children grow older, faith is usually characterized by questioning, doubt, searching, and experimentation. "Searching faith requires that we explore alternatives to our earlier understandings and ways, for people need to test their own tradition by learning about others. It is only then that they are able to reach convictions that are truly their own."[23]

Young people at this searching stage need to be allowed to explore. At the same time, they need to "be encouraged to remain in the faith community during their intellectual struggle, experimentation, and first endeavors at commitment."[24]

A final stage of faith development is "owned faith." Westerhoff remarks,

> Due to the serious struggle with doubt that precedes it, owned faith often appears as a great illumination or enlightenment, but in any case it can be witnessed in our actions and new needs. Now people most want to put their faith into personal

and social action, and they are willing and able to stand up for what they believe, even against the community of their nurture.[25]

Steve Wamberg notes that the apostle Paul was a prime example of "owned faith." Once he came to faith in Christ, he was eager to put his faith into action. He took the opportunity time and again to stand up for his belief in Christ, even against the Jewish faith community that had nurtured him.[26]

Parents and teachers can encourage and enhance owned faith by[27]:

- Connecting Scripture with everyday life
- Asking open-ended questions that demand mature thought
- Addressing a broad range of relevant and current topics
- Challenging those with owned faith to daily express their faith in practical ways
- Encouraging daily Bible reading and prayer
- Encouraging biblical action in response to social needs

Once again, *faith development is a process.* The better we understand the process of developing faith in children, the better we can help children optimize their experience and understanding of God as they grow.

IS THERE A 4/14 WINDOW OF RECEPTIVITY?[25]

We acknowledge that faith typically *grows* like a tree and has many stages, growing along with the physical and psychological maturity of the child. Interestingly, evidence suggests that *if* children are going to make significant, long-term life-changing decisions to follow Christ, those decisions will often be made before the age of 15. To put it another way, there is a 4/14 Window of receptivity for children and young people to make a firm decision to follow Christ. If a young person has not made such a decision before the age of 15, it is highly unlikely that he or she will make such a life-changing "conversion" decision at any time in their future.

Recently, important confirmation that this is true (at least in the USA) has come from the well-known church researcher George Barna. In his book *Transforming Children into Spiritual Champions*,[29] Barna presents results of extensive research related to faith decisions in the U.S. He reports that 93 percent of 13-year-olds in the U.S. consider themselves to be Christian, though only about 34 percent of them really have an understanding of what it means to be a Christian.[30] However, if people are going to become a Christian, they are far more likely to make that decision by the age of 13 than after that age. Barna states that:

> . . . the probability of someone embracing Jesus as his or her Savior was 32 percent for those between the ages of 5 and 12; 4 percent for those in the 13-18 range; and 6 percent for people 19 or

older. In other words, if people do not embrace
Jesus Christ as their Savior before they reach their
teenage years, the chance of their doing so at all is
slim.[31]

As he reports these surprising statistics, Barna urges,

> Consider the facts. People are much more
> likely to accept Christ as their Savior when they are
> young. Absorption of biblical information and prin-
> ciples typically peaks during the preteen years. . . .
> Habits related to the practice of one's faith develop
> when one is young and change surprisingly little
> over time.[32]

The need for strategic ministry to children is apparent.
We must adapt our ideas about children and their spiritual
capacities to match both their growth and their potential. "The
implication of these findings is clear," says Barna. "Anyone
who wishes to have significant influence on the development
of a person's moral and spiritual foundations had better exert
that influence while the person is still open-minded and impressionable—in other words, while the person is still young."[33]

What should we teach the children God has put in our care?
I often suggest Dr. James Dobson's *Checklist for Spiritual
Training*,[34] a set of targets at which to aim. These five Scriptural
concepts should be consciously taught, providing the foundation on which all future doctrine and faith will rest. Dr. Dobson
acknowledges that many of the items require maturity that

children lack and we should not try to make adult Christians out of our immature youngsters. However, we agree with him that we can gently urge them toward these goals during the impressionable years of childhood.

Concept 1 is the great truth, "Love the Lord your God with all your heart and with all your soul and with all your strength" (Mark 12:30). Children need to learn to know God through your example, the Bible and prayer—to begin. Only by knowing God will they learn to love Him completely.

Concept 2, Jesus said, is like the first: "Love your neighbor as yourself" (Mark 12:31). Our challenge is to teach children to understand and empathize with others, even in the midst of a self-centered world.

Teaching children the practical and relational importance of obeying God is the heart of **Concept 3, "Teach me to do your will; for you are my God" (Psalm 143:10).**

Helping children revere God—and to listen to the Holy Spirit—are core ideas in **Concept 4, "Fear God . . . for this is the whole duty of man" (Ecclesiastes 12:13).**

Nurturing children in generosity, responsibility and healthy self-denial are key elements in **Concept 5: "But the fruit of the Spirit is . . . self-control" (Galatians 5:22-23).**

These concepts are covered in greater detail in the study guide developed for this book. But you certainly have the possibility of using this checklist as is to frame your own specific strategy for faith development in the children you know.

Wouldn't it be great if we could prepare this generation of children to say at the age of accountability, "Here I am, Lord, send me!"?

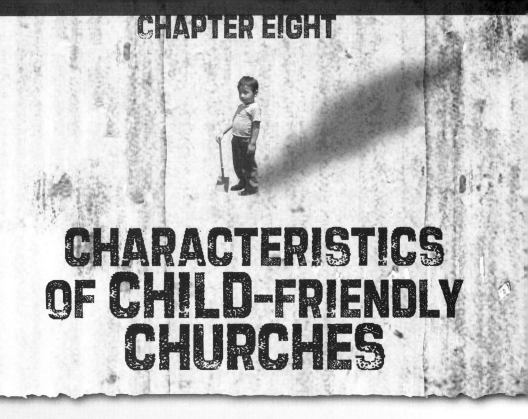

CHAPTER EIGHT

CHARACTERISTICS OF CHILD-FRIENDLY CHURCHES

This is what the Lord Almighty says: "Once again men and women of ripe old age will sit in the streets of Jerusalem, each with cane in hand because of his age. The city streets will be filled with boys and girls playing there."
Zechariah 8:4-5

In the Penang Child Theology Consultation in 2006, a question was posed to the participants: "Where is the 'heart' of the Church?"[2] The exercise was to reveal how well the global church fared in placing the child in the midst. A litany of responses was gathered in that consultation. It proves a point that where other things, programs, or important people are placed in the "midst" instead of the child, the Church fails to treat children the way God intends them to be treated. In summary, the consultation gathered the following information:[2]

- The church is often adult-oriented.
- Children are treated as spiritually inferior.
- Children may be seen as a means to an end (e.g., children's ministry is seen as an apprenticeship for future pastors).
- Churches use children as "ornaments" during festive seasons such as Christmas or Easter.
- Churches are schizophrenic in the attitude toward children—they are called "Junior Church" but not allowed to take part in communion or vote or otherwise have a significant role.

We have seen that the Church has a biblical responsibility and mandate to care for children both inside and outside of churches. And we know that the Church (along with the parents) has a biblical responsibility to teach the children. We also know that children learn far better in child-friendly environments.

This chapter provides suggestions of the characteristics of a child-friendly church environment. It also offers a checklist of actions a church may take to make it friendlier toward children. We will first look at the basic things a child ought to be able to expect from a church. Then we will examine ways to improve the friendliness of church programs, facilities, and staff. Finally, we will touch on the responsibilities toward children of church "hierarchies"—the national fellowships, the denominations, and the local churches.

A CHILD-FRIENDLY WORLD WHERE A CHILD CAN LOVE AND BE LOVED; CAN THE CHURCH HELP?

"The overriding need of every child," Dr. Keith White writes, "is to be loved by, and to love, one or more significant adults."[3] He lists five basic needs of a child, which, if not met, will impair the capacity of the child to experience and express love. "If none of these are met over a substantial period of a child's early years, the likelihood is that the child will be emotionally scarred and impaired."[4] These fundamental needs, summarized below, are to be met primarily in the home. However, the sensitive church, seeking to improve its ministry and child-friendliness, will also be an important resource in meeting these needs.[5]

The primary need of a child is **security** through a place for relationship, exploration, play, and development. No intervention will have any effect unless children know they are safe.

Children also need to be assured of their **significance**, that they are someone precious because of who they are. Every child needs to know that there is at least one adult who is committed to them unconditionally. Any program for child development/care is nothing if this is absent in the treatment of children and their relationships.

Children need **boundaries** to feel safe, to develop, and to relate with others appropriately. Often what comes to mind as we think of boundaries are *rules and discipline*. But even more important than boundaries are the values and principles that characterize and govern a person's life. Biblically, children (like the rest of us) are created for **community** and relationships. Are our churches providing that community?

Children need to exercise their **creativity.** They are essentially creative and creators. I have watched with delight (and sometimes envy!) as children in the poorest neighborhoods create toys from scraps of wood, plastic, rubber, and paper. It's no wonder: As created in the image of God, children must be given opportunities to create, to make, and to shape. A church can provide safe and age-appropriate materials, from crayons to modeling clay to papier-mache, to encourage children to express their creativity. Children can also be effective actors and dramatists, too!

Beyond these five basic needs, there are things specific to churches that children should expect. Combined together, these elements can help us enhance, increase, and improve its overall ministry to children and create a more child-friendly environment.

BASIC THINGS THAT CHILDREN SHOULD GET FROM THE CHURCH

What are the basic things that a child should expect from a church? The following would seem to be important for all churches and for all children.[6]

Children should expect church to **teach them the Word of God.** God demands from the Church that children grow up hearing and learning about the love of God for them and worshiping Him in a way compatible with their age and capability. The logical outcome is that a church will also **make disciples of children.** Each child shall be encouraged and given an opportunity to become a disciple of Jesus through the teaching from the Word of God, commensurate with age and capability.

Children should also expect church to regularly support them in **prayer.** The prayer items of the church should often include children's issues. Teachers, parents, and staff alike should pray by name for the children they reach. Children should also be enabled to grow in **love and care** that a church affords them.

Churches should provide a "listening ear" to the children, so they should be free to share their views, needs, hurts, hopes, and dreams. In like manner, children should expect to be integrated into church life through **opportunities to participate in ministry.** The church should enable children to serve in their homes, the church, and in their community.

Children should also expect a church to offer **child–friendly church facilities.** This includes safe places for children to play and be "childlike," and **appropriate classrooms.** Where possible, churches should provide child-size tables and chairs and colorful things on the walls at child-eye level (preferably things that the children themselves have produced).

A child-friendly church also offers **qualified children's teachers** and **age–graded classes and curricula.** The church should ensure that children receive regular, sound, biblical education that is based on their age and capabilities. As part of its education initiative, a church should also engage in **family equipping and preparation** that educates, encourages, and equips parents to raise their children in accordance with the Word of God. They should proactively **protect children from harmful traditions** and other things that defile their consciences and their faith.

As noted above, these are simply the basic expectations we believe a child should expect from church. We address these more fully in the study guide for this book. These issues form the core of any church's outreach to children.

MAKING CHURCH PROGRAMS MORE CHILD-FRIENDLY

The above items are the minimum that children should expect from their church. You and your church colleagues can no doubt add many other things, some perhaps very specific items relevant to your church.

Beyond these, there are measures that a church may take to make the programs and the church meeting place more nurturing, profitable, interesting, and safe for the child. Again, your church may build its own more extensive checklist that will stimulate thinking and help it respond to children's needs in your own context and the particular environment of your church.

The worship services should be meaningful to children and not just adult experiences in which children must conform to adult standards. Many churches, especially in the "majority world," do not have the luxury of space and facilities to accommodate children in the main service. Many, however, make a genuine effort to place the children in the midst. For example, some have designated a family worship service on a communion Sunday. The important point is that the children know they are welcome.

Children should be talked to and listened to—before, during, or after church—about their worship experience. The children should be asked what they want to be done for them in the church, and they should participate in the decision-making.

The church *may* do a child's sermon or provide other kinds of instruction in the worship service at the child's level and that include the children and help them to know that they are noticed and valued. I say *may* do a child sermon, but you may find that there are good reasons *not* to do child sermons. (See this book's study guide for more thoughts on this issue.)

The agenda items of the church elders' meetings and annual church programs should include matters relating to children and how to improve the church's ministry to children.

The Bible classes and teaching materials should be age-graded and suitable for the age and maturity of the children. In today's electronic-oriented world Sunday school materials, where possible, should be interactive and employ a variety of multi-media resources.

The budget of the church should provide funds for significant child ministries, including materials, teacher training, activities, and rituals.

The church should emphasize **rituals**—Christmas, Easter, other special church days, birthdays, Sunday school graduations, anniversaries and remembrances—and make them a big deal for the children. Also, the church should have **designated days and times to bless children** in its annual program.

The pastor should be a regular visitor to the children's ministry and should know many of the children by name.

These simple tactics, when implemented, can launch any church into a more effective ministry to children and youth.

MAKING CHURCH FACILITIES MORE CHILD-FRIENDLY

I have been saddened at times when I visit churches in overseas contexts that host projects and activities for children, yet make no provision to turn the compound into a place where a child would want to be. I have seen churches with almost daily child activities that lack child-sized tables or chairs, and have nothing on the walls that is colorful or attractive to children. Worse still, I have seen compounds that are neither clean nor safe for children.

Many churches, of course, have very limited space and have to "make do" in many ways. But in any church, much can be done to make the church meeting place safe, attractive, warm, and welcoming. In churches where facilities have multiple uses (perhaps on different days of the week), the appearance of the church can be modified on the children's days so they feel welcome and at home. At the very least, the church should strive for the following. (Again, you and your church colleagues can add to this list.)

Ensure that the buildings and grounds are safe for the children. Allow no exposed sharp corners or objects; no broken furniture; no rough edges, exposed wiring, open drains; or other problems that endanger the physical safety of the children. **Seek to make the church meeting place attractive**, clean, and friendly for children and childhood.

Have classrooms for Bible classes for children that are decorated and equipped to appeal to children.

Have space specifically for children to play (even playground equipment), to work, color, play with their hands, and to have fun.

These ideas may seem too practical to have any overt spiritual value. Yet we must remember that our calling is to provide holistic Christian ministry to the children whom God so highly values.

MAKING CHURCH STAFF MORE CHILD-FRIENDLY

No church will have a meaningful program for its children unless it gives close attention to the recruiting, equipping, and supporting of the caregivers it places in charge of its ministry to children.

A primary function of a church is to provide a place where adults can teach and disciple children to help them understand what it means to be a follower of Jesus. The success of the church in fulfilling this obligation is dependent on the quality and commitment of the staff, teachers, and other caregivers. Sadly, the careless church will often assign its least qualified persons to work with the children—those who have little biblical understanding, no awareness of child learning styles, no understanding of child behavior, discipline, or nurture.

Here, briefly, are a few guidelines to help a church improve the child-friendliness of its staff.

The church must insist on purity among leaders. Church leaders and staff are models for the children. They must understand that they are modeling all the time, whether their example is positive or negative. Children are always watching.

The people assigned to teach children should be trained and experienced. The church should invest in regular training courses for all its teachers and caregivers. Children's Bible classes should be monitored and evaluated on a regular basis by a body set up for this purpose.

The leaders and staff of the church should look at children's potential (not just their current behavior). They should learn to see and appreciate each child as a work in progress, not as a finished product.

The church leaders and staff should support the child's family. They should provide regular and varied parenting classes and support for parents in difficult situations, (e.g. for the parents of rebellious children). The church should seek to provide resources for the home, in the form of classes, books, videos, tapes, and other materials.

The church should have regular family-together activities, to provide intergenerational interaction, and to avoid overscheduling children's or youth activities at the expense of family time.

The staff should be trained in child protection (see the section on child protection in this book), and should be able to recognize the symptoms of neglect and abuse amongst children. In turn, **the church should seek to have trained people to help children who have been abused, mistreated, or "on the streets."**

In the first edition of this book, I included a checklist to rate your church programs, staff, and facilities on child-friendliness. My friends with the VIVA Network in Uganda have developed that checklist further and have allowed me to use it in slightly adapted form on the following pages.[7]

RESPONSIBILITIES OF THE CHURCH AT ALL LEVELS

Shiferaw Michael, a brilliant, passionate advocate for children in Africa, has done much work with the churches in Ethiopia and elsewhere. Over a period of several months, Mr. Michael brought the church leaders together at all levels—national fellowships, denominational leadership, and local church leaders. He asked the question we asked above: "What should a child expect from the church?" One of the more significant outcomes of his exercise was the Covenant for

CREATING A CHILD FRIENDLY CHURCH

Name of church		Pastor or Person in Charge	

AIM 1: There is a vision for children's work	**Yes**	**No**	**Unsure**	**Possible evidences**
There a common vision for children's work in the church				Vision Statement for Children's Ministry
Children's work is regularly on church leadership agendas				Minutes of meetings
We view children as real people, who have spiritual needs, and who have a role to play in our church				Interviews

AIM 2: Training of workers and child protection is being implemented	**Yes**	**No**	**Unsure**	**Possible evidences**
We recognize that we have a biblical responsibility to work with children.				Interviews
Children's workers have been trained on how to teach children from a Christian perspective				Dated records of training
The church has an appropriate and monitored child protection policy				Child Protection Policy
All staff and volunteers in the church have signed a child protection declaration form				Child Protection Declaration Forms
All activities in the church are properly supervised and approved by the church leadership				Interviews

AIM 3: The church building offers a safe environment	**Yes**	**No**	**Unsure**	**Possible evidences**
Group meeting areas are clean and safe				Tour of facilities
A first aid box is kept on church premises and can be accessed by all leaders				Location of first aid box
Details of emergency contacts are displayed where all people can see them				Location of notices

AIM 4: Nurture groups are available for children and young people	**Yes**	**No**	**Unsure**	**Possible evidences**
The church provides age appropriate Sunday or mid week groups for young people and children				Church programme
There are opportunities for children to seek God through the scriptures, teaching, and their personal experiences				Interviews
There is regular prayer with and for children and young people				Interviews
The church supports children with special needs.				Tour of facilities; report of interventions
There is a realistic budget for children's work				Annual budgets or accounts

AIM 5: There are opportunities for children to engage in worship in the church	Yes	No	Unsure	Possible evidences
Some services are designed to be for all ages				Service records
Services are planned in a way that children are appropriately engaged in spiritual development				Interviews
Children's leaders and children are involved in planning and leading child friendly services				Interviews
AIM 6: Suitable facilities for under 5s are available	Yes	No	Unsure	Possible evidences
A special area is allocated for parents/carers to care for babies and very young children				Tour of facilities
Young children have access to engaging activities or appropriate toys and books				Tour of facilities
Christian parenting support is offered				Church programme
AIM 7: Children and young people are involved as equal members of the church community	Yes	No	Unsure	Possible evidences
Children and young people listened to and consulted on church matters				Interviews
We include children in our attendance figures				Attendance lists
AIM 8: There are outreach opportunities	Yes	No	Unsure	Possible evidences
The church's outreach programs include opportunities for children to participate				Interviews
The church is working with the local community officials to raise standards of child protection and awareness				Meeting records
The church helps prevent and delay problems through support of widows; heath care; parenting courses; feeding; family transition; income generating opportunities; etc...				Annual report
The church continues to be involved in the child's life by promoting self sustainability for young people e.g. discipleship; vocational training; education; etc...				Child records

Adapted from Clibborne, Isobel Booth, Mim Friday, and others.
Viva Network resources, Kampala, Uganda.

Churches on Ministering to Children.[8] This document detailed the responsibilities of each level of church. It set out minimum standards, which each level should seek to provide or achieve in order to better minister to the children and families they serve.

The result of their planning was written up in the form of a signed covenant. By actually getting responsible church leaders to sign their names, they created a higher level of commitment to actually do what they know they ought. The covenant details specific actions that leaders at each level will take. By observing and measuring what the churches have agreed to do, responsible Christians working with children will be able to gauge the extent to which the provisions have actually been carried out at each level. It is hoped, too, that the leaders will allow themselves to be held accountable to carry out what they have agreed in writing to do.

Key to the Covenant for the Churches are the obligations suggested for each level of the church. These are the responsibilities of the national fellowships or national alliances, the responsibilities of the denominational leadership, and of course, the responsibilities of the church at the local level.

The objectives of the Covenant are:

- To highlight the importance of, and the biblical basis for, ministry to children.
- To encourage the church to give attention to holistic child ministries.
- To call the evangelical fellowship of a given country, the denominations, local churches, Christian

agencies, and Christian schools to action on behalf of needy children.

- To create standards that will help the church to measure its ministry to children.

COVENANT ON MINISTERING TO CHILDREN

The following is an adaptation of Michael's work on the responsibilities of a church at each of the levels listed.

Responsibilities of the National-Level Fellowship(s) of Churches

A. Focus on Children

The fellowship of denominations shall:

- Prepare its nationwide vision and mission for child ministry.
- Establish a children's commission that will give overall guidance and coordination on matters relating to children.
- Have a department responsible for children's ministry.
- Make provision for children's ministries in its plans, programs, budget, constitution, and by-laws.
- Gather and analyze complete information regarding its children, and disseminate the same to all concerned on a regular basis.
- Carry out studies regarding harmful cultures, attitudes, and practices, and designate ways to eliminate them.

- Be an advocate for children among all its churches, in society, government, and all other institutions.

B. Training and Encouragement

The fellowship of denominations shall:

- Organize trainings and encouragement programs to denominations to enable them to focus on children.
- Devise strategies and prepare materials for use by the denominations.

C. Preparation of Children's Bible Study Materials

The fellowship of denominations shall:

- Conduct and encourage the preparation of children's Bible study books and materials.
- Produce, collect, and disseminate writings, tapes, videotapes, and other materials that help churches increase understanding of children.

Responsibilities of Denominations

A. Focus on Children

Each denomination shall:

- Prepare its vision and mission for children's ministries throughout the denomination.
- Give high priority to children's ministries as required by the Bible.

- Establish a committee to give overall guidance and coordination on matters relating to children's ministries.
- Have a department responsible for children's ministries.
- Include children's ministries in its activities, plans, programs, budget, constitutions, and by-laws.

B. Compiling Information on Child Needs and Resources to Address Them

Each denomination shall:

- Gather and analyze complete information regarding its children, and disseminate the same to all concerned on a regular basis.
- Carry out studies regarding harmful cultures, attitudes, and practices, and designate ways to eliminate them.

C. Training and Encouragement

Each denomination shall:

- Organize various training and encouragement programs with and for the children's workers in each of its churches.
- Assist its churches in the acquisition of studies, writings, videos, and other resources to equip them in their ministries to children.
- Provide appropriate child protection training and protocols/guidelines in each of their churches.

D. Child Ministry Curriculum in Bible Schools

Each denomination shall:

- Ensure that its own Bible schools include children ministry in their curriculum.
- Ensure that its own Bible schools give training and consultancy to people serving children in especially difficult circumstances.

E. Children's Teachers

Each denomination shall ensure that the teachers of children have proper training to teach children.

Responsibilities of Local Churches

A. Focus on Children

The local church shall:

- Have a mission and vision statement for child ministry.
- Give the same focus to children as it gives to its other ministries.
- Establish a committee that will give overall guidance and coordination on matters relating to children.
- Include children's ministry in its activities, plans, programs and budget.

B. Child-Friendly Church Facility

The local church shall seek to make its facilities and classrooms attractive, clean, friendly, and safe for children and childhood.

C. Children in Especially Difficult Circumstances

Each local church shall take concrete action with respect to the care and protection of rights of the children in especially difficult circumstances in cooperation with the individuals and organizations in its area.

D. Compilation of Information About the Needs of Children and the Resources to Address Those Needs.

Each local church shall:

- Gather and analyze complete information regarding its children.
- Carry out studies regarding harmful cultures, attitudes, and practices, and designate ways to eliminate them.

E. Training of Parents

Each local church shall:

- Educate and train parents/guardians and youth on their responsibilities regarding children.
- Educate and encourage parents to raise children in accordance with the Word of God, and in a way that protects them from harmful aspects of culture that defile their consciences and their faith.

F. Age-Graded Classes

Each church shall:

- Ensure that children attend age-graded classes.
- See to it that the syllabus takes into consideration the age and capabilities of children.

G. Advocate for Children

Each local church shall advocate for children in its community.

Michael provides places for all involved to sign. In this way, the commitment to make the church a child-friendly place is both shared and public.

That's just how it should be, isn't it?

CHAPTER NINE

CHILD PROTECTION IN CHURCH ENVIRONMENTS

Love does not delight in evil but rejoices with the truth. It always
protects, always trusts, always hopes, always perseveres.
1 Corinthians 13:6-7

Concern for children is the cornerstone of holistic child development. We are clearly opposed to all forms of child exploitation, including child labor, child prostitution, and all other forms of physical, emotional, and sexual abuse.

It is a shame to have to discuss the question of child protection in the context of churches' ministries to children. The vast majority of people with whom we work hold the same core values we do. However, we must not be naive. It is possible that there are those who would seek to use involvement in a church-based child program for their own personal motives, which may be perverted rather than pure. As I wrote this manuscript, I saw a story about a convicted pedophile found working in an orphanage set up to care for children after the December 2004 tsunami in Sri Lanka—apparently to gain access to the children. It does happen.

These guidelines are intended to help us ensure that the staff, donors, volunteers, or other personnel in our churches and child-focused programs are not involved in child exploitation of any kind. All churches or organizations caring for children should develop training activities to ensure that all those in and around our program understand the critical nature of this problem and ways to prevent it. The emphasis here is on prevention of sexual abuse, but the concern includes prevention of other kinds of abuse as well.

PROTECTING CHILDREN FROM OURSELVES

One of the most pervasive and offensive forms of child exploitation is the sexual abuse of children by adults. In Asia, the perverted desires of thousands of tourists who seek pleasure from prostitutes—even young child prostitutes—have spawned a multi-billion dollar sex industry. In several countries, girls and boys ages 9 and younger are sold into prostitution by their parents desperate for money or deceived by traffickers preying on young children. Homeless children, living on the streets, are recruited by pimps to sell their bodies for sex and survival. They are not only physically raped and plundered, but also psychologically scarred for the rest of their lives.

Who are the pedophiles? The pedophile is rarely a stranger. It is usually someone who knows the child, such as a parent or babysitter, or someone in authority, such as a teacher or youth worker. They are often people of standing in the community, and no one would dare to believe accusations of a child against such people. The abuse of children is mostly *not* the violent, commercial, spontaneous abuse in sex bars and hotels catering to sex tourists. It is the abuse that happens after an adult gains the confidence of youngsters in order to abuse that is so difficult to detect.

Even court judgments rarely deter the people who engage in child exploitation through a children's organization or ministry. If they fail in one organization, they join another one. But make no mistake here. The U.N. Convention on the Rights of the Child urges all states to prevent:

- The inducement or coercion of a child to engage in any unlawful sexual activity,
- The exploitative use of children in prostitution or other unlawful sexual practices, and
- The exploitative use of children in pornographic performances and materials.

The laws on child sexual abuse are different in every country. It may be necessary that legal counsel review any policies and procedures so they are consistent with the laws in your country. Law enforcement and child protection agencies in many countries may have materials that can be useful in adapting these guidelines to national situations.

RECOGNIZING CHILD ABUSE[1]

Physical abuse of children often leaves signs on the child's body. Caregivers will sometimes try to excuse injuries as the result of normal childhood accidents. There is a difference between the injuries that children get as a normal function of rough play and injuries often symptomatic of physical abuse. Child development professionals will learn to recognize the difference. The picture[2] below is an illustration comparing the location (on the left) of typical playground injuries and the location of injuries as the result of physical abuse.

The table on pages 194-195 is a summary of the physical and behavioral symptoms of several kinds of abuse.[3]

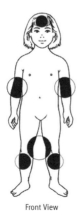

Front View

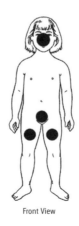

Front View

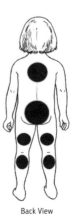

Back View

GENERAL GUIDELINES FOR PROTECTING CHILDREN

There are several proven, common-sense guidelines that are effective in protecting both the children you serve and your ministry from injury due to child abuse.

Screen visitors to your child activities or projects. Many church projects have local or foreign donors or sponsors who occasionally want to visit the program they support. Visitors and donors should be informed of your church's concern to avoid exploitation of children. They should understand that any personal information you seek about them is for prevention purposes. The approach should be positive: "Here is what we are doing to protect the children whom you help us assist."

Screen and carefully select the staff who work with children. Establish, review, and reinforce recruiting and employment policies and procedures, particularly for your staff who work with children. This includes development of behavioral guidelines for all staff. A responsible staff member who has been trained to screen potential staff should interview individuals applying for positions. If permissible by law, the interviewer should ask direct questions designed to identify applicants who may present a risk in this area and, therefore, should not work for a child-focused organization.

Implement staff behavior guidelines. Even if organizations use reasonable care in selecting staff or volunteers, it is still possible that children might be harmed, if employees who work with children are not properly supervised. The risk of harm to children and organizational liability can be reduced by staff observance of behavior guidelines.

TYPE OF ABUSE	PHYSICAL SIGNS	BEHAVIORAL
PHYSICAL ABUSE	Bruises or welts in various stages of healing or other visible injuries that appear on a child recurrently and cannot be explained by developmentally expected behavior	Explanation for a physical injury that is inconsistent with the injury, or the child's developmental age
	Unexplained or multiple broken bones, especially a broken rib, severe skull fracture, or other major head injury	Persistent or repetitive physical complaints of unclear cause, such as headache or belly pain
		The parent/caregiver reports that a significant injury was self-inflicted, or the child reports being injured by a parent or other caregiver.
	Burns or injuries in the shape of an object used to cause the injury such as bite marks, hand prints, cigar or cigarette burns, belt buckle markings; burns from immersion in scalding water or other hot liquids	The parent/caregivers have delayed seeking appropriate medical care.
	Unexplained or repetitive dental injuries	
	Failure to grow at the expected rate in a child who seems hungry and eager to eat when offered food	

TYPE OF ABUSE	PHYSICAL SIGNS	BEHAVIORAL
SEXUAL ABUSE	Pain, itching, bruises, or bleeding around the genitalia; stained or bloody underclothing	Bizarre, too sophisticated, or unusual sexual knowledge or behavior for the child's age, such as asking others to do sex acts, putting mouth on sex parts, trying to have intercourse
	Venereal disease	Child reports sexual abuse by a parent or adult
	Difficulty walking or sitting	
	Discharge from the vagina or urine openings	

TYPE OF ABUSE	PHYSICAL SIGNS	BEHAVIORAL
EMOTIONAL ABUSE	Delayed physical, emotional, or intellectual development that is not otherwise explicable	Impaired sense of self-worth, depression, withdrawal
	Habits such as rocking, sucking on fingers in excess of expectation for developmental stage	Extremes of behavior, such as overly aggressive or passive, apathetic, empty facial appearance, decreased social interaction with others, phobias, generalized fearfulness, fear of parent

TYPE OF ABUSE	PHYSICAL SIGNS	BEHAVIORAL
NEGLECT	Constant hunger, begging for food or hoarding food; fatigue or listlessness; poor hygiene such as dirty hair, skin, and clothes; inappropriate dress	Lack of supervision for long periods of time, inappropriate to the child's age or developmental stage
	Malnutrition or failure to thrive not explained by physical illness	
	Delayed seeking of professional attention for physical or dental problems	
	Impairment of parent or caregiver due to substance abuse, physical or mental illness	

TYPE OF ABUSE	PHYSICAL SIGNS	BEHAVIORAL
ANY TYPE OF ABUSE	Substance abuse; unexplained absences from the child care program	Over- and under-compliance of the child; lack of selectivity in friendly approach to adults; developmental regression, such as a previously toilet-trained child reverting to incontinence; sleep and appetite disturbances; depression; self-destructive behavior; excessive/inappropriate fears

Again, these guidelines are grounded in biblical common sense. First, any suggested behavior guidelines and principles involved should apply to all staff and volunteers who work with minors and children. Second, staff should avoid any appearance of inappropriate conduct. For example, it may be culturally acceptable for an adult to invite a child or minor to his or her home for a meal or a visit, but this may be perceived by others as wrong, and therefore should be avoided. In any case, more than one adult should usually be present at all times with children to make the child feel more comfortable and to protect the staff from false accusations of child abuse.

Psychologists point out that it is natural for children, especially adolescents, to develop emotional feelings for adults they admire and respect. They often express these feelings by flirting, flattering, hugging, or even making suggestive comments. Volunteers or staff who encounter such experiences should be careful that they do not put themselves into a compromising or vulnerable position. Therefore, if staff members feel uncomfortable about relationships with a minor, they should consult a peer, talk to their supervisor, or seek professional counsel. Following this line of thought, staff members should use good judgment, wisdom, and caution in becoming personally involved with children and minors who have emotional and psychological problems.

To keep these guidelines intact, we advise our child development centers to practice this simple and practical list of specific dos and don'ts:

- All volunteers, staff, sponsors, and project workers must be entirely professional in their relationship

with minors and children, while at the same time demonstrating Christian love and care.

- Volunteers, staff, sponsors, and project workers must not stay overnight alone with one or more children whether in the staff member's home or elsewhere.
- Workers must not hire minors as "house help" or provide shelter for minors in the staff member's home.
- Volunteers, staff, donors, and project workers must not fondle, hold, kiss, cuddle, or touch minors in an inappropriate way.
- Staff and project workers should notify the appropriate supervisor before spending time alone with a minor in an unsupervised situation.

REPORTING PROCEDURES FOR ALLEGED SEXUAL MISCONDUCT

Make no mistake: It is never pleasant when allegations of sexual misconduct arise. This is why it is crucial to have clear procedures in place for reporting such allegations.

An effective reporting procedure of alleged sexual misconduct enhances the effort to protect children from sexual or other abuse. Child abusers will not be prone to remain in an environment where workers are trained to report suspicious behavior. All staff should understand that discreet and confidential reporting of suspicions of sexual abuse, suspected incidents of child abuse, or inappropriate behavior is critical to abuse prevention and protection of children. Reporting represents a caring attitude. It is not an act of disloyalty. Workers should be alert to physical signs of abuse and molestation, as well as behavioral and verbal signs that a child may exhibit.

In a situation of suspected child abuse or molestation in an activity or project, the following reporting procedures should be followed:

1. Internal Reporting Procedures

If a staff member knows that a child has been molested, or reasonably suspects abuse, or hears allegations of abuse, he or she should:

    a. Immediately report the incident to the supervisor in charge of the activity or the most senior person at the project.

    b. Take careful notes of what has been observed or heard and any action taken. These notes should be dated, signed, and kept securely.

    c. Do not however, confront the accused or prejudge the situation.

2. External Reporting Procedures:

In many countries, there may be legal requirements that mandate reporting procedures to government or law enforcement authorities in suspected cases of child abuse. Except in emergencies, a report should be made first to senior management, then to government authorities as required or as appropriate. With the exception of legally mandated reporting, no one outside of the organization should be contacted or informed until formal internal reporting steps have been completed and until instructions from senior management are given for appropriate external reporting. Under no circumstances should a staff member speak to the media concerning any allegations.

SIX PRINCIPLES OF RESPONDING TO ALLEGATIONS OF ABUSE

A church's response to any allegations of child sexual abuse should be based upon the following principles:

1. All allegations will be taken seriously and will be handled responsibly by the appropriate person.
2. Sexual abuse of children will not be tolerated. Volunteers and staff members should understand this basic principle at the time of their employment.
3. Each situation must be handled forthrightly with due respect for the privacy of both the child and the individual whose behavior is at issue.
4. Adequate care for the well-being of any child who has been abused or suspected of having been abused will be a primary concern.
5. The child should not be held responsible, unless the facts indicate otherwise.
6. Any staff member accused of child abuse will be treated with concern for his or her privacy and legal rights. Church

leadership should act in ways that respect the dignity and worth of every person, including the children.

We put the above in a checklist in the *Future Impact Study Guide*. The list also specifically details the kinds of things that must be included in any Child Protection Policy that you may implement in your church or childcare programs.

Any inkling or rumor of child abuse must be followed up to protect the children you serve, and in some cases innocent staff members. This is a most difficult issue in child ministry. Yet if we learn to deal quickly and directly with it, we can truly change children's lives for the better.

THE CHILD AND MISSION

OVERVIEW

The Church has traditionally done an adequate job of caring for children already in the churches. Many churches, especially in the West have Sunday school, VBS, camps, and other programs. Some of these focus on reaching unchurched children, though more often it is those already at least marginally part of the church who participate, and the programs generally emphasize spiritual transformation. In the West, few of these programs present the opportunity or motivation to reach out to the fully unchurched child and those from other religious backgrounds. For our purposes here, such interfaith ministry is part of what we call *Mission*, and we now introduce the Mission component of our *Future Impact* study.

Just as we have done in previous sections, we want now to put the child "in the midst" in relation to Mission. In this section we ask, *How does ministry to the child relate to mission and the Mission of the Church?* Or better, *How does Mission include the child?* Are children the *Great Omission* in missions strategies? How can cross-cultural ministry to children be sensitive, ethical, and effective? How can children be both objects of Mission and resources for missions?

To explore these issues, we will first acquaint ourselves with some of the core issues arising from historical and contemporary missions. We will apply these to the matters of cross-cultural (interfaith) mission to children. We will reflect on the ethics of child evangelism in a cross-cultural setting. Then we will broadly examine the matters of children as agents for missions as well as child ministries and overall mission strategy, with special attention to the 4/14 Window.

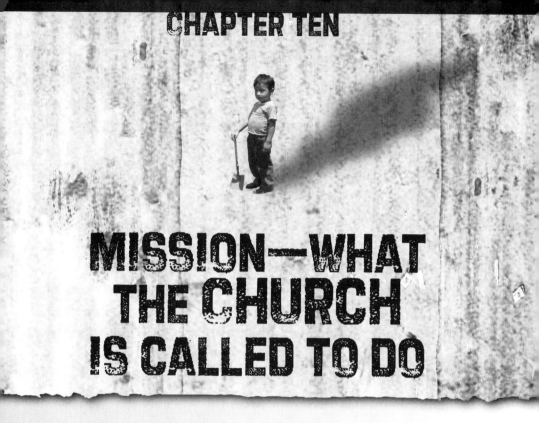

CHAPTER TEN

MISSION—WHAT THE CHURCH IS CALLED TO DO

All this is from God, who reconciled us to himself through Christ and gave us the ministry of reconciliation: that God was reconciling the world to himself in Christ, not counting men's sins against them. And he has committed to us the message of reconciliation.
2 Corinthians 5:18-19

Most churches give some attention to missions. Many have a missions Sunday once a year and often invite a missionary to speak, usually showing pictures and challenging the church to give to missions. I have often been one of those speakers. Having done so, many churches will feel they can then get back to the real work of "doing church." Have you ever thought

that perhaps the main reason for the existence of the Church is to do missions, or to send missionaries?

So what is Mission? (Just as we used a capital "C" in referring to the worldwide Church, so we often use a capital "M" when referring to global Mission or the Mission of the Church. We will use the small "m" when referring to specific mission work or missionary activity.) The word *mission* is not used in the Bible. (Incidentally, neither are other familiar Christian terms like *rapture* or *Trinity*.) The word *mission* has many uses in contemporary English—diplomatic mission, peace-seeking mission, mission to outer space, or mission impossible! However, the kind of mission we are interested in here is the Mission of God or of the Church.

In his fine book *What is Mission?*,[1] Andrew Kirk helps us understand the significance of Mission. Kirk's definition of Mission is: "The purposes and activities of God in and for the whole universe."[2] "No one," he writes, "falls outside its compass. It perseveres even when opposed, rejected and misinterpreted."[3] God's purpose has always been to redeem mankind and re-establish His rule on earth. His means for doing this is what we call "Mission."

If we are in agreement with Kirk, we will agree, then, that Mission is at the heart of the Church. "The Church," says Kirk, "is missionary by definition. [R]ather than think of it as one aspect of its existence, it is better to think of it as defining its essence."[4] Mission is quite simply, though profoundly, what the Christian community is sent to do.

Note that because this Mission is for the *whole* universe, and thus for *whole* people, it is a *holistic* mission. God desires to bring "positive change in the whole of human life materially, socially, and spiritually."[5] While this section may address primarily the spiritual aspect of the person, let us be clear that Mission in the biblical sense is holistic—always addressing the needs of the whole person. Children need to embrace their "true identity as human beings created in the image of God," enjoying His abundance in all areas of life. The Bible does not encourage a divide between evangelistic mission and physical mission, but instead blends both into the fullness of the truth of the gospel.

Certainly a child's spiritual well-being is important, for without a relationship with God, children have no hope of becoming fully who God wants them to be. But *whole* children have bodies, minds, and emotions; they exist in spheres such as a family, school, work, society, and other structures. Each of these aspects of a child is equally important.

It is not enough to preach salvation and only talk to children who are suffering; "an empty stomach has no ears." If we only focus on teaching children to pray, read the Bible, and say they are Christians, we only teach them part of the gospel. Mission to children involves responding to their physical and social as well as their spiritual needs.

OVERVIEW OF MISSION IN THE BIBLE

Some people think that the foundation for Mission is the Great Commission found in Matthew 28:19. The fact is, the rationale for Mission is found throughout the Bible. God's choosing of Abraham was a selection of one nation to communicate His message to others. God's covenant with Abraham was that He would bless Abraham and that all nations would be blessed through him. As recorded in Genesis 12:2-3, "I will make you into a great nation and I will bless you; I will make your name great, and you will be a blessing. I will bless those who bless you, and whoever curses you I will curse; *and all peoples on earth will be blessed through you*" (emphasis added).

From the beginning, Abraham's descendants had the responsibility of blessing the nations. Throughout the Exodus and the conquest of the Promised Land, through the judges and all of the kings, God continued to be faithful to His covenant. His purpose was that His name was being exalted among the nations. The blessing was never only for Israel but, from the beginning, for the nations. And it was never only limited to spiritual blessings. God's intention for all His people was that they would thrive holistically.

Understanding God's mission brings into focus the goal in ministry with children: that they would be transformed wholly into who God created them to be, embracing their unique identity and purpose.[6]

A *VERY* CONCISE HISTORY OF MODERN MISSIONS

The *Perspectives on World Mission*[7] suggests three overlapping eras of missions in the last 200 years. These years are the time frame of what is called *Modern Missions*.

The **First Era** of Modern Missions (1792–1910) began with William Carey, the "Founder of Modern Mission." In 1791, Carey wrote an article called "An Enquiry into the Obligations of Christians to use 'Means' for the Conversion of the Heathens." He argued that in order for the missionary endeavor to be successful, mission societies or sending agencies were needed to provide prayer and financial support to send out missionaries. (These societies were the *means* to which he referred.)

Soon after, *means* were established. The Baptist Missions Society, with William Carey as its first missionary, was formed. Although this society was rather weak and provided only the minimal support Carey needed to get to India, it inspired the formation and activities of many other societies on both sides of the Atlantic.[8]

William Carey had a very holistic view of mission, for during his 42-year missionary career in India, he translated or supervised the translation of Scriptures into 37 languages, established over 200 schools (over half for girls who had traditionally were often not allowed to go to school), did much to improve Indian crops and farming, and established many medical missions and health facilities.

Mission to the coastlands of Africa and Asia characterized the **First Era**. It saw the establishment of denominational agencies. Most of the missionaries were British or European. The era was characterized by an astonishing demonstration of love and sacrifice on the part of those who went out. Very few missionaries survived. Generally, missions during this time were characterized by very high quality and holistic mission strategies. In fact, some of the health and educational systems set up during that era are still bearing fruit today!

The Second Era (1865–1874) featured missions into the interior of mission fields. The impetus was Hudson Taylor's bold vision that the peoples of the interior of China needed to be reached. The organization that he founded—China Inland Mission—eventually served more than 6,000 missionaries. Over 40 other interior mission agencies were formed, including Africa Inland Mission, China Inland Mission, and Sudan Interior Mission. North Americans became more prominent in missions during this era. The idea of *faith* missions was common—that is, nondenominational missionaries who raised their own support.

In both the first and second eras of missions, ministry to children figured prominently. Strangely, however, mission historians often overlook this aspect. For example, the respected historian Kenneth Scott Latourette documents the history of the spread of Christianity in a comprehensive and sweeping way, but one must look very hard to see discussions of credible mission efforts directed toward children and youth.

Interestingly though, his work has frequent references to the impact of Christian schools in mission efforts. A large number of African political leaders came out of the Christian school systems set up in almost all African nations during the first part of this century. Presidents Kenyatta, Moi, Kaunda, Nyerere, Boigne, and scores of others—not to mention virtually all the leaders of the African church—are among those whose lives were impacted by this early mission strategy in Africa.

To some extent, the same was true in Asia. For example, Latourette observes the importance of Christian schools in India:

Protestantism's approach to India was varied. . . . Some of it was through schools. . . . They ranged from village schools which, to members of the depressed classes, were doors of hope to a world of larger opportunity, through secondary schools, to colleges of university grade.[9]

Latourette notes too that the leader "who did most to shape the ideals of revolutionary China between 1911 and the late 1940s was Sun Yat-Sen, an avowed Christian who owed most of his formal education to Christian schools."[10] Other examples could be cited.

One can also get a sense of the importance of Christian schools in the mind of some of the Marxist leaders in the fact that, where Communism took over, one of the first restrictions was on Christian schools. Referring to the takeover by the communists in China, Latourette writes:

Religious instruction of youths under 18 years of age in groups of more than four was forbidden . . . Special theological courses were still allowed, but only by express permission of the state. No believer was permitted to teach in a state school.[11]

The long-term presence of Christian schools in Korea contributed to the dramatic growth of Christianity in that nation, Korean pastor Nam Soo Kim notes. He points out that foreign missionaries came to Thailand and Korea at about the same time, around 1885. Both countries were and continue to be closed societies and difficult to penetrate. Today, the Christian population in Thailand remains less than 1 percent, while over 30 percent of Koreans are Christians. What made the difference? The missions strategy in Korea included establishing Christian schools. There was no such meaningful mission effort in Thailand. Rev. Kim reports that these original Christian schools in Korea have now graduated more than 350,000 students, and are among the most prestigious universities of Korea.[12]

For a variety of reasons, the mission emphasis on schools was largely abandoned after the end of the colonial era. The relief and development focus of many evangelicals may have absorbed some of the energies formerly devoted to ministry through schools. These new efforts were not, however, normally targeted toward children and youth. Obviously, we cannot and should not try to start Christian schools—at least not on a national scale. But the question we must ask is, *With what have we replaced the mission emphasis on children and youth in schools? How are we growing the next generation of Church and national leadership?*

The Third Era of missions (1974–present), like the previous two, was inspired by key visionaries: Cameron Townsend. Townsend was a "third era" missionary working in Guatemala, trying to distribute Spanish Bibles. He noticed that most of the Indians did not speak Spanish. One asked him, "If your God is so smart, why can't He speak our language?"[13] Good question! The problem inspired Townsend to start his own mission, Wycliffe Bible Translators. At first, Townsend estimated that there were probably 500 or so unreached tribal groups in the world. Now we know that there are more than 5,000! Wycliffe continues to grow, focusing particularly on tribal groups and languages. Today, Wycliffe has over 6,000 missionaries and by far the highest number of Ph.D.s and other highly trained personnel.

Also, as had happened in the earlier eras, the third era spawned many new missions agencies and organizations. This era saw the rise of many *service missions*, such as Missionary Aviation Fellowship and gospel recordings. The early 1950s also marked the launch of the first of many relief and development organizations, including World Vision and Compassion International.

As early Christian missionaries traveled to different parts of the world, their service to children frequently included schools, hospitals, and orphanages. At times these programs were flawed, requiring children to be "extracted" from their communities and cultural identities. Children were sometimes forced to learn new languages, dress codes, and value systems. Sometimes the Western understandings of childhood, as a time of innocence, playfulness, and freedom, clashed with other cultural views of childhood. But children were not neglected or omitted. Missionaries understood the need to grow the next generation of Christians.

THE RECENT GROWTH OF CHRISTIANITY

When contemplating Satan's hold on so much of the 10/40 Window and other parts of the world, it's easy to get discouraged about the progress of global evangelism. Looking at the decline in committed Christianity in the Western world can also be discouraging. However, there is considerable reason for hope. Indeed, many Christians tend to have a very myopic view of what God is doing. In fact, people movements are taking place around the world, and the Holy Spirit is obviously winning battles in diverse places around the globe.

Revivals have been sweeping across the globe. Since the 1930s, the "center of Christianity" has been slowly shifting southward and eastward. The decades of the '40s, '50s, and '60s were a time of massive revivals throughout Africa, to the point where now the vast majority of Africans south of the Sahara claim to be Christians.

The 1970s was the decade of enormous increases in evangelicalism in Latin America. There are now more evangelicals in Brazil than there are in all of Western Europe. The 1980s saw Christianity sweep through many parts of Asia. The 1990s and first decade of the 21st century have seen the Korean Church become one of the most active and evangelical churches in the entire world. The number of Korean missionaries being sent out per capita is the greatest of any country. There are now more Asian Christians than Western Christians.

However, there is another way to look at the growth of Christianity that also offers hope. That is, the ratio of Christians to non-Christians in the world has been steadily increasing and this is especially true in the last few decades. In the time of Apostle Paul, the ratio of Christians to non-Christians was predictably and infinitesimally small. A generous estimate would put the ratio at one Christian to every 100,000 or 200,000 non-Christians by the end of the first century. Even in 1792, at the dawn of the modern missionary age when William Carey went to Asia, the ratio of Christians to non-Christians was still very small.

Now, however, the number of Christians to non-Christians has dramatically risen. More than 30 percent of the world now calls themselves Christians (roughly one out of every three), and another 40 percent have been evangelized; that is, they have had an opportunity to hear Christ. This means that two out of every three people in the world are either Christian or have had an opportunity to hear the gospel. Looked at in this way, the remaining task of sharing the gospel with the unreached is less daunting than it has been at any time in history.

THE GROWTH OF NON-WESTERN MISSIONS

The previous brief summary of missions history is decidedly Western. However, the global Mission movement is by no means only Western. Over the past quarter century, the growth in the number of non-Western missionaries and missions organizations, while less well-documented, has nevertheless been dramatic. In fact, it is now estimated that non-Western missionaries outnumber Western missionaries.[14] In Asia, it is exciting to see the enthusiasm and commitment of a huge number of

Indian, diaspora Chinese, Filipinos, Koreans, and other nation-alities responding to the missionary calling.

Larry Pate[15] lists several essential mind-sets that must be in place to ensure that this growth of global missions is encouraged and supported. These include:

1. The non-Western Church—Asian, African, and Latin American—must learn to understand itself in a global context.
2. Global cooperation in missionary training is vital. Many Two-Thirds World missionaries are sent to the field with little or no training, and others wait months or even years for a training opportunity.
3. Global models of support must shift toward the Two-Thirds World. Western missions agencies need to incorporate many Two-Thirds missionaries into their organizations, allowing them complete international status and equal opportunities for leadership. Non-Western mission-sending agencies and missionaries need to be supported.
4. Informational resources must be decentralized. This is among the goals of such international agencies as Global Mapping International, DAWN Ministries, and OC International.
5. Western missionaries must be prepared to shift roles. Many tasks in which Western

missionaries have traditionally been engaged must increasingly fall into the hands of non-Western leaders.

The expansion of the non-Western missionary movement does not mean that there are no longer valid roles for Westerners in missions. Harold Fuller of SIM[16] has outlined four stages of missionary roles in relation to the Mission Church. These apply to Western and non-Western missionaries.

Stage One, the **Pioneer** stage, requires the gift of leadership along with other gifts. Because there are few or no believers during this stage, the missionary must lead and do much of the work himself.

Stage Two, the **Parent** stage, requires the gift of teaching. The young church has a growing child's relationship to the mission. But the *parent* must avoid paternalism.

Stage Three, the **Partner** stage, is rather delicate. It requires change from a parent-child relationship between the missionary and the young church to an adult-adult relationship. It is difficult for both parties to change but essential to the church becoming a mature "adult."

Stage Four, **Participant**: A fully mature church assumes leadership. As long as the mission remains, it should use its gifts to strengthen the church to meet the original objectives of the Great Commission. Meanwhile the missionary should be involved in stage one elsewhere.

FIVE IMPORTANT MISSIOLOGICAL CONCEPTS[17] (AND THEIR RELEVANCE TO CHILDREN)

The first and most important missiological concept is the **Great Commission** found in Matthew 28: "Go into all the world and preach the gospel." In view of the rapid secularization of the USA and Western Europe, the rapid spread of Islam, New Age, and other false religions, it is difficult to believe that the Great Commission is any closer to being fulfilled than it ever was. However, as we have seen, that is a short-sighted view. A broader understanding of what God is doing throughout the world helps put things into perspective. It also can give us a much more positive outlook on the status of world Christianity and the prospects of fulfilling the Great Commission.

Of course, children are included in this Great Commission. In Matthew 19:14 Jesus said, "Let the little children come to me and don't hinder them." We know that this "coming to Jesus" was not just physically approaching Jesus as He was teaching His disciples, but also allowing and encouraging them to come to Him in faith. Note that the children are not made or forced in any way to come to Jesus, but rather simply permitted. Indeed, we often see that children willingly and happily come to Jesus when given the opportunity.

The second concept to consider is **looking at the world in people groups.** A people group may be defined as an ethnic or racial group speaking its own language and having its own traditions, history, customs, and language. As missionaries and missions organizations have begun to think about people

groups instead of just national boundaries, they have been able to target their efforts much more specifically and effectively to individual groups within countries. This has revolutionized the way missiologists look at the unfinished evangelism task.

As we noted in chapter one, children are not a "people group" according to the normal missiological definitions. But looking at children as a people group helps us find common characteristics, just like we do among adult people groups, which enable us to better present the gospel to meet their felt needs.

Children are an *enormous* people group nearly two billion strong and growing, especially in the parts of the world where the gospel is least known. They are a *suffering* people group: 26,000 under 5 die every day. Children are an *unwanted* people group, as indicated by the appallingly high rates of abortion, and equally shocking problem of street children around the world. They are a *victimized* people group, often subject to trafficking, exploitation, and other forms of abuse.

But most important for our present discussion, we know that children are a *receptive* people group, a fact to which we will return below. Sadly, from a missions perspective, children have usually been a *forgotten* people group. Historically, there has been a curious relative lack of attention given to children as either objects of or agents for mission.

The third useful missiological concept is **the distinction between evangelized and unevangelized peoples.** For missiological purposes, a group is evangelized if most people have had an "adequate" opportunity to hear and respond to the gospel. This does not mean that all or even most of the individuals have accepted Christ. It does mean that there are enough churches, missionaries, radio programs, available Bible portions or translations, or other Christian resources for them to become Christians if they want to. "Unreached" people are groups who have not had that opportunity, for whatever reason, to respond to the gospel.

For example, the percentage of committed Christians in France is very low. It is also very low in Thailand. However, France is an evangelized country, and Thailand is not. Why? Because in France, almost everyone has heard the name of Jesus. Anyone who wants more information about the faith, or who wants to become a Christian can find other believers to help, a Bible in his/her language and lots of other resources. The same is not true in Thailand. Many (perhaps most?) have never heard of Jesus. Further, churches are not extensive enough to provide an adequate opportunity for an interested Thai to receive Christ.

Many missions groups today have begun to change their focus to concentrate more on unreached or unevangelized people groups. And among those populations, as among all others, children and young people will be the most receptive.

The fourth concept is the **10/40 Window**, proven to be very helpful in viewing an area of the world that is largely unreached and very poor. This window is from the 10th to the 40th latitudes, stretching roughly from West Africa across through the Middle East, South Asia, and Southeast Asia, including Indonesia. There are at least six reasons why the 10/40 Window is significant.[18]

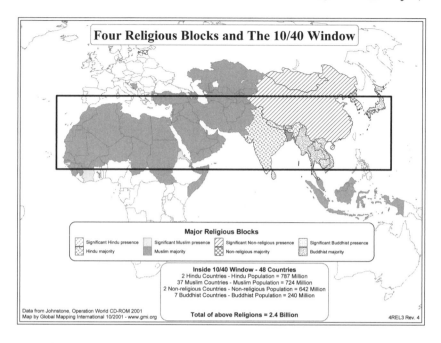

Four Religious Blocks and The 10/40 Window

Major Religious Blocks

Significant Hindu presence   Significant Muslim presence   Significant Non-religious presence   Significant Buddhist presence

Hindu majority   Muslim majority   Non-religious majority   Buddhist majority

Inside 10/40 Window - 48 Countries
2 Hindu Countries - Hindu Population = 787 Million
37 Muslim Countries - Muslim Population = 724 Million
2 Non-religious Countries - Non-religious Population = 642 Million
7 Buddhist Countries - Buddhist Population = 240 Million

Data from Johnstone, Operation World CD-ROM 2001
Map by Global Mapping International 10/2001 - www.gmi.org

Total of above Religions = 2.4 Billion

4REL3 Rev. 4

A. The historical and biblical significance of this part of the world. Ancient biblical history was worked out in territories marked by the 10/40 Window. In the 10/40 Window, Christ was born, lived His life, and died on a cross. Indeed, it was not until Paul's second missionary journey—and toward the end of biblical record—that events of divine history occurred outside of the territory identified by the 10/40 Window.

B. Most of the world's unevangelized people live in the 10/40 Window. In fact, while this is only one-third of the total land area of the world, almost two-thirds of the world's people live in the 10/40 Window.

C. The 10/40 Window is the heart of the world's non-Christian religions. There are 28 Muslim countries, one Hindu country (including a population of almost a billion people), and eight Buddhist countries including a population of over 230 million people.

D. The poorest of the poor live in the 10/40 Window. More than eight out of ten of the poorest of the poor—who on the average have a gross national product of under $500 per person per year—live in the 10/40 Window.

E. The quality of life for persons is the lowest in countries in the 10/40 Window. One way of measuring the quality of life has been to combine three variables: life expectancy, infant mortality, and literacy. More than eight out of ten of the people living in the 50 countries of the world with the lowest quality of life also live in the 10/40 Window.

F. The 10/40 Window is a stronghold of Satan. As we look back through the pages of history, we discover in the record of the prophet Daniel evidence of a territorial stronghold by the spiritual forces of evil (Daniel 10:13).

The fifth concept to consider is **the 4/14 Window.** In fact, missiologist Luis Bush is now calling the 4/14

Window the "core of the core" in missions. Dr. Bush is heading up a whole new movement "to open hearts and minds to the idea of reaching and raising up a new generation from within this vast group—a generation that can experience personal transformation and, as a result, become agents for global transformation."[19]

One thing that missiologists talk about frequently is the receptivity of people. That is, how receptive is a particular group to hearing the gospel and making a commitment to Christ? Children and young people are the most receptive segment of the population in very many societies, regardless of religious background or affiliation.

Many missions have taken a short-sighted view of their evangelism efforts—Christ is coming soon; therefore, we have to evangelize the adults. They often do not have time to evangelize the children and "grow" the church. However, if older populations are so unreceptive, serious mission organizations must certainly give more attention to the segment of the population that is receptive.

THE CHILD AND MISSION

Why this lengthy explanation of missions and missiology in a book about children? The reason is that children are (or should be) very strategic in reaching the unreached and furthering God's kingdom. Children figure prominently (or should) in each of the key missions concepts noted above.

The Great Commission applies to children as well as to adults. Children, more than any other people group, are receptive to the gospel. Nearly half of the population of every country within the 10/40 Window is also in the 4/14 Window. Where the churches are growing, most of the new converts are under the age of 18. Children are both objectives of, and resources for, Mission in the non-Western world.

Consider Selome, who takes part in a children's church outreach near her guardian's home in Ethiopia. Selome began attending the outreach with other local children several years ago. Her mother died within months of giving birth to Selome. Her father could not afford to take care of Selome and found a guardian for her miles away from the land he farms. As they do with every parent or guardian, the church talked over the outreach's gospel teaching and Bible study with Selome's guardian before inviting Selome to the outreach.

As Selome became more familiar with the Good News, she decided to become a Christian. Her decision came at a time when the church organized a children's outreach that not only *reached* children, but also was *led* by children at certain points. Selome has become an active communicator of the gospel through singing, leading short lessons, and talking to children her age about what it means to be a Christian *from a child's point of view*. Once an objective of outreach, Selome has become a resource for outreach.

Christian mission with children is vibrant and widespread today. The worldwide Christian movement serves more than

20 million children through approximately 25,000 workers. Many ministries participate in truly holistic mission, not simply concerned about children's souls, but also their minds, bodies, and relationships.

The reality of the strategic importance of children has changed how the organization with which I work, Compassion International, thinks about growth strategies. At the top of the list of criteria today is the missiological criteria. That is, *Where can we not only help needy children but also help the emerging church and also be strategic in furthering God's kingdom?*

Compassion's reflections on our role in furthering the kingdom have changed us a great deal. The staff in each country knows the language of unreached peoples and evangelism. They are more aware of what God is doing both around the world and in the country in which they work. Most of the new children enrolled into existing projects or children enrolled into new projects are from unsaved families and our overall growth is largely from unsaved and non-Christian populations. The directors and staff in each country know who the unreached peoples are.

Thus, we are not just helping the poor or even the poor within churches. Rather, we are challenging the churches to have a vision beyond themselves and further God's kingdom by deliberately strategizing to enroll non-Christian children so that they and their families can come to Christ.

GIVE ME CHILDREN, OR I'LL DIE!

In the first verse of Genesis 30, there is a remarkable, plaintive cry from Rachel, the barren wife of Jacob. Desperate to avoid the stigma of barrenness, Rachel repeatedly prays that God will give her children. So desperate was she for children that she cries out, "Give me children, or I'll die!"

This heart-rending cry should be on the lips of every leader in the Church today: "Give me children, or I [we, the Church] will die!"

Anyone who goes to Europe as a tourist sees the vast but empty cavernous cathedrals in every major city. Thousands of people traipse through these cathedrals marveling at the astounding arches and domes and the exquisite stained glass windows. If they are there at the right time, they might see 30 or so elderly believers taking communion or silently praying. The immense and inspiring cathedrals of Europe are architectural wonders, yet they are nothing more than awe-inspiring museums today. These magnificent churches of Europe are either dead or dying.

Why? The church in Europe did not cry out, "Give me the children, or we will die!" They did not win the hearts of the children, and the churches died.

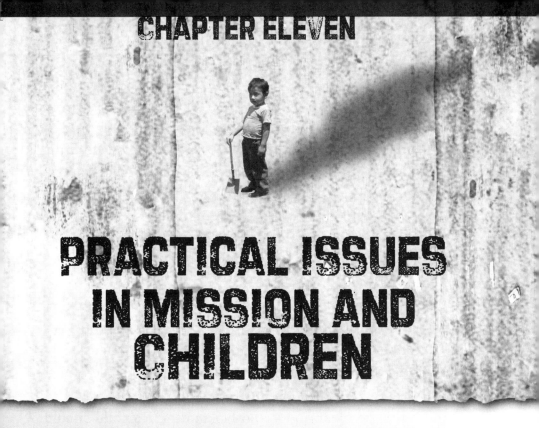

CHAPTER ELEVEN

PRACTICAL ISSUES IN MISSION AND CHILDREN

People will come from east and west and north and south, and will take their places at the feast in the kingdom of God. Indeed there are those who are last who will be first, and first who will be last.
Luke 13:29-30

Jesus' remarks in the above verses are just some of many verses peppered throughout Scripture that indicate the Good News would impact people everywhere. The gospel was never meant for one culture, but for all. Issues arise, however, whenever the gospel crosses cultural boundaries.

The questions of conversion and faith development in cross-cultural or interfaith evangelism are very different from the same matters in the Christian context. Ministry to children may be a remarkably effective way to find sensitive inroads into unreached communities and people groups. But interfaith evangelism, especially the interfaith evangelism of children, has very significant issues and implications. Just as cross-cultural missionaries must study the cultures and the context of the adult peoples to whom they minister, so those who would do inter faith mission with children must be extremely wise, sensitive, and cautious in holistic ministry to children from non-Christian contexts.

Clearly, just because children tend to be very receptive to the gospel does not mean that we can be careless in how we approach them or their parents. Indeed, that heightened receptivity should cause us to be even more cautious and discerning, for the possibility of exploitation is also heightened.

And let us be clear about another matter. **No child should be subjected to religious teaching and training without the knowledge and consent of the parents.** Just as caring Christian parents would seethe over attempts to influence their own children, so parents of non-Christian children will have the same protective impulse. They deserve the full respect and care that the gospel requires. God is not divisive, deceitful, or secretive, and neither should we be especially in any dealings with the children and families of other faiths.

KEY ISSUES IN INTERFAITH EVANGELISM WITH CHILDREN

A common argument against cross-cultural or interfaith child conversions is that children are not psychologically mature enough to make an informed decision or to choose their own religion. Hence, directing a child toward a particular religion is not ethically correct. Some Christians even suggest that it is unethical to evangelize children! Their view is that we should evangelize only parents and, in turn, parents will evangelize their own children. However, this position is not scriptural.

The biblical pattern of evangelism is to proclaim the gospel to everybody. No one is excluded. It is neither ethical nor fair that one large section of the population only hears the gospel if another section responds favorably to it. Evangelism, or providing Christian training, to children of non-Christian parents is neither exploitative nor unethical. We emphasize again, however, the particular sensitivities and ethical considerations involved in interfaith spiritual ministries to children.

CONVERSION OR PROSELYTISM?[1]

Proselytism is seeking a change of another's religion under the dominating influence of the stronger powers, under duress, or when it is economically or socially advantageous to do so. Charges and accusations are sometimes made about proselytizing among children. Laws in many countries prohibit proselytizing. We sometimes also hear accusations of "forced conversions." And some countries are now making laws against any conversion from one faith to another.

While it is true that some people may be brainwashed into accepting false teachings, and some children may feel compelled to acquiesce when invited to receive Christ, in reality, it is impossible to force a conversion. True conversion refers to a deep inner spiritual change within an individual that, by definition, is always voluntary.

However, it is also true that sincere, sensitive evangelism may be misunderstood by the peoples and keepers of non-Christian faiths. It is vitally important then, as noted above, that Christian training should not be provided to the children without the awareness and permission of the parents.

We must remember, too, that most non-Western peoples tend to come to Christ as family groups or clans. All major decisions are group decisions—and no one decides until the whole group is ready to decide. A church worker in child evangelism efforts needs to understand such people movements. Seeking the conversion of an individual child may not only put the child at risk of ostracism or worse, but may also be culturally insensitive as it is contrary to the way any decision is made in that society.

WHAT ABOUT "BUYING CONVERTS"?

Much legitimate criticism has been lodged against "buying converts," and the dangers of creating "rice Christians." It is possible to coerce a child (or adult) into making a declaration of faith in response to receiving a bowl of rice or other attractive material goods. They may do this because they are desperate or simply in order to ensure that the flow of material goods is not interrupted. Naturally, such "converts" may denounce their declarations of faith when the need is met. And

they may be quite willing to "convert" again once more food or other assistance is offered.

But just as it is impossible to force a conversion, it is also impossible to buy a convert. No responsible Christian would insist on a decision under such circumstances, nor believe that any declaration under such duress truly reflects the change of heart that brings a person to faith.

Nonetheless, this possibility is what has led some Christian relief and development agencies to separate totally their humanitarian activities from whatever Christian witness in which they might engage. Indeed, some organizations with sound Christian credentials at their international level may not even be known to be Christian at the local level in non-Christian environments. They may accommodate or water down the Christian message out of sensitivity to their non-Christian hearers. And this is the danger. Christian holistic child development can exclude careful attention neither to the physical *nor* spiritual needs of the children and families. How can Christians provide material love and care for children and not share the Good News, which can transform the lives of children both now and forever?

Dr. Bryant Myers provides helpful insights on the matter of Christian witness in non-Christian environments. He notes,

> We must witness because witnessing is a central feature of our faith commitment; it is not an option. Yet how we witness raises a difficulty and a challenge. The difficulty is that everyone—Christian or non-Christian—is witnessing all the

time anyway. The only question is to what or to whom are they witnessing.[2]

The how of Christian witness is often the challenge. The familiar quote attributed to St. Francis of Assisi, "Preach the gospel everywhere and all the time; use words if necessary," is a helpful and holistic guideline. Suggesting that we are only witnessing if we are proclaiming Christ and seeking converts is a truncated and dichotomized gospel. That Christian witness must be present, and that it must be sensitive, contextually attentive, and non-manipulative is axiomatic.

Finally, at another level, we should note that the motivation that pushes a person toward the threshold of faith may not be nearly as important to God as the fact that the person is so motivated to place their faith in Christ. Many people's motivations may be somewhat suspect. In the long run, it is more appropriate to affirm and nurture a person who has made a decision to follow Christ, rather than critique the motives contributing to that decision.

EVANGELISM OR EXPLOITATION?

All this said, Christians engaged in meeting the spiritual needs of children are often criticized by non-Christians who see evangelism, or any "tampering" with local beliefs, customs, and practices as a form of exploitation.

How do we respond to this accusation? Do the methods we employ make this accusation legitimate? Are we acting as

brokers who baptize children into denominations or as ambassadors for the purposes and glory of God? Are our ministry efforts rooted in the holistic well-being of the child?

In our statements and activities with non-Christians, we must be clear about our unwavering conviction that children have spiritual as well as physical, emotional, and mental needs. While exercising sensitivity, we must also stand unapologetically committed to spiritual as well as physical transformation. We must exercise a non manipulative integrity and respect in our evangelism without softening the gospel and the truth of the children's need for it. Children need an authentic encounter with Christ to experience the fullness of life that God intended for them.

As noted above, parents of any faith will feel strongly that a child belongs to the religion of their parents. Thoughtful, ethical evangelists will acknowledge and support the absolute necessity of sensitivity in this important matter. At the same time, a distinction should be made between simply viewing children as property of their parents or treating children as persons who have rights of their own. The most basic exegesis of the Great Commission, and indeed the foundation for any mission, is that we are to take the gospel to all people, including children, with the intention and expectation that they will become followers of Christ.

Evangelism and Christian training with children of non-Christian parents is neither exploitative nor unethical provided there is understanding and acceptance on the part of the parents. In ministry to children, we must always be *particularly* sensitive to the proper time, place, manner, and approach for overt evangelism. Inattentiveness to the situation and circumstances may make overt evangelism *in that time, place, and manner* insensitive or even unethical.

CAUTIONS FOR CHILD EVANGELISM IN SENSITIVE SITUATIONS

Honest and transparent evangelism and Christian training with children of non-Christian parents, is important and appropriate. However, there are circumstances that may make overt evangelism improper or even unethical. Here are a few principles, probably obvious and well understood, which I believe are valid and important for those ministering to children in sensitive, non-Christian environments.

Children should not be subjected to religious teaching and training without the knowledge and consent of the parents. In fact, some Christian workers, including myself, believe that in most sensitive situations *church leaders should not baptize a child until the parents are also ready to be baptized* in order to ensure that the child has support and encouragement in his or her new faith.

Christians should not pressure children for conversion in situations where the children and/or their parents are completely dependent on the financial and/or material support of Christians. This may occur in orphanages, children's homes, day care centers, refugee camps, social aid projects, and communities heavily sustained by Christian development efforts. Children are so conscious of their powerlessness that they are likely to accept any conditions attached to the support they are provided with. Surely, the gospel may be presented to children in these situations but with sensitivity and caution.

It is improper to seek the conversion of children with a patronizing attitude that distances oneself from the painful realities that the children are experiencing. The sensitive caregiver should relate empathetically to suffering children, who are extremely vulnerable and have no control over their circumstances. The approach must be one of identification and compassion.

It is improper to present the gospel to children in a way that undermines, despises, or denies the validity of their culture. A common historical problem in missions is that Christian conversion sometimes becomes synonymous with cultural conversion. God created cultures. Just as every culture has aspects that must be rejected or redeemed, so every culture has aspects that can be affirmed and celebrated. We must be aware of cultural factors while at the same time not allowing them to undermine the power of the gospel.

It is improper and may be unethical to guide children to become Christians in instances where they do not have a proper understanding of what it entails. Especially in circumstances where a commitment to Christ may involve ostracism, rejection, persecution, or suffering, the consequences of a commitment to follow Christ must be clearly presented in a manner commensurate with understanding and maturity level of the child.

STRATEGIC MISSION WITH CHILDREN

We have already discussed the 4/14 Window and the reality that most people who make decisions for Christ do so between the ages of 4 and 14. From what you learned in chapter ten, you now know that the idea of the 4/14 Window is piggy-backed on the concept of the 10/40 Window. This is intentional, of course. I believe that both concepts are important for mission strategists today.

This "Window within the Window"[3] lets in the light not just on the churches and missions, but also on the very foundations for the future of the Church. Each time I speak to Christian groups on this subject, I conduct my own unofficial survey. I ask, "How many of you made your first significant decision to follow Christ before you reached your 15th birthday?" Overwhelmingly, my results confirm this important missiological fact. These informal results in non-Western populations generally yield a figure of between 50 and 70 percent.

Obviously, their answers depend somewhat on how becoming a Christian is defined, and many Christians have more than one experience involving a faith commitment, as the commitment to follow Christ ripens and matures as a person grows older. But what then shall we say? Perhaps only 60 percent of Christians make their decision for Christ during these pliable years, or perhaps only 50 or 60 percent. What should this say to missions leaders today?

The reality of the 4/14 Window was once again confirmed at the 2004 Lausanne Conference held in Pattaya, Thailand. There, Paul Eschelman, the person primarily responsible for the Jesus Film worldwide, asked the 1,700 or so participants of

the consultation to stand if they had made their first decision to follow Christ before the age of 15. At least 80 percent of that group rose to their feet.

CHILDREN, CHURCH GROWTH, AND LEADERSHIP DEVELOPMENT

Children warrant not only ministry to address their physical needs, but the attention of missiologists as well in development of effective mission strategies. Church planters frequently recognize the importance of ministry to children. All too often, however, the recognition is given because ministry to children is believed to open the door to their parents. It often does, but when ministry to children is done for this reason, it is often starved of resources. A ministry to children should be done *because of the value of children as children in the eyes of God*. In the process, many of those families involved—both the children and the adults—will come to Christ.

Children are the Church of the future. They are also the Church of today.

In their enthusiasm for development of global evangelism strategies, Christians sometimes act as though we do not have time to wait for young Christians to mature into their place of leadership. This is a shortsighted approach. Clearly we must affirm that we can still afford to grow the Church.

Today's children are still tomorrow's leaders. Just as we as parents know that it takes at least 18 years to "develop" our own children, so, likewise, child development is a long-term proposition. Maturity in future Christian leadership requires strategic and sustained investments in the Christian nurture of children today.

There is a tendency to stereotype ministries and missions to children, saying that ministry to children is not serious missions or it is the work for the less able or creative missionaries. Child ministries *are* a very effective way to achieve church growth, to develop new Christian leadership, and an effective way to reach adults and unreached peoples. Therefore, it is crucial not only that missions groups and missions thinkers do not ignore children and youth, but also that they do not stereotype ministries to children. Children are not insignificant. Missions groups should re-examine mission strategies that suggest a bias toward ministry to adults only. They should practice a holistic mission, which includes the children and youth.

CHILDREN AS AGENTS OF MISSION

The reality of the 4/14 Window means that including children in mission strategies is important for serious missions work today. However, children must not be thought of only as possible objects of evangelism and missions. As we have also seen, both Scripture and experience show us that children have far more spiritual capacity than they are often given credit for. They can hear and obey God's word in their lives, and they can minister to others. In the Bible, they participate fully in the faith communities. Again and again they are chosen as God's instruments when adults or adult institutions fail.

Pete Hohmann writes,

> Kids have a tremendous spiritual capacity. They can bring joy to God's heart. They can hear and obey God. They can minister to others. However, children are dependent on adults to equip them to do these things. Our lack of vision for the spiritual capacity of children can cause us to do things that actually harm or stunt the spiritual growth of children. Children are dreamers. They are idealists; they always have faith in a better tomorrow. No wonder Jesus told us to be like little children. God often accomplishes His greatest purposes through children.[4]

As we have seen, God was not hesitant to use children as His messengers or instruments seemingly when the task is so important it can't be entrusted to adults. Perhaps God knows that children will not rob His glory. Perhaps He just knows they are listening.

When God needed great generosity, He chose a child. Throughout Scripture, we see that nearly every time a child is mentioned, God is doing something important. In one case, He fed 5,000 people. He could have done it in any number of ways, but He did it for that little guy just to show, I think, His respect for children and that anyone who will give God everything he has, He can multiply it far beyond their wildest expectations. Can you imagine when the little boy got home? Surely his mother said, "How was your lunch? And don't make up one of your wild stories again!"

When God wanted to test commitment, He chose a child. When Peter was in the courtyard, the first person to come to him to test his faith was a servant girl. The Lord must have said, "I'm going to give Peter every opportunity to succeed." If you cannot share your faith with a child, *who can you share it with*? This little girl said, "Aren't you one of His followers?" And Peter failed. "No. No, little girl, I am not."[5]

Children still need to be challenged. A look at the resources for Sunday school teachers will reveal many topics about how God will bless believers but virtually nothing on equipping children for outreach or challenging them for service or missions.

I am told that on the day I was born, my father carried me in his arms and prayed that I would someday be a missionary. Our family tradition says that he did the same for all of his six children. Occasionally, when I speak in Asian missions conferences, I ask how many of the Asian parents carried their very young children in their arms praying that they would be become missionaries. Only very rarely has anyone been able to say that he or she had. Much more often, the question is a shock. How could we possibly pray that our children would undertake such risk and hazards? But children who are prayed for in that way then have that dream nurtured throughout their childhood, very often may make such a commitment.

Children usually live up (or down) to our expectations of them. As I used to say to my son, "Think you can, think you can't—either way, you will be right." Many children and young people become bored with Christianity. The problem for some may be that they have not been given opportunities to put their

faith into action. Their ideas and beliefs remain untested and, therefore, are not integrated into their own faith in a meaningful way.

Children and young people—the 4/14ers—have much to offer. Dr. Bambang Budijanto calls them *clean energy* and an *untapped force for mission.*[6] Children and young people love to be challenged. But much of what passes for children's ministry in churches today is geared toward entertaining rather than equipping or challenging them. We must ask, "What are our children not doing and not learning while they are being entertained?"

While in their late teen years, Alex and Brett Harris wrote a book called *Do Hard Things*. The Harrises note that "Being considered a good teen only requires that we don't do bad stuff like taking drugs, drinking, and partying. But is it enough to know of the negative things we don't do?"[7]

Dr. William Damon notes,

> . . . contrary to what some adults think, [children and youth] really do not need to come home after their six-hour day and "cool out" in front of the TV. They do need to have their energies fully and joyfully engaged in worthwhile pursuits. . . . By systematically underestimating the child's capabilities, we are limiting the child's potential for growth. In withholding from children the expectation to serve others . . . we are preventing them from acquiring a sense of social and personal responsibility. . . . Paradoxically, by giving the child purposes that go beyond the self, an orientation to

service results in a more secure belief in oneself
can contribute much to positive social change.[8]

So how can we challenge our children to be involved in missions? At least in the following ways:

Children can be effective in praying for others. Because of their sincere faith and believing hearts, children may be uniquely able to make a difference through prayer. One of the most powerful moments at the Congress on World Evangelization in Pretoria, South Africa, in 1997 was the children praying confidently and competently for all the conference participants. "Because of their sincere faith and believing hearts, children are uniquely able to make a difference through prayer. . . . Since children think concretely, God often communicates His will to them through pictures in their mind as they pray."[9] Esther Ilnisky and her Esther Network details and documents the role of children as prayers and prayer warriors.[10]

Children can share their faith. They often have a greater boldness in sharing than many adults. Patricia, a 12-year-old girl living in the slum community of Santa Mesa in the Philippines, is a prime example of this. Her neighborhood has a reputation for being "home base" to growing numbers of thieves, gangs, and prostitutes. Patricia saw the seeds of disrespect and bad habits in the children of Santa Mesa. In response, she began a weekly Bible time for the 5- to 10-year-olds in her neighborhood. She has a simple explanation for what she does: "I don't want them to grow up to be criminals, but to know about Jesus."

As Patricia's example demonstrates, **children can make a difference through community outreach.** Outreach in the community is the perfect classroom of life that builds character in children. Outreach is where children test out their ideas and beliefs, and discover what is real and who has the power.

Children can make a difference through involvement in world missions. Unless we impart a biblical worldview to our children, society will impart its default worldview: self-gratification. God's purpose in the Bible is to make His name known to every tongue, tribe, and nation.

Sylvia Foth, in her excellent book on giving children a heart for missions called *Daddy Are We There Yet?*, suggests the following ways to help children feel they are a part of something significant:[11]

- **Work to develop real ministry skills.** Help children develop skills—listening, prayer, encouragement, generosity—they will really need to minister to others, regardless of where they live in the world. Though a children's project may be a baby step, make it significant so kids are part of something bigger than themselves.
- **Work to give children real information about the real world.** Even younger children can't fully understand the complex issues facing our planet; they can have seeds of truth planted early that will not need to be weeded out later. Watch for myths like, "All children from other countries are poor." "Missionaries are

only from England or America." "Our country is more Christian than others." "The world is already reached." Of course, if you work with children, you will need to inform yourself first. That way, you're giving healthy and true information to the children.

- **Let children create their own projects.** Especially as children move into the pre-teen years, they will have the desire to help meet the needs in the world on their own. Pre-planned missions projects can be great options—offering printed prayer cards, videos, and project ideas. However, at some point, children will be ready to make their own project to help missionaries or needy people around the world. Let them pray, listen for God's direction, and learn to obey from the heart.

- **Teach children about the difference between Christian service and kindness and other service and kindness.** There should be a difference between a child's school helping project and a Christian project. How is Jesus' love different than any other love on the planet? How will people know we are sharing Jesus' love with them? Our project will be different because we add prayer, because we make a long-term commitment to help, because we sacrifice to serve, or because it helps people to hear about Jesus for themselves. Talk about it together.

"Equipping kids to minister requires a lot of effort," writes Pete Hohmann. "But can we afford not to? Kids who minister to others are excited about their faith. They acquire a proven knowledge of God through real-life (classroom of life) experiences. These experiences become the building blocks of character. Children who minister to others also find a purpose in life that is greater than themselves."[12]

I couldn't have said it better myself.

AVENUES FOR ADVOCACY

OVERVIEW

We begin this final section of *Future Impact* by looking at the concept of advocacy. Advocacy is a legal term referring to pleading to someone in a position of responsibility or authority on behalf of something or someone whose rights are being violated or whose voice is not being heard. There are many different ways for doing advocacy. Speaking out can take many different forms. Sometimes advocates are loud and intrusive. We will look at avenues for advocacy for Christians, especially from a nonconfrontational point of view. One important tool used by advocates for children around the world is the Convention on the Rights of the Child, or CRC, produced by the United Nations (U.N.) and ratified by most of the countries of the world. This tool is so well-known that many organizations use it as a starting point for all of their work with children. It is so well known that the Church needs to be very familiar with it, and understand its provisions, its strengths, and its weaknesses. Therefore, in chapter thirteen, we will examine the useful aspects of this tool, and raise some of the questions about it asked by some Christians from a biblical standpoint.

Networking goes hand in hand with advocacy. We have shown the importance of the Church worldwide in responding to the needs of children. But many of the churches and ministries caring for children operate largely on their own. So as we conclude this book, we will see how effective and extensive networking can help ministries encourage one another, combine efforts, and avoid overlap—all crucial aspects of maximizing both our present and future impact in ministry and mission to children.

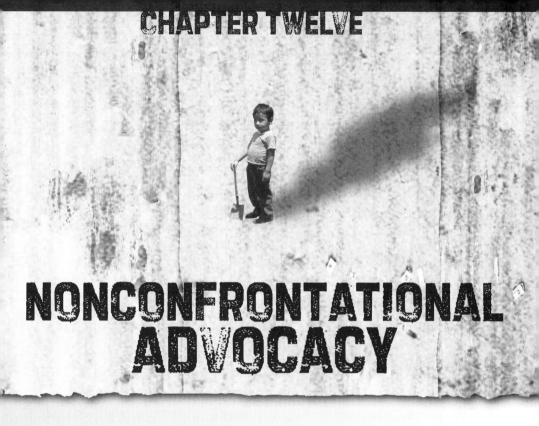

CHAPTER TWELVE

NONCONFRONTATIONAL ADVOCACY

Speak up for those who cannot speak for themselves, for the
rights of all who are destitute. Speak up and judge fairly;
defend the rights of the poor and needy.
Proverbs 31:8-9

Advocacy takes its roots from the legal profession. Advocacy means to speak for, act for, or defend someone or something before someone else—and it is a vital activity of God's people. Advocacy seeks to influence and change people, policies, and structures on behalf of the poor or those who have no voice.

It is part of the role of the Church to do advocacy through speaking out against injustice, defending the cause of the poor, holding those in power to account, and empowering people to speak out for themselves. It is clear from the Bible that God expects Christians to be concerned about—and raise their voices on behalf of—the poor.

This expectation has been a part of the faith community from Old Testament times. Lamentations 2:19 states, "Arise, cry out in the night, as the watches of the night begin; pour out your heart like water in the presence of the Lord. Lift up your hands to him for the lives of your children, who faint from hunger at the head of every street." Deuteronomy 10:17-18—part of the Law of Moses—says, "For the LORD your God is God of gods and Lord of lords, the great God, mighty and awesome, who shows no partiality and accepts no bribes. He defends the cause of the fatherless and the widow, and loves the alien, giving him food and clothing."

Moses was no stranger to advocacy. He frequently had to intercede for the grumbling Israelites as God led them out of captivity in Egypt. Exodus 32:10-14 provides one such example:

> But Moses sought the favor of the LORD his God. "O LORD," he said, "why should your anger burn against your people, whom you brought out of Egypt with great power and a mighty hand? Why should the Egyptians say, 'It was with evil intent that he brought them out, to kill them in the mountains and to wipe them off the face of the earth'? Turn from your fierce anger; relent and do not bring disaster on your people. Remember your servants

Abraham, Isaac and Israel, to whom you swore by your own self: 'I will make your descendants as numerous as the stars in the sky and I will give your descendants all this land I promised them, and it will be their inheritance forever.'" Then the LORD relented and did not bring on his people the disaster he had threatened.

Another (perhaps surprising) episode of an Old Testament leader being an advocate is Abraham speaking on behalf of the notorious Sodom and Gomorrah. Genesis 18:23-32 records,

Then Abraham approached [the LORD] and said: "Will you sweep away the righteous with the wicked? What if there are fifty righteous people in the city? Will you really sweep it away and not spare the place for the sake of the fifty righteous people in it? Far be it from you to do such a thing-- to kill the righteous with the wicked, treating the righteous and the wicked alike. Far be it from you! Will not the Judge of all the earth do right?" The LORD said, "If I find fifty righteous people in the city of Sodom, I will spare the whole place for their sake."

In the New Testament, Jesus Himself was a frequent advocate for children and for the poor. When He placed the child in the midst (Matthew 18:1-3), when He accepted the anointing by the "sinful woman" (Luke 7:36-50), when He associated with the unvirtuous woman at the well (John 4:5-29), He was being their advocate. Immediately after calling His disciples, Luke records seven "advocacy" encounters (between chapters five to eight) Jesus had with the poor and the outcast.

NONCONFRONTATIONAL ADVOCACY

Anyone can be an advocate. One needs not be a professional or an expert. An advocate is someone with a strong opinion, someone who actively strives to influence others in the same way. Advocacy is done directly by those affected by injustice or on their behalf. Many child advocacy organizations specifically target public policy or governments to change or enact laws to benefit children. This is a viable and important component of child advocacy that has done much good for children worldwide.

A more aggressive form of advocacy involves action or activism. Methods often include lobbying government officials or those who make laws and policies. It may be done through demonstrations, marches, holding placards, and raising voices in public places. Sometimes advocacy is done through actions such as obstructing access to facilities through sabotage or other kinds of disruption. Yet this more visible and upsetting kind of advocacy often draws more attention to the method of advocacy than the issues affecting children. This is why we encourage the strategies and actions of *nonconfrontational advocacy*.

Nonconfrontational advocacy involves speaking out or enabling others to find their own voices to raise awareness.

It includes actively challenging people with not just facts and figures, but a distinct call for change. It may involve enabling others to make changes and using experience to train and equip those willing to make those changes. Almost always it involves prayer, education, research, training, encouraging, networking and other means of highlighting and addressing issues.

AVENUES FOR NONCONFRONTATIONAL ADVOCACY

There are a number of ways to practice nonconfrontational advocacy. Each of the following focuses on the *issues* that demand advocacy for children, rather than *methods* that might diffuse that focus.

Prayer is one obvious avenue for advocacy. Prayer is pleading to someone in authority (God), on behalf of those whose rights are trampled or whose voice is not being heard, in our case, children. Lamentations tells us to "Arise, cry out in the night, as the watches of the night begin; pour out your heart like water in the presence of the Lord. Lift up your hands to him for the lives of your children, who faint from hunger at the head of every street" (2:19).

Any time then when we lift up our children in prayer, we are being their advocates. Whether it is in the preparation of the strategy or in its implementation, we want and need the Lord to be a part of our activities. Our own advocate, the Holy Spirit, prays on our behalf and stands before God speaking on our behalf.

Vision casting broadens the scope of one's advocacy through inviting others to see things the way you do, or to see things from a different perspective. I love the frequent admonishment in Isaiah to "lift up your eyes and look around" (Isaiah 49:18).

Vision casting can mean teaching church members about the biblical foundations of children and ministry to children (the Great Commission). It might engage teaching and sharing a biblical view of poverty and human development. It often means teaching and speaking about the needs, neglect, and nurture of children—the nature and scope of challenges children in poverty face, the potential of children, the role of the Church and Christian community in the discipleship and development of children, and the current state of the responses of the Church and Christian community to children.

Speaking out means finding and creating opportunities to speak out about the needs of children and challenging churches to action. Here it can also mean lending our voice to challenge those in responsible positions to protect and nurture children.

Of course, advocacy involves more than just speaking out about children. Part of what we have to say, we will learn through **research**. Research will give us better understandings of the needs, neglect, and nurture of children—the nature and scope of the challenges and threats to children worldwide. It will provide a context in which child development takes place and the root causes of poverty: injustice, exploitation, hopelessness, effects of modernity and post-modernity. It brings to light both relevant child/adolescent law and current theory and practice of child development and children's issues around the world. It actively engages the existing literature on child development and what is available in each country.

Networking helps people and organizations learn best practices, remain motivated and encouraged, and enhance coordination and planning of child development efforts. It involves sharing of best practices and coordinating efforts for better efficiencies. In many cases, networking includes information about large national and international child development organizations and their programs.

Equipping and training interested parties is another strategic tool in nonconfrontational advocacy. Those with expertise and resources in Christian holistic child development, biblical foundations, program administration, and resources can share with others. One powerful way that Christians work together is in taking opportunities to train and equip individuals and groups in those and other areas who directly impact children in need.

ADVOCACY AND DEVELOPMENT GO TOGETHER

You have heard it said, "Give a child a fish; feed him for a day. Teach a child to fish; feed him for a lifetime." But what if the child has no access to the pond? What if the water has been polluted upstream? What if the wealthy forces the child to turn over the fish to him? What if other things keep people from using the skills and abilities they already have? Often development does not get to the root of the problem. Advocacy often deals with the structural aspects of poverty, exploitation, and injustice that address more directly some of these issues.

Advocacy can be a forerunner for child development. John the Baptist was a forerunner of the ministry of Jesus. In the same way, advocacy activities can prepare the way for your church to do significant child development work—work that is grounded in a deep understanding of the needs and issues facing children.

Advocacy can strengthen child development programs. You cannot share what you do not have. Many churches doing development work struggle with the issue of ownership. Some have not caught the mission and vision of ministry to children. This is partly due to sowing the seed before properly preparing the seedbeds. Advocacy activities can help church members understand how they are part of a very significant harvest.

It's not always easy to talk about the everyday threats some children face. There are systemic problems like the lack of services, healthcare, education, and sanitation. Children often suffer first under conditions of government corruption and abuse of power in the military and police. Discrimination and subsequent mistreatment impact millions of children daily. Child pornography, child trafficking, and child prostitution outrage most people.

The ugliness of all these issues (and others) could easily make child development among the poor seem overwhelming. Yet the good news is that a stable child development presence can help overcome the negative effects of every single issue discussed by child advocates. In a way, advocacy provides the crucial voice for child development.

It should be obvious that advocacy activities can be risky and dangerous. The people involved in corruption and exploitation may not take kindly to interference and raising awareness about their activities. "Hit and run" advocacy—speaking out on someone's behalf then leaving them to deal with the consequences—is obviously not a helpful strategy. Violence, isolation and ostracism, damaged reputations, and economic loss are all very real risks for both the advocates and those being advocated for. Clearly, the effective advocate will be cautious, wise, and sensitive.

ADVOCACY IN COMPASSION INTERNATIONAL

While Compassion International shares the common definitions of advocacy, we intentionally do not define our child advocacy as being in the public policy realm. We do not lobby governments, seek legislative changes in the courts, nor join the many United Nations groups working to do the same throughout the world. First and foremost, we define ourselves as child advocates. Whatever we do and say is for the defense of and intercession for children.

Advocacy is our mind-set. Compassion International views advocacy as a mindset that can influence all the ministries in the church. Advocacy as a mind-set allows us to be in regional and global discussions on child and missions issues and positions us to take our place in a variety of forums on child issues.

Viewing ourselves as advocates encourages us to lift up our eyes and to view our ministry not just as administrators on behalf of children, but also as advocates for children—speaking out and acting on their behalf. As such, advocacy allows us to multiply our ministry rather than just add to it. It also enables us to improve and increase the ministry of other Christians on behalf of the needy children around the world.

As advocates for children, we're compelled to speak to those within and outside the Compassion family to encourage and equip them in effective ministry to children. Advocacy is an integral part of staff and donor and partner development.

For Compassion, advocacy is really about championing the cause of children through mobilizing the worldwide Christian community on their behalf. This involves using our voice and experience to educate, to motivate, and to bring about changes in the hearts, minds, and strategies of the Church and her people. Our approach is church-focused and noncon-frontational. Our objective is to challenge the global Church to greater involvement and effectiveness on behalf of needy children. Our advocacy ministries seek to:

Increase: Motivating and equipping the Church and others for greater involvement on behalf of children.

Improve: Training and equipping the Church to greater effectiveness in their ministries to children.

Inspire: Affirm and encourage existing Christian ministries to needy children, and influence other churches and individuals to appropriate and rewarding ministries on behalf of needy children.

EXPANDING THE DEFINITION OF ADVOCACY FOR COMPASSION

Compassion International defines child advocacy as follows: *Child advocacy for Compassion is the ministry of raising awareness of the needs, neglect, nurture, and potential of children in poverty and challenging and enabling those within our influence to greater involvement and effectiveness on behalf of children.*

An expansion of this definition helps clarify the breadth and depth that advocacy, by anyone, on behalf of children can have.

Advocacy: For Compassion, the most synonymous concept for advocacy is that of being a champion. We champion the cause of children in poverty and become the champions for individual children.

Ministry: Our mission statement declares that we exist as advocates. Advocacy both characterizes who we are and directs what we do.

Raising awareness: We raise awareness through personal and public means of communication and education. We must have good information and research as a basis of this communication.

Needs: With poverty come a lack of opportunities and options and innumerable barriers to the development of children.

Neglect: The concept of neglect includes the failure of caregivers and protectors to provide what is necessary for healthy development and also includes many types of abuse, oppression, and injustice.

Nurture: Children need to be nurtured to develop healthily. There are basics of good child development that can be taught and applied across circumstances and cultures.

Potential: Each child has incredible potential, which good development helps to unfold. In addition, children are a great resource to their families and communities.

Children in poverty: Our target population is children in poverty. Children are the most powerless group in society. Children in poverty generally have the greatest obstacles to their development.

Challenging: Advocacy needs to move people to action. We cast the vision and challenge others to help us fulfill it.

Enabling: We enable others to engage in more effective child development through facilitation, training, equipping, and the provision of materials.

Those within our influence: We can be effective only with those within our influence. We focus on those closest to Compassion (staff, sponsors, donors, church partners) and work out from that sphere of influence to an ever-widening influence on the worldwide Church. We do not seek to directly influence governments or secular authorities.

Greater involvement: The goal is not just awareness of the issues but greater activity on behalf of children in need. We share what we are doing, what others are doing, and how people can get involved.

Effectiveness: Activity without effectiveness is pointless. We challenge and equip others to engage in the most effective interventions with the least amount of redundancy.

WHAT YOU CAN DO AS AN ADVOCATE

Let's note a few things that every person can do to make advocacy a mind-set.[1]

- Be well-informed about the situation of children in general and in your community in particular.
- Educate families, churches, and the community about different initiatives on behalf of children around the world.
- Lead a life at home, at church, and in your community that respects the worth of children.
- Pray about matters affecting children; be as specific as possible.

- Network with those who work for children and assist them in any way you can.
- Support the work of your church or other child-focused ministry, and encourage others to join in making the world a safer place for children.

These simple ideas become a powerful foundation of advocacy when put into practice. Whatever you do, never under-estimate the power of a well-placed word or deed on behalf of a child who needs it. This is the very heart of advocacy.

CHAPTER THIRTEEN

THE UNITED NATIONS CONVENTION ON THE RIGHTS OF THE CHILD

Do not envy the oppressor,
and choose none of his ways.
Proverbs 3:31

Christians and the Church are certainly not alone in their concern about the needs of children. Children also benefit from the activity of many secular NGOs, governments, and the United Nations. We turn our attention now to some of the major secular initiatives and documents promoting the welfare of children.

Foremost among these is the U.N. Convention on the Rights of the Child, or simply the CRC. The CRC is the most respected statement regarding the protection and provision for children. The CRC is a U.N. document ratified in the 1990s by all but two nations in the world (Somalia and the USA). Its origins go back to a visionary Christian named Eglantyne Jebb. Early in 1920, she oversaw the creation of the International Save the Children Union, which combined organizations from various countries working together to relieve child suffering in Europe.

Eglantyne wanted to raise the awareness of children's needs around the world. She developed a statement that captured her vision of rights for all children:

> I believe we should claim certain rights for the children and labour for their universal recognition, so that everybody—not merely the small number of people who are in a position to contribute to relief funds, but everybody who in any way comes into contact with children, that is to say the vast majority of mankind—may be in a position to help forward the movement.[1]

Within a year, Eglantyne Jebb's Declaration of the Rights of the Child was adopted by the League of Nations and achieved lasting international significance. The present U.N. Convention on the Rights of the Child is derived from Eglantyne's original statement.

The CRC spells out the basic human rights that children everywhere—without discrimination—have a right to survival, for an opportunity for full development, to protection from harmful influences, abuse and exploitation, and to participate fully in family, cultural, and social life.

By ratifying the CRC, national governments have supposedly committed themselves to protecting and ensuring children's rights. They have agreed to hold themselves accountable for this commitment before the international community.

Earlier in this text we referred to another well-known UNICEF publication, *The State of the World's Children* (SOWC). Each year, the SOWC highlights some issues relating to the welfare of children. The main purpose of the publication, however, is to monitor the extent to which the various governments are making progress towards implementing the CRC and in improving the overall welfare of its children. And progress is being made. We have seen for example, over the years, the number of children dying every day coming down. A few years back, SOWC reported that over 42,000 children were dying every day. Most recent figures indicate that the number is about 24,000.

CONTENT AND INTENT OF THE CRC

A *convention* is an agreement between countries to obey the same law. When a government ratifies a convention, it means that it agrees to obey the law written in that convention. The CRC is considered the most powerful legal instrument for the recognition and protection of children's human rights. It has 54 articles in all.

The basic provisions of the convention are in three different categories. They are:

- Protection (protecting children from harm)
- Provision (providing what children need to live and develop)
- Participation (engaging children in their world)

An extensive list of the provisions of the CRC is in the study guide for this book.

The CRC is a constructive document that can be a valuable tool for Christians and churches as they reflect and strategize for the care for children and holistic child development. It articulates many of the threats facing children, providing a helpful framework for church and community awareness and action. It is also a promising step forward in challenging governments to take the legal, structural, and supportive actions necessary to secure children's well-being.

Through these properly governmental responses, CRC thus becomes a channel in holding the governments accountable to do their part. The extent to which some governments are more responsive to the needs of children, as evidenced by general improvements in the welfare of children in some sectors and in some areas, is encouraging. Sadly, though, in the places where children suffer the most, the governments tend to be most neglectful of their obligations in spite of their signatory commitments.

SOME CHRISTIANS' CONCERNS ABOUT THE CRC

While the CRC is the most widely used and accepted document in use today, not all Christians are enthusiastic about the CRC. The official reason why it has not been ratified by the USA is the provision of Article 41, which states that wherever national standards for protection of the child are higher than those in this convention, the higher standard shall always apply. The USA argues that such protections do exist in the USA. However, an unofficial reason that the CRC has not been ratified by the US is at least partly due to resistance or opposition on the part of influential Christians there. (Many American legislators also feel that current USA federal laws uphold the rights of children sufficiently.) Some Christian workers have been reluctant to use the CRC, either because of their own concerns or their understanding that some like-minded Christians have reservations about it.

Some of these concerns, along with the respective responses, are shown below.

The general objection to the CRC among many Christians has to do with the biblical emphasis on responsibilities and obligations rather than upon rights. Christian maturity *defers* any rights we may have in the interest of others as exemplified by both Jesus and Paul. As Paul Stephenson notes,

> [R]ights are not simply to be claimed or enforced, but are the result of active responsibility to God for others. In his letter to the Ephesians,

Paul sums this up in verse 21: "Submit to one another out of reverence for Christ." By acting out God's intentions for humanity, human rights, e.g., harmonious, loving and just relationships between people can be achieved.[2]

Following this line of thought, many Christians are concerned that **the CRC gives away too many parental rights.** There is a perceived conflict between the CRC and parental rights—an over-empowerment of children and that these rights are anti-family and erode positive Christian values. Some Christians, for example, feel that Article 3 transfers God-given parental rights and responsibilities to the State:

Article 3: Best interests of the child
All actions concerning the child shall take full account of his or her best interests. The State shall provide the child with adequate care when parents, or others charged with that responsibility, fail to do so.

Further, some feel that articles 12, 13, and 14 tend to institutionalize rebellion by vesting children with various fundamental rights that advance notions of the child's autonomy and freedom from parental guidance:

Article 12: The child's opinion
The child has the right to express his or her opinion freely and to have that opinion taken into account in any matter or procedure affecting the child.

Article 13: Freedom of expression

The child has the right to express his or her views, obtain information, and make ideas or information known, regardless of frontiers.

Article 14: Freedom of thought, conscience and religion

The State shall respect the child's right to freedom of thought, conscience and religion, subject to appropriate parental guidance.

As we respond, these concerns must be given careful consideration. These provisions have, in fact, been used by some to challenge parental authority—especially in some Western world contexts. We should note, however, that in several places the CRC is careful to specify that the role of the State is subordinate to that of the parents. In the introduction to the CRC, UNICEF argues,

> . . . the Convention specifically refers to the family as the fundamental group of society and the natural environment for the growth and well-being of its members, particularly children. States are obliged to respect parents' primary responsibility for providing care and guidance for their children and to support parents in this regard, providing material assistance and support programs.[3]

Article 5 in the CRC emphasizes that "States . . . shall respect the responsibilities, rights, and duties of parents . . .

to provide . . . appropriate direction and guidance in the exercise by the child of the rights recognized by the convention." Further, Article 18 states that "Parents have joint primary responsibility for raising the child, and the State shall support them in this. The State shall provide appropriate assistance to parents in child-raising." The CRC creates no hindrances to the discretion of parents to make choices about how they raise their children.

A second common concern is that **the CRC emphasizes rights that the child may not be mature enough to handle.** The articles causing concern include these:

Article 14: Freedom of thought, conscience and religion

The State shall respect the child's right to freedom of thought, conscience and religion, subject to appropriate parental guidance.

Article 15: Freedom of association

Children have a right to meet with others, and to join or form associations.

Article 16: Protection of privacy

Children have the right to protection from interference with privacy, family, home and correspondence, and from libel or slander.

Article 17: Access to appropriate information

The State shall ensure the accessibility of information to children . . . from a diversity of sources, and it shall encourage [dissemination of] information of . . . benefit to the child, and take steps to protect from harmful materials.

In response, the CRC seeks respect for children—but not at the expense of the human rights or responsibilities of others. The CRC confirms that children have a right to express their views and to have their views taken seriously and given due weight, *but it does not state that children's views are the only ones to be considered.* The convention also explicitly states that children have a responsibility to respect the rights of others, especially those of parents. The convention emphasizes the need to respect children's "evolving capacities" but does not give children the right to make decisions for themselves at too young an age. This is rooted in the common-sense concept that the child's path from total dependence to adulthood is gradual.[4]

A third concern is that **the CRC may make loving discipline including spanking in the home a form of child abuse,** as per the article here.

Article 19: Protection from abuse and neglect
The State shall protect the child from all forms of maltreatment by parents or others responsible for the care of the child.

The Committee on the Rights of the Child, the U.N. body that monitors compliance with the CRC, said this means physical punishment or the spanking of children, at home as well as at school, is prohibited.

In response, this is also a legitimate concern—especially for those, (including myself) who believe that *loving, physical discipline* is appropriate and sometimes necessary for training of a young child. It is unfortunate that there is so little teaching of adults about proper physical discipline. Indeed, spanking is often done in anger and does, in fact, at times step over the line into a form of physical abuse.

I believe that many of the parents who are concerned about the limitations this article may place on their training of their children do know how to properly use physical correction. They use it in an *infrequent, controlled, and loving* manner, which affirms the child while discouraging unwanted behaviors, establishes the necessary boundaries that a child needs, and puts the parent in the proper role of shaping the will of the child without damaging the spirit.

I believe churches need to include child training and discipline in parental training classes, and provide counsel and support for parents in this difficult and often confusing responsibility. Parents who understand the proper use of spanking should not be hindered (or worse—even prosecuted) from using it in a private, and again, *loving* manner. Nevertheless, in the general absence of such training, it is best to discourage spanking if parents do not have this understanding. Moreover, in today's society, I certainly would not advocate physical discipline of children by anyone other than loving, insightful parents (for example, school teachers or other caregivers).

Another concern is that **the whole discussion of "rights" may not be culturally appropriate (especially in Asian cultures).**

Another dividing line between Christian and secular rights is the underlying God-centeredness of the Christian concept. Modern secular rights theory can be rooted in an individualistic (and even self-centered) approach. For Christians, the God-centeredness of rights dictates that their focus is not on claims for self, but on the desire to serve others in accordance with the teaching of Christ. Indeed, Scripture calls us consistently to think of the rights of both neighbors and strangers.[5]

Unlike in the West, which emphasizes the individual, the core of Asian values is community-oriented, hence, the emphasis on respect of elders, care for the extended family, and filial piety. Under normal circumstances, such cultural practices naturally protect the well-being of the child. Therefore, the issue of "rights" does not arise.

In response, anyone seeking to implement the CRC must respect the culture of each family structure. It must be contextualized in each situation, while at the same time preserving its intent. It cannot let "this is just our culture" provide an excuse for continuation of harmful cultural practices. Moreover, when traditional structures are broken and the child loses his protection, CRC rises above the culture (whether Asian or Western) of the child to speak on his behalf in order to restore his basic human "rights."

Another concern is **the practical fallout of biblical vs. secular rights.** From a secular standpoint, rights are self-centered. Rights for Christians are God-given and cannot be given or created by people or laws.

In response, there *is* an essential difference between secular rights language and that of biblically based, God-given rights. Secular rights are based in a presumed "contractual" relationship between an individual and the wider society. Biblical rights are God-given and bound up with His desire for a transformed and just society.[6] So where man-made legal rights correspond with God-given rights, they should be supported. Those that do not should not be supported.

What then shall we say? As noted above, my own feeling is that the CRC is useful and a helpful tool for Christian groups. Seen in their most positive light, the intent of the CRC can certainly be affirmed by all Christians. Moreover, the scope of the articles is very helpful, demonstrating the wide range of aspects of the child's life, experience, and environment where attention and provision is necessary by loving care-givers. Further, I believe that, again, seen in their best light virtually all of the articles of the CRC will find Scriptural support. Indeed, several Christian groups have given thought to Christian versions of the Rights of the Child, some of which provide extensive biblical support for each of the rights.[7]

Finally, it is probably true that the CRC features prominently in the majority of secular programs caring for children. Given this pervasiveness, and given our commitment to encourage better care for children everywhere and at all times, Christian practitioners seeking to be well informed in the global arena of child care and protection must be very familiar with the CRC.

THE MILLENNIUM DEVELOPMENT GOALS (MDG)

We now turn our attention briefly to another global secular initiative for the protection of and provision for children: *The*

Millennium Development Goals. Governments around the world have set targets for poverty reduction and development, among many other concerns. Such targets, while not always achieved, are well intentioned and have great influence on governments who participate in the community of nations.

The Millennium Development Goals were formulated at the Millennium Summit in September 2000, based on agreements from world conferences organized by the U.N. in the previous decade. The goals have been accepted by many as a framework for measuring overall national development progress.

The goals focus on the efforts of the world community on achieving significant and measurable improvements in people's lives. They establish yardsticks for measuring results, not just for developing countries but also for rich countries. These yardsticks provide evaluative standards that help to fund development programs and inform the multilateral institutions that help countries implement them.[8]

The major goals and targets, standards, or indicators are the following:

Goal 1—Eradicate extreme poverty and hunger.
- Target 1: Halve, between 1990 and 2015, the proportion of people whose income is less than $1 a day.
- Target 2: Halve, between 1990 and 2015, the proportion of people who suffer from hunger.

Goal 2—Achieve universal primary education.
- Target 3: Ensure that, by 2015, children everywhere, boys and girls alike, will be able to complete a full course of primary schooling.

Goal 3—Promote gender equality and empower women.

- Target 4: Eliminate gender disparity in primary and secondary education preferably by 2005 and in all levels of education no later than 2015.

Goal 4—Reduce child mortality.

- Target 5: Reduce by two-thirds, between 1990 and 2015, the under-5 mortality rate.

Goal 5—Improve maternal health.

- Target 6: Reduce by three-quarters, between 1990 and 2015, the maternal mortality ratio.

Goal 6—Combat HIV/AIDS, malaria, and other diseases.

- Target 7: Have halted by 2015 and begun to reverse the spread of HIV/AIDS.
- Target 8: Have halted by 2015 and begun to reverse the incidence of malaria and other major diseases.

Goal 7—Ensure environmental sustainability.

- Target 9: Integrate the principles of sustainable development into country policies and program and reverse the loss of environmental resources.
- Target 10: Halve, by 2015, the proportion of people without sustainable access to safe drinking water and basic sanitation.
- Target 11: Have achieved, by 2020, a significant improvement in the lives of at least 100 million slum dwellers.

Goal 8—Develop a global partnership for development.

- Target 12: Develop further an open, rule-based, predictable, nondiscriminatory trading and financial system (includes a commitment to good governance, development, and poverty reduction— both nationally and internationally).

These goals resonate with many issues of justice and mercy outlined in the Scriptures. Some of the issues involved invite controversy, but that does not mean we have to avoid them. Rather, we must continue in our biblical role as light and salt before a watching world and the God who created it.

A WORLD FIT FOR CHILDREN (WFFC)

The final widely recognized secular document encouraging the protection for provisions for children for our consideration is called *A World Fit for Children*. At the U.N. Special Summit on Children held in 2002, this declaration was signed and adopted by 180 nations.

The document reaffirms the leaders' obligation to promote and protect the rights of each child and acknowledging the legal standards set by the CRC. All of society is called upon to join a global movement to build a world fit for children, based on a ten-point rallying call that also formed the core of the Say Yes for Children campaign.

The plan of action sets out three necessary outcomes: the best possible start in life for children, access to a quality basic education, including free and compulsory primary education, and ample opportunity for children and adolescents, to develop their individual capacities.[9]

A summary of the 10 principles and objectives of *A World Fit For Children* provisions is shown below:

1. **Put children first.** In all actions that affect children, the best interests of the child will be one of the first things we think about.

2. **End poverty: Invest in children.** We promise once again to make a major reduction in poverty within a single generation. We all agree that to get rid of poverty we must invest in children and realize their rights. Immediate action must be taken to stop the worst forms of child labor.

3. **Leave no child behind.** Every girl and boy is born free and equal in every way. All forms of discrimination affecting children must end.

4. **Care for every child.** Children must get the best possible start in life. The survival, protection, growth, and development of healthy and well-nourished children is the most important start to human development. We will make real efforts to fight diseases and major causes of hunger. We will take care of children in a safe environment so that they can learn and be physically, mentally, emotionally, and socially healthy.

5. **Educate every child.** All boys and girls should be able to have and complete a primary education that is free, something all children must attend and of good quality. Boys and girls should have equal access to primary and secondary education.

6. Protect children from harm and exploitation. Children must be protected against any acts of violence, abuse, exploitation, and discrimination, as well as all forms of terrorism and hostage taking.

7. Protect children from war. Children must be protected from the horrors of war. Using international law, children living in areas occupied by another country must also be protected.

8. Combat HIV/AIDS. Children and their families must be protected from the terrible impact of HIV/AIDS.

9. Listen to children and ensure their participation. We believe that children and adolescents can help to build a better future for everyone. We must respect their rights to express themselves and to participate in all matters that affect them, according to their age and maturity.

10. Protect the earth for children. We must protect our natural environment with its huge variety of life, its beauty and its resources, all of which make human life better both now and in the future. We will do everything we can to protect children from the effects of natural disasters and environmental problems.

As noted above, I believe each of these documents is generally useful for Christian caregivers. While Christians will test the provisions against Scriptural teachings—as well we should—I believe we can all profit from consideration of their lofty intent.

The commitments made or implied generally are not in conflict with Christian commitments on behalf of children. Their scope helps us understand the depth and breadth of the holistic child development issues, as well as possible intervention strategies. And given how widely disseminated are the *Convention on the Rights of the Child*, *The Millennium Development Goals*, and *A World Fit for Children* documents, it is not possible for Christian practitioners to be fully conversational in the global arenas of child care without familiarity with these documents.

CHAPTER FOURTEEN

NETWORKING ON BEHALF OF CHILDREN

So we, being many, are one
body in Christ, and individually
members of one another.
Romans 12:5

Hand in hand with advocacy is the important work of networking. We have shown the importance of the Church worldwide responding to the needs of children. And the Church has indeed responded massively and compassionately over the years and across the continents.

At the same time, despite the large numbers of church-run and church-based programs and projects aimed at meeting the needs of children very many of those operate largely on their own. Many lack basic know-how and information: *Who does what and where? Who can help me? Who has done this before? How do I do this?* Most lack encouragement, support, and fellowship.

Yet matters of management, caring for staff, liaising with donors, governments, authorities, and others in the community are essential to effective programming on behalf of children. Effective and extensive networking is part of the response to these and other challenges.

BENEFITS OF NETWORKING

Isolation is a troubling and discouraging problem for many ministries to children. The work is hard in any case. Trying to do it alone is harder still. Many ministries do not know what help or encouragement may be available in their own community or town. **Being effectively connected**[1] is one key benefit of networking.

> When Christians are not linked together, every new situation that arises, no matter how common, must be dealt with as though for the first time. Devising teaching plans, approaching local authorities for resources, finding prayer support, tracking down sources of food, funding and equipment,

dealing with legal problems, enforcing discipline
and figuring out how to handle emotional upsets
with staff and children with each new problem the
wheel is reinvented in an attempt to find solutions.
Without the experience and accumulated wisdom
of others to draw on, mistakes are made that could
have been avoided.[2]

Maximizing the use of resources is a related benefit of
networking. Some places have overlapping work with children
while many other areas have none. It is not uncommon to find
similar ministries working or considering work in the same
barrio or community. At the same time, there are so many
areas that have no helping ministries. Networking is crucial to
ensure that the gaps are covered and the overlap is minimized.
It is important that we maximize the use of our resources and
minimize duplication of efforts.

Networking often **improves development practice.** Many
church based programs or projects, while doing the best they
can, lack either resources or capacity to operate profession-
ally. As Christians we need to do more than simply care for
children in need—we need to do it with professionalism and
real expertise. Networking can help ministries access and
implement the training, resources, and best practices needed
to operate with excellence.

Networking encourages the **development of professional
standards.** *What does good Christian childcare look like?
What does it involve? How is it achieved?* Networking can
help bring people and organizations together to establish and

agree upon professional ministry standards. Once standards have been established, the networked ministries can hold one another accountable and together pursue higher levels of excellence.

Networking usually makes **quality training more accessible.** There is a vast need for training and capacity building among Christian childcare workers. Most childcare workers are eager for expertise and advice. The problem is providing it. When churches and organizations are networked together, they can begin to identify similar needs for training. Networking can then link together the expertise, materials, and other resources with those needing the equipping.

Networking shows appreciation. It demonstrates the unity in the body of Christ.[3] It often reduces a spirit of competition and encourages a spirit of sharing.[4] Further, networking encourages accountability to those who share the same vision and understand the constraints.[5]

Networking protects attitudes. It encourages humility in larger organizations when they acknowledge that they do not have all the answers but can learn from others.[6] And networking helps smaller organizations to feel they are making a contribution beyond their own limited resources.[7]

Networking demonstrates fellowship. It often encourages greater stewardship and efficiency by joining together to share facilities, reducing duplication, and limiting waste.[8] Networking helps support and lift up those who are struggling in the task.[9] It allows us to rejoice in success from wherever it originates.[10]

Networking improves effectiveness. Networking recognizes that we live in a complicated world and that only by working together and sharing our combined God-given wisdom and resources will we accomplish the task.[11] It also allows us to brainstorm together, share varying approaches, evaluate different strategies, learn from the mistakes and successes of others, and provide some benchmarking for future activity.[12]

Finally, networking almost always **provides better care for caregivers.** Patrick McDonald points out that Christian ministries are not known for their care for caregivers:

> A very serious, but often unrecognized, problem for people in the frontline of ministry to children at risk, is lack of practical, emotional, and spiritual support. Inability to find time for fellowship with other Christians or for personal renewal and lack of prayer backing leads to discouragement and early burn-out. Some carry on but begin to lose the vision they once had for helping these children and end up investing all their resources into just surviving the next crisis.[13]

Networking offers so much for both the context and implementation of ministry to children. The Viva Network is living proof.

VIVA VIVA!

The global Christian movement involved in caring for

children at risk has a very strong ally in the Viva Network. Viva Network is a global movement of Christians caring for children at risk. It seeks to enhance and expand existing efforts by connecting and mobilizing all Christians to meet the challenge of helping hurting children. This is done through a variety of networking initiatives, which give Christians working with children at risk opportunities to find others involved in similar work. They encourage and challenge each other, share ideas, information and resources, engage in joint ventures, and launch new initiatives on behalf of children at risk. These networking initiatives take place locally, regionally, and internationally.[14]

This remarkable ministry has established more than 40 national networks around the world. Viva has been the impetus for many sub-networks and child-related initiatives of all kinds. They have helped launch training, materials development, forums, conferences, research, and whole new ministry directions, such as the Child Theology Movement and Understanding God's Heart for Children.

The goals of the Viva Network are to improve the quality of care for children, increase action on behalf of children, and influence decision-makers to be a more effective voice for children. They do this in numerous ways:

- By establishing networks at all levels,
- By linking people and groups wanting to help children, and linking those with common needs or interests, through individual contacts, conferences and forums,
- Developing or facilitating the development of training and equipping opportunities at all levels,

- Providing resources such as the journal *Reaching Children at Risk*,
- Developing ministry databases and other kinds of mapping on all aspects of ministry to children and identifying and following key trends pertaining to the global effort to care for children,
- Mobilizing new efforts to reach children at risk worldwide,
- Being national and local advocates for children.

I highly recommend Viva Network as a place to begin your journey into networking on behalf of children in need. You might also consider the value of contacting churches in your area to find out what is being offered to benefit the children near you. Check out www.viva.org for more information.

Children don't need ministries that stand alone as though other Christians didn't exist. They need connected, congruent ministry so the Church can reach as many of them as possible. Only then will we optimize their future impact to advance God's kingdom in their generation.

CONCLUSION

He took a little child and had him stand among them. Taking
him in his arms, he said to them, "Whoever welcomes one of
these little children in my name welcomes me; and whoever
welcomes me does not welcome me but the one who sent me.
Mark 9:36-37

How can we optimize and maximize the future impact of today's children for God's kingdom?

We began this study by doing what Jesus did – placing a
child in the midst. Jesus Himself said that children are both a
sign of, and heirs to, the kingdom. If Jesus was serious about
the well-being of the child, then we too must take the respect
and care for children seriously, and understand their role and
biblical significance. We saw that all children are at risk, from
either poverty or prosperity, and that childhood is marred by
suffering and exploitation or squeezed into adulthood by our
commercialism and materialism.

We found that, contrary to what some people believe, the
Bible actually has a great deal to say about children. They are
neither hidden nor ignored; neither insignificant nor periph-
eral. Rather, they feature prominently in the unfolding story of
God's *new way.* Children were frequently His agents, instruments, His models and His *means.*

Recognizing the importance of children in God's perspective,
we then turned to issues relating to the holistic development

of children. How can we ensure that all children enjoy the *fullness of life* that is God's intent for all children? Concern for the needs, neglect and nurture of all children is seen throughout Scripture, and God expects it to be a focus for our concern as well.

Children suffer greatly from poverty. Poverty is not just a matter of physical deprivations but is, in fact, most fundamentally a *spiritual* problem. We noted how the worldviews of *animism* and *secularism* lead children and families toward hopelessness, poverty and destruction. In contrast a biblical worldview, *consistently followed and acted upon*, leads similarly in the opposite direction – towards lives of wholeness, abundance and hope.

Since poverty is a spiritual problem, addressing poverty is the *particular* responsibility of Christians and of the Church. We found that the Church is God's instrument not only the salvation, redemption and reconciliation of the *whole* person, but the *whole* of creation as well. In spite of this clear biblical mandate, there have long been *debates* and *dissensions* in the church about its dual roles of evangelism *and* social action (or holistic ministries).

Next we placed the *child in the church*. How can we make the church a more child-friendly place? Often we have misunderstood the place, and underestimated the contribution of children and little ones. At all levels, the church has a responsibility to work toward more child-sensitive approaches and ministries. Much can be done to make church programs, facilities, and staff more child-friendly. We looked at a model of how faith grows in children, and how the church can promote and encourage that faith development.

Though painful, we acknowledged that even in church contexts, children may be vulnerable to abuse and exploitation. The church has an enormous responsibility to *protect* the children in its care. We provided an overview of child protection protocols to protect the children and ministries from devastating incidents of child abuse within our walls.

Our conviction is that ministry to children is the most fruitful kind of mission. Historically, through the establishment of mission schools, whole generations of future African and Asian leaders grew up with Christian training. While Christian schools may not be viable mission models today, we asked, "What new strategies can mission agencies use today to reach and grow the next generation of global leaders?" The reality of the 4/14 Window means that ministry to children and young people must feature prominently in any credible modern mission strategy.

Moreover, children are not only objects of mission, but also important and effective *agents* and instruments for mission. Joseph, Moses, Miriam, Samuel, Naaman's Samaritan servant girl, Esther, David, Josiah, and Jeremiah were all His agents and emissaries in Scripture. When God needed great faith and great courage, when He needed a pure, clear, channel for His message, when He needed vision, when He needed great creative genius, when He needed great generosity – He chose a child. Likewise, children today need to be viewed as resources *for* mission, and challenged and released to become risk-takers for God.

Finally, with *the child in the midst*, we looked at the need to "…speak up for those who cannot speak for themselves, for the rights of all who are destitute" (Proverbs 31:8-9). Christians need to find their voice – to do *child advocacy* by speaking out against injustice, defending the cause of the poor, holding those in power to account, and empowering people to speak out for themselves. Advocacy may take many forms – prayer, education, research, training, encouraging, networking and other means. All these may serve to highlight and address the issues facing children.

It is my prayer that *Future Impact* helped you develop your understanding of the meaning and nature of the relationships between child, church, and mission. More than that, I hope it has:

- **Informed** about children's issues, and about their needs, neglect and nurture; about the Church's role in caring for them, and how they are an integral part of God's design for ministry, mission and furthering His kingdom.
- **Inspired** to understand children from a biblical perspective and to view ministry and mission to and with children as more legitimate, profound and strategic than you had before.
- **Influenced** to seek to improve your own and your church's ministries to children and to seek, in turn, to influence others in the same direction.

Releasing children from poverty
Compassion
in Jesus' name

About Compassion International

Compassion International is a Christian holistic child-development ministry working to release over one million children from poverty. More than 50 years of child-development experience have shaped Compassion's understanding of children and childhood as critically important for individual, family, community and national transformation.

The Compassion Difference

- **Christ Centered.** Each child has an opportunity to hear the gospel in an age-appropriate and culturally relevant way.
- **Child Focused.** Engaging each child as a complete person, we protect and nurture each child in all aspects of their growth.
- **Church Based.** We partner with local Christian churches to equip them for ministry with children.
- **Committed to Integrity.** We are dedicated to delivering excellent programs with complete integrity.

Compassion's Mission Statement

In response to the Great Commission, Compassion International exists as an advocate for children, to release them from their spiritual, economic, social and physical poverty and enable them to become responsible and fulfilled Christian adults.

Publishing at Compassion

God nurtures a very special relationship with the poor and the oppressed. Those without the power to change their lot. Nowhere do forces of poverty and oppression do more harm than in the lives of the world's poorest children.

That's why Compassion publishes books to help Christians understand the destruction poverty inflicts. To see the potential of children crushed in its grip. And to unleash the overwhelming power of the Church to free children—one by one, village by village, nation by nation.

When Christians spend themselves in the development of a child, they are invested in the purpose of God. These books inform that cause and inspire action. These books enable the Church to experience God's call of releasing children from poverty in Jesus' name.

The Blue Corner

Every book that rolls off the press through Publishing at Compassion bears a symbol of God's intent. Our blue corner points back to Leviticus 23:22.

> When you reap the harvest of your land, don't reap
> the corners of your field or gather the gleanings.
> Leave them for the poor and the foreigners.
> (MSG)

This symbol is a reminder to leave a "corner of our lives" on behalf of the poor.

PROFILE OF VIVA NETWORK

A Movement of Christians Caring for Children at Risk

Viva exists to change the lives of children by enabling people to work together. The problems faced by children at risk are vast, and so the solutions we offer must be just as big. We need to revolutionize whole cities and regions in order for children's lives to be meaningfully transformed. Only if we work together can we see this ideal become a reality.

AIMS

We want those Christians helping vulnerable children to work in partnership, thus having a wider area of impact, and we want them to strive for excellence, thus having a deeper and longer lasting impact. This will lead to real solutions to the problems faced by vulnerable children, as together we not only react to the need but proactively tackle the root issues.

OVERALL STRATEGY

1) Locate—who, what, and where

The Christian response is large but fragmented. In any given location, we must identify the needs of the children, find the existing response, uncover the gaps, and spot the potential areas for collaboration.

2) Connect—bringing people together

Through the development of local networks we link the many different projects, churches, and organizations in a geographic area responding to children. This builds collective identity, allows people to share contacts, know-how, and support, and begins to give communities a voice.

3) Equip—making people stronger

Through the networks we build excellence into all areas of child development and care, through training, resourcing, and developing standards for projects, workers, leaders, and influential decision-makers.

4) Innovate—offering real solutions

As we build up the local networks, bringing people together and making them stronger, they can increasingly put into action larger and more significant joint programs. They can then much more effectively address and prevent issues such as trafficking, HIV, street life, and forced labor.

Viva presently engages about 43 Christian networks representing more than 8,000 projects and 25,000 workers. As these Christians work together, the lives of over one million children are being transformed.

MALAYSIA BAPTIST THEOLOGICAL SEMINARY

Vision and Philosophy of the M.A. HCD at the
Malaysia Baptist Theological Seminary

The M.A. in Holistic Child Development (HCD) is an international program based on a partnership in Asia between Malaysia Baptist Theological Seminary (MBTS) and Compassion International to provide graduate level training for church leaders, as well as practitioners in children's ministries.

PROGRAM GOAL

The program goal is to enable Christians to become humble lifelong learners with and through children placed in their lives and work, whether Christians serve as advocates, parents, pastors, careers, team leaders, trainers on behalf of children in the life, ministry, and Mission of the Church.

PROGRAM OBJECTIVES AND COMPETENCIES

On completion of the HCD program, the student will have responded to the challenge to embark on a paradigm shift through the agency of children. They will be equipped to hear, see, and understand children differently as God intended, and so be able to:

- **Reflect** on childhoods and families and the potential nurture and needs of children in light of history, Scripture, culture, and theology **(Theology/ Anthropology)**.

- **Analyze** the experiences and potential of children in the light of ideologies, systems, structures, and globalization with particular reference to poverty and marginalization in families, communities, and nations **(Sociology/Theology)**.

- **Examine** relevant theoretical approaches to childhood, the impact of negative factors on child development, and formulate appropriate intervention strategies **(Child Development/ Psychology/Theology)**.

- **Explore** and understand the strategic importance of children in church and Mission and in furthering the kingdom of God **[Mission /Theology].**

- **Integrate** the knowledge and skills of HCD necessary to be competent and compassionate advocates as leaders, pastors, teachers, parents, and caregivers in their areas of responsibility to listen, to counsel, and to speak out on behalf of children **[Personal Growth/Leadership /Theology].**

DAN BREWSTER

Dan Brewster is the Director for International Academic Programs for Compassion International. In this role, he has primary responsibility for advising and consulting with seminaries and Christian institutions about programming in holistic child development. In his more than 25 years with Compassion, Dan has served as advocacy director in Asia, the Africa area director, director for program develop-  ment, and the first international director for advocacy. He has traveled to over 100 countries and has been involved in planning and monitoring child and family development or relief projects in more than fifty countries.

Dan has a doctorate in missiology from Fuller Seminary. He has written and taught widely, promoting and managing Christian holistic child development ministries and programs. Dan and his wife Alice live in Penang, Malaysia, and have three grown children.

NOTES

SECTION ONE
THE CHILD IN BIBLICAL PERSPECTIVE

1. UNICEF, "Child Survival and Health," 2009, http://www.childinfo.org/mortality.html.

1: WHY CHILDREN?

1. Population in April 2010: 6,816,207,233 (6.8 billion); "International Data Base Information Gateway," U.S. Bureau of the Census, http://www.census.gov/ipc/www/idb/worldpopinfo.php.

2. Patrick McDonald, Foreword to *Celebrating Children*, edited by Glenn Miles and Josephine-Joy Wright (Carlisle, Cumbria: Paternoster Press, 2003), xv.

3. David Gordon and others, *Child Poverty in the Developing World*, (Bristol, UK: The Policy Press, 2003), http://aa.ecn.cz/img_upload/65636e2e7a707261766f64616a737476/ Child_poverty.pdf.

4. UNICEF, "State of the World's Children," (2009), The State of the World's Children Statistics section says that

globally, 9,216,000 children under age 5 died in 2007. http://www.unicef.org/sowc09/docs/SOWC09_Table_1.pdf.

5. UNICEF, "State of the World's Children," 2004.

6. UNICEF, "State of the World's Children," 2009.

7. "Fullness of Life and Dignity of Children in the Midst of Globalization with a Focus on Children." Report of the Diakonia and Solidarity Team of World Council of Churches/Christian Conference of Asia Inter-Regional Consultation, Mumbai, India, 2004, 7.

8. William R. Mattox, guest editorial, *Colorado Springs Gazette Telegraph*, March 10, 1991.

9. Alissa Quart, *Branded: The Buying and Selling of Teenagers* (New York: Basic Books, 2003), 8.

10. Tom Hayes, *Jump Point: How Network Culture is Revolutionizing Business* (New York: McGraw-Hill, 2008) Kindle edition, Loc. 2494-2501.

11. Ibid., Loc. 1205-10.

12. Ibid., Loc. 2511-22.

13. Susan Greener, "The Effects of Failure to Meet Children's Needs," *Celebrating Children* (Carlisle, Cumbria: Paternoster Press, 2003), 130.

14. Wess Stafford, foreword to *The 4/14 Window: Raising up a New Generation to Transform the World*, by Luis Bush, (Colorado Springs, CO: Compassion, 2009), 6.

15. Vinay Samuel, "Some Theological Perspectives on Children at Risk," *Transformation* 14, no. 2 (1997): 27.

16. Katherine Copsey, "What is a Child?" *Celebrating Children*, (Carlisle, Cumbria: Paternoster Press, 2003), 8.

17. Ibid., 9.

18. Ibid.

2: WHAT THE BIBLE SAYS ABOUT CHILDREN

1. I am indebted to my friend Dr. Keith White for many of the understandings of the themes concerning children in the Old and New Testaments, as well as Glenn Miles for some of the approach taken and biblical examples in this chapter.

2. Wendy Strachen and Simon Hood, eds. "Evangelization of Children." *Lausanne Occasional Paper* 47 (2004): 11, 12.

3. See Psalm 127:3.

4. See Hosea 11:1, Matthew 18:2-3.

5. See Matthew 18:4.

6. See Deuteronomy 6, 11.

7. See Psalm 68:5; James 1:27.

8. See Matthew 18:5-6, 10.

9. See Psalm 8:2.

10. See Matthew 21:15.

11. See Isaiah 11:6.

12. See Matthew 19:13-15.

13. See Luke 7, 8.

14. See Mark 10.

15. See Luke 18:17.

16. See Matthew 18:12-14.

17. Keith White, "A Little Child Shall Lead Them: Rediscovering Children at the Heart of Mission." Paper presented to the Cutting Edge conference, De Bron, Holland, 2001, 1.

18. See Matthew 11:25.

19. See Luke 17:2.

20. Among the other passages are Psalm 10:18, 68:5, and 82:3.

21. For one example, see Proverbs 22:6.

22. See Proverbs 22:15, 29:15.

23. See Joshua 4:6

24. See Ezra 10.

25. See Nehemiah 12:43.

26. See Matthew 21:16.

27. See Matthew 11:25.

28. See 2 Timothy 3:15.

29. See Psalm 119:9.

30. See 1 Timothy 4:12.

31. See 2 Timothy 2:22.

32. Wess Stafford, *Too Small to Ignore* (Colorado Springs, CO: Waterbrook, 2005), 216.

33. See 2 Kings 5:3.

34. Esther Menn, "Child Characters in Biblical Narratives: The Young David (1 Samuel 16-17) and the Little Israelite Servant Girl (2 Kings 5:1-19)" in *The Child in the Bible*, Marcia Bunge, ed. (Grand Rapids, MI: Eerdmans, 2008), 343.

35. Ibid.

36. See 2 Kings 5:13-15.

37. See Deuteronomy 6: 4-6.

38. This brief look at Old and New Testament themes surrounding children are summarized from Keith White, "A Little Child Shall Lead Them: Rediscovering Children at the Heart of Mission," (2001): 4-6.

39. Ibid., 4.

40. Ibid., 5.

41. See Matthew 15, Mark 7.

42. See Matthew 17, Mark 9, Luke 9.

43. See John 4.

44. See Matthew 9, Mark 5, Luke 8.

45. White, 5.

46. See Mark 5:37, 40b.

47. See Matthew 19:13, Mark 10:13, Luke 18:15.

48. This brief look at Old and New Testament themes surrounding children are summarized from Keith White, "A Little Child Shall Lead Them," (2001): 4-6.

49. Ibid., 6.

50. Donald Kraybill, *The Upside Down Kingdom* (Scottsdale, PA: Herald Press, 2003), 21.

51. See John 3.

52. Keith J. White, "A Little Child Shall Lead Them. Rediscovering Children at the Heart of Mission" Paper presented to the Cutting Edge Conference (De Bron, Holland: 2001), 1.

53. Ibid.

54. Ibid, 8

55. See Ephesians 6:1-4.

56. See Colossians 3:20

57. See Deuteronomy 21:18-21, 24:16, 2 Kings 14:5-6.

58. See Luke 20:9-19.

59. See Luke 15:20-24.

60. See 1 Thessalonians 2:11-12.

61. See Exodus 20:12, Deuteronomy 5:16.

62. See James 1:27.

3: THE MINISTRY OF CHILD DEVELOPMENT

1. See Amos 8:4-7, 5:10-15.

2. See Amos 4:1.

3. John B. Wong, *Christian Wholism: Theological and Ethical Implications in the Postmodern World* (Lanham, MD: University Press of America, 2002), 189.

4. Ibid., 14.

5. Ibid., 2.

6. Ibid.

7. Keith White, "The Contribution of Child Theology to the HCD Course and Beyond," Unpublished paper presented at the Holistic Child Development conference (Chiang Mai, Thailand, 2007), 11.

8. Dewi Hughes, *The God of the Poor* (UK: OM Publishing, 1998), 6.

9. Ibid., 5.

10. Part of the discussion that follows is taken from Dan Brewster and Gordon Mullenix, "Development: Bounded, Centered, or Fuzzy?" *Together* 50 (April-June 1996): 10-13.

11. For this reason I will argue in chapter six that it is *only* Christians who in reality can truly do Christian holistic development.

12. James Yen, "Credo of Rural Reconstruction," International Institute of Rural Reconstruction.

13. See Matthew 16:13-17.

14. Following are a few references to such examples: Matthew 18:1-6—a child; Matthew 18:10-14—a lost sheep; Matthew 19:22-30—the encounter with the rich young ruler; Luke 18:15-17—the disciples' negative reaction to people bringing their children to Jesus; Luke 21:1-4—the poor widow's offering.

15. See Matthew 18:1-6; Luke 11:1-13.

16. See Matthew 9:9-10.

17. Following are a few references and related examples: Luke 11:1-13—prayer; Luke 18:1-18—perseverance; Luke 21:1-9—sacrificial giving.

18. See John 9:16-17.

19. See Matthew 9:35-38, 11:4-6, John 10:37, 38, 11:41, 42, 14:11.

20. See Matthew 19:13-15.

21. See John 8:12.

4: A SPIRITUAL UNDERSTANDING OF POVERTY

1. Bryant Myers, *Walking with the Poor* (New York: Orbis Books, 1999), 66.

2. Ibid., 67

3. I am indebted to my late colleague Dr. Don Miller in an undated and unpublished paper called "Child Development" for this analysis of poverty as a lack of wholeness.

4. CIA World Factbook. "Country Comparison: Total Fertility Rate," https://www.cia.gov/library/publications/the-world-factbook/rankorder/2127rank.html.

5. Ben Wattenberg, *Fewer* (Chicago: Ivan R. Dee, 2004), 85.

6. Jayakumar Christian, *The God of the Empty-Handed.* (Monrovia, CA: MARC, 1999), 30.

7. Ibid., 30.

8. Compassion Program Field Manual, 2006, 3.

9. Charles Kraft, *Anthropology for Christian Witness* (New York: Orbis Books, 1996), 52.

10. Darrow Miller, *Discipling Nations: The Power of Truth to Transform Cultures* (Seattle, WA: YWAM Publishing, 1998), 38.

11. Ibid., 39.

12. Ibid., 40 ff.

13. Ibid., 41.

14. See Romans 1:18-22.

15. I am indebted to Darrow Miller for most of the insights in this section, from his book *Discipling Nations*.

16. See 1 Timothy 2:3-4.

17. Ibid., 95-96.

18. Darrow Miller, *Discipling Nations* (Seattle, WA: YWAM Publishing, 1998), 38.

SECTION TWO
THE CHILD AND THE CHURCH

5: THE ROLE OF THE CHURCH

1. Genesis 1:4, 10, 12, 18, 21, 25, 31.

2. Wolters, 42.

3. Arthur F. Holmes, "Toward a Christian View of Things" in *The Making of a Christian Mind*, ed. Arthur Holmes (Downers Grove, IL: InterVarsity Press, 1985), 20.

4. Wolters, *Creation Regained*, 58.

5. Bob Moffitt, *If Jesus Were Mayor* (Phoenix: Harvest Publishing, 2004), 61.

6. I am indebted to Bob Moffitt and his fine book *If Jesus Were Mayor* for some of these thoughts on the "mystery" of the role of the church.

7. Bambang Budijanto, "The Ecclesia of Jesus Christ," Unpublished paper, 9.

8. Ibid., 6.

9. My friend Dr. Keith White has a simplified definition of the kingdom of God. He suggests that substituting

the phrase "God's way of doing things," when we see "kingdom of God" in Scripture, helps to make the meaning clear and simple.

10. Rodney Stark, *The Rise of Christianity* (San Francisco: HarperOne, 1997), 212.

11. Stark, *The Rise of Christianity*, 212.

12. Moffitt, 38.

13. Stark, *The Rise of Christianity*, 212.

14. Moffitt, *If Jesus Were Mayor*, 104-105.

15. Timothy Chester, *Awakening to a World of Need* (Leicester, UK: InterVarsity Press, 1993), 62.

16. Ibid., 63.

17. Ibid.

18. Quoted by Bob Moffitt, *If Jesus Were Mayor*, 106.

19. Bong Rin Ro, "The Perspectives of Church History from New Testament Times to 1960," in *In Word and Deed: Evangelism and Social Responsibility*, ed. Bruce J. Nicholls (Carlisle, Cumbria: Paternoster Press, 1985).

20. Hughes, *The God of Poor*, 13-14.

21. John H. Westerhoff III, *Living in the Faith Community* (Minneapolis: Winston Press 1985), 78-79.

22. Tokumboh Adeyemo, "A Critical Evaluation of Contemporary Perspectives" in *In Word and Deed: Evangelism and Social Responsibility*, ed. Bruce Nicholls (Carlisle, Cumbria: Paternoster Press, 1985), 48-57.

23. Lausanne Covenant, (Lausanne, Switzerland: International Congress on World Evangelization, July 1974), 23.

24. Meg Crossman, quoted in Moffitt, *If Jesus Were Mayor*, 114.

25. I am indebted to Dr. Bambang Budijanto and his paper "The Ecclesia of Jesus Christ" for the thoughts in this section.

26. See Luke 6:20.

27. See Matthew 5:10.

28. See Mark 10:14-15.

29. While a centurion might not live an unpleasant life as compared to the other categories on the list, first he came to Christ representing his slave, and second as a Roman soldier, he was not part of the mainstream Jewish community.

30. Budijanto, 12.

31. Ibid., 12

32. See Luke 18:17.

33. See Matthew 18:4.

34. Ralph D. Winter, "Two Structures of God's Redemptive Mission," in *Perspectives on the World Christian Movement: A Reader*, eds. Ralph D. Winter and Steven C. Hawthorne (Pasadena, CA: William Carey Library, 1999).

6: WHY CARE FOR CHILDREN IS THE PARTICULAR RESPONSIBILITY OF THE CHURCH

1. Gothard, Bill, *Advanced Seminar Textbook* (Oakbrook, IL: Institute in Basic Life Principles, 1986), 358.

2. See 2 Peter 1:5.

3. Moffitt, *If Jesus Were Mayor*, 37-39.

4. The thoughts in this portion are drawn from the booklet by Dr. Alemu Beeftu called *God Heard the Boy Crying* (Colorado Springs, CO: Compassion, 2001).

5. See Genesis 21:9-21.

6. See Genesis 21:19.

7. See Genesis 21:20.

8. See 1 Kings 17:20.

SECTION THREE
THE CHILD IN THE CHURCH

7: FAITH DEVELOPMENT IN CHILDREN

1. Roy Zuck, *Precious in His Sight* (Grand Rapids, MI: Baker, 1996), 21-22.

2. McConnell, Douglas, et. al. (Colorado Springs: Authentic Publishing, 2007) 225.

3. Clifford Ingle, ed., *Children and Conversion* (Nashville, TN: Broadman Press, 1970), 12.

4. Ibid.

5. Ibid., 62.

6. Honeycutt, Roy L. Jr., "The Child within the Old Testament Community" in *Children and Conversion*, ed. Clifford Ingle (Nashville, TN: Broadman Press, 1970), 33.

7. Ibid., 35.

8. Ibid., 25.

9. William Hendricks, "The Age of Accountability" in

Children and Conversion, ed. Clifford Ingle (Nashville, TN: Broadman Press, 1970), 94.

10. Zuck, *Precious in His Sight*, 18.

11. Matthew 11:25.

12. Sylvia Foth, *Daddy, Are We There Yet?* (Mukilteo, WA: Kidzana Ministries, 2009), 158.

13. Ibid., 158.

14. Ibid., 159.

15. Copsey. 9.

16. Ibid., 9, 10.

17. Steve Wamberg, *Youth and Faith Development* (Prepared as a Continuing Education Training Module for Compassion International, January 2004), 4. I am indebted to Mr. Wamberg for most of this discussion on faith development in children.

18. See 1 Peter 2:2.

19. Ibid., 6.

20. John Westerhoff, *Will Our Children Have Faith?*, revised edition (Harrisburg, PA: Morehouse Publishing, 2000), 88-89.

21. John Westerhoff, *Will Our Children Have Faith?*, revised edition (Harrisburg, PA: Morehouse Publishing, 2000). I am indebted to Steve Wamberg for this summary as well.

22. Ibid., 92.

23. Ibid., 94.

24. Ibid., 95.

25. Ibid., 95.

26. Wamberg, 14.

27. Ibid., 15.

28. Dan Brewster, "The 4/14 Window: Child Ministries and Mission Strategies" in *Children in Crisis: A New Commitment*, ed. Phyllis Kilbourne (Monrovia, CA: MARC, 1996). This section on the "4/14 Window of Receptivity" is taken from a paper presented to the Lausanne Congress on World Evangelization in Pattaya, Thailand, October, 2004 by Daniel Brewster and Patrick McDonald called "Children: The Great Omission?" (Oxford: Viva Network, 2004).

29. George Barna, *Transforming Children into Spiritual Champions* (Ventura, CA: Regal, 2003).

30. Ibid., 33.

31. Ibid., 34.

32. Ibid., 41.

33. Ibid., 47.

34. James Dobson, *Dr. Dobson Answers Your Questions*, (Carol Stream, IL: Tyndale, 1992), *slightly abridged.*

8: CHARACTERISTICS OF CHILD FRIENDLY CHURCHES

1. John Collier & Associates, *Toddling to the Kingdom* (UK: The Child Theology Movement, 2009), 204.

2. Ibid., 205.

3. Keith White, "An Integrated Biblical and Theoretical Typology of Children's Needs" in *Celebrating Children*,

eds. Glenn Miles and Josephine-Joy Wright (Carlisle, UK: Paternoster Press, 2003), 123.

4. Ibid., 123.

5. Ibid., 123-126.

6. Some of these are an adaptation from *Covenant on Ministering to Children*, an unpublished document by Shiferaw Michael used to help African churches understand their responsibilities toward children.

7. Isobel Booth Clibborne. Mim Friday, and others. Viva Network, Kampala, Uganda.

8. Shiferaw Michael, *Covenant on Ministering to Children.* Unpublished. Compassion Africa area document, 2002.

9: CHILD PROTECTION IN CHURCH ENVIRONMENTS

1. This section on recognizing child abuse is from *The Compassion Guidelines for Child Protection*, "Protecting Children from Abuse," April 2003.

2. Kostelnik, "Guiding Children's Social Development" in *Child Abuse and Neglect: A Self-Instructional Text for Head Start Personnel* (Washington, D.C.: U.S. Government Printing Office, 1977). Taken from Head Start Bureau and Children's Bureau, U.S. Department of Health, Education and Welfare.

3. _____"Caring for Our Children" in *National Health and Safety Performance Standards- Appendix K* (American Academy of Pediatrics, 2002), 420.

SECTION FOUR
THE CHILD AND MISSION

10: MISSION: WHAT THE CHURCH IS CALLED TO DO

1. Andrew Kirk, *What Is Mission?* (Darton, UK: Longman & Todd Ltd., 1999), 25.

2. Ibid.,25.

3. Ibid., 29.

4. Ibid., 30.

5. Myers, *Walking with the Poor*, 3.

6. Myers, *Walking with the Poor*.

7. Meg Crossman, ed. *Worldwide Perspectives* (Pasadena, CA: William Carey Library, 1995), 5-1.

8. Ibid., 5-4.

9. Kenneth Scott Latourette, *A History of Christianity (Vol. II): Reformation to the Present A.D. 1500 to A.D. 1975* (San Francisco: Harper Collins, 1975), 1353.

10. Ibid., 1317-8.

11. Ibid., 1397-8.

12. Nam Soo Kim, Notes from sermon delivered at 4/14 Window conference in Debre Zeit, Ethiopia, April 27, 2010.

13. Crossman, *Worldwide Perspectives*, 5-10.

14. Larry Pate, "The Changing Balance in Global Mission" in *Worldwide Perspectives*, ed. Meg Crossman (Pasadena, CA: William Carey Library, 1995), 15-14, 15-15.

15. Ibid., 15-16.

16. Harold Fuller, "Stages of Missionary Roles" in *Worldwide Perspectives*, ed. Meg Crossman (Pasadena, CA: William Carey Library, 1995), 5-6.

17. These five missiological concepts are adapted from Dan Brewster, *Compassion's Role in Furthering the Kingdom* (Unpublished paper, 1995).

18. Adapted from Luis Bush, *Getting to the Core of the 10/40 Window*, (Wheaton, IL: Evangelism and Missions Information Service, 1996), 1-7.

19. Luis Bush, *The 4/14 Window* (Colorado Springs, CO: Compassion International, 2009), x.

11: PRACTICAL ISSUES IN MISSION AND CHILDREN

1. I am indebted to Sujitha Siri Kumara, a friend from Colombo, Sri Lanka for some of the thoughts in this section. His paper presented in my class on Child, Church and Mission at the Malaysia Baptist Theological Seminary in June 2003, helped shape many of my points.

2. Bryant Myers, *Walking with the Poor*, 17.

3. Portions of this section are adapted from Dan Brewster, "The 4/14 Window: Child Ministries and Mission Strategies" in *Children in Crisis: A New Commitment*, ed. Phyllis Kilbourne (Monrovia, CA: MARC, 1996).

4. Pete Hohmann, *Kids Making a Difference* (Instant Publisher, 2004). From correspondence regarding the pre-publication manuscript.

5. I gratefully acknowledge Dr. Wess Stafford of Compassion International for these examples.

6. Bambang Budijanto, "Children: New Energy in Mission," in *Emerging Missions Movements* (Colorado Springs, CO: Compassion. 2010), 47.

7. Alex Harris and Brett Harris, *Do Hard Things* (Colorado Springs, CO: Multnomah Books, 2008) 97.

8. Ibid., 86.

9. Ibid.

10. Esther Ilnisky, *Let the Children Pray* (Ventura, CA: Regal, 2000).

11. Ibid. 203

12. Peter Hohmann, *The Great Commissary Kids* (Springfield, MO: Boys and Girls Missionary Crusade, 1997), 21.

SECTION FIVE
AVENUES FOR ADVOCACY

12: NON CONFRONTATIONAL ADVOCACY

1. Adapted from *Compassion Child Advocacy Frequently Asked Questions* (Compassion International, 2004).

13: THE UN CONVENTION ON THE RIGHTS OF THE CHILD

1. Save the Children, "Eglantyne Jebb," http://www.

savethechildren.ca/en/who-we-are/international-alliance/377 (accessed March 2, 2010).

2. Paul Stephenson, "The 'Rights' of the Child and the Christian Response" in *Celebrating Children*, eds. Glenn Miles and Josephine-Joy Wright (Carlisle, UK: Paternoster Press, 2003), 57.

3. UNICEF, "Convention on the Fights of the Child: Promoting and protecting rights for children," http://www.unicef.org/crc/index_30168.html (accessed March 2, 2010).

4. Ibid.

5. Edna Valdez, ed. *Protecting Children: A Biblical Perspective on Child Rights* (Monrovia, CA: World Vision, 2002), 14. See also Proverbs 31:8, 9; Luke 20: 46, 47.

6. See Psalm 11:7; 33:5; 106:3; Proverbs 29:7; Isaiah 1:17; 5:7; Hosea 12:6; Amos 5:15-24; Micah 3:1; Zechariah 7: 9, 10.

7. See for example the Spanish version "Liturgia y Derechos Humanos del Movimiento Ecuménico por los Derechos Humanos," done by the Latin American Council of Churches in 1984.

8. United Nations, "Millennium Development Goals," http://www.developmentgoals.org/About_the_goals.htm (accessed March 2, 2010).

9. United Nations, "A World Fit for Children," http://www.unicef.org/specialsession/wffc/ (accessed March 2, 2010).

14: NETWORKING ON BEHALF OF CHILDREN

1. No discussion of the networking of Christian child care workers can be done without noting the contribution of Patrick McDonald and the Viva Network. Most of the points that follow are from his book *Reaching Children in Need*, and/or other materials from Patrick and the Viva Network.

2. Patrick McDonald, *Reaching Children in Need*, (Eastbourne: Kingsway Publications, 2001), 81.

3. See John 17:20-23.

4. See 1 Corinthians 1:12-13; Colossians 4:16.

5. See Luke 19:12-27

6. See 1 Corinthians 4:6, 7, 18

7. See 1 Corinthians 12:21-25.

8. See Titus 3:14.

9. See Isaiah 34:1-4.

10. See Philippians 1:12-14.

11. See Ecclesiastes 4:9-12.

12. See Proverbs 13:10.

13. Ibid., 88.

14. Viva Network, "About Viva," http://www.viva.org/about-viva.aspx (accessed March 2, 2010).

REFERENCES

Aaron, Audrey, Hugh Hughes and Juliet Grayton. *Child-to-Child*. London: Macmillan Press, 1979.

Adeyemo, Tokumboh. "A Critical Evaluation of Contemporary Perspectives." *In Word and Deed*, edited by Bruce Nicholls. Carlisle, Cumbria: Paternoster Press, 1985.

Albert, Linda and Michael Popkin. *Quality Parenting*. New York: Random House, 1987.

Atkins, Andy and Graham Gordon. *Advocacy Study Pack*. UK: TEARFUND, June 1999.

Barna, George. *Transforming Children into Spiritual Champions*. Ventura, CA: Regal, 2003.

Beasley-Murray, G.R. "The Child and the Church." *Children and Conversion*, edited by Clifford Ingle. Nashville, TN: Broadman Press, 1970.

Beeftu, Dr. Alemu. *God Heard the Boy Crying*. Colorado Springs, CO: Compassion International, 2001.

Boice, James Montgomery. "Children's Worship," *ChristiansUnite Articles*. http://articles.christiansunite.com/article2544.shtml.

Boyle, Renita. "A Liturgy of Hope." A Summary of the Consultation Proceedings of the Consultation on Children at Risk. Oxford, UK: January 1997.

Brewster, Daniel. "Compassion's Role in Furthering the Kingdom." Unpublished paper, 1995.

Brewster, Daniel. "The 4/14 Window: Child Ministries and Mission Strategies." *Children in Crisis: A New Commitment*, edited by Phyllis Kilbourne. Monrovia, CA: MARC, 1996.

Brewster, Daniel. "True Compassion with Strings." *Religious Broadcasting* (April 1995).

Brewster, Daniel and Gordon Mullenix. "Development: Bounded, Centered or Fuzzy?" *Together 50* MARC Publications (April-June 1996): 10-13.

Brewster, Daniel and Heather McCloud. "Protecting Children from Ourselves." Presentation made at the Cutting Edge III Conference, Le Bron, Holland, March 2001.

Budijanto, Bambang. "A Reflection on the 'Association' Factor for Holistic Mission." Reflection paper for Lausanne, 2004.

Bush, Luis. *Getting to the Core of the 10/40 Window*. Wheaton, IL: Evangelism and Missions Information Service, 1996.

"Caring for Our Children." *National Health and Safety Performance Standards — Appendix K* American Academy of Pediatrics, 2002.

Chester, Timothy. *Awakening to a World of Need*. Leicester, England: InterVarsity Press, 1993.

"The Child in South Asia: Issues in Development as if Children Mattered." New Delhi: UNICEF, 1988.

Choun, Robert and Michael Lawson. *The Complete Handbook for Children's Ministry*. Nashville, TN: Thomas Nelson, 1993.

Compassion Child Advocacy Frequently Asked Questions. Compassion International, 2004.

Copsey, Katherine. "What Is a Child?" in *Celebrating Children*. Carlisle, Cumbria: Paternoster Press, 2003.

Crossman, Meg, ed. *Worldwide Perspectives*. Pasadena, CA: William Carey Library, 1995.

Dawn, Marva. *Is It a Lost Cause?* Grand Rapids, MI: Eerdmans Publishing, 1997.

Dobson, James. "Dr. Dobson Answers Your Questions" *Focus on the Family* 20 no. 1 (1996).

Doherty, Sam. *Why Evangelize Children?* (Northern Ireland: Child Evangelism Fellowship, 1996).

"Evangelism and Social Action." *Lausanne Occasional Papers* no. 21. Grand Rapids Report, 1982.

Fuller, Harold. "Stages of Missionary Roles." In *Worldwide Perspectives*, edited by Meg Crossman. Pasadena, CA: William Carey Library, 1995.

Fuller, Harold. "Fullness of Life and Dignity of Children in the Midst of Globalisation." Report of the WCC/CCA

Inter-Regional Consultation. Mumbai, India (January 2004): 21-25.

George, Timothy. "You Must Be Born Again but at What Age?" *Christianity Today* (March 1, 1999).

Gordon, Graham. *Advocacy Toolkit Vol. 1. Under-standing Advocacy*. Teddington, UK: TEARFUND, 2002.

Gordon, Graham. *Advocacy Toolkit Vol. 2, Practical Action in Advocacy*. Teddington, UK: TEARFUND, 2002.

Gothard, Bill. *Advanced Seminar* Textbook. Oakbrook, IL: Institute in Basic Life Principles, 1986.

Grant, Wilson. *The Caring Father*. Nashville, TN: Broadman Press, 1983.

Hendricks, William. "The Age of Accountability." *Children and Conversion*, edited by Clifford Ingle. Nashville, TN: Broadman Press, 1970.

Hewlett, Sylvia. *When the Bough Breaks*. New York: Basic Books, 1991.

Holmes, Arthur F. "Toward a Christian View of Things." *The Making of a Christian Mind*, edited by Arthur Holmes. Downers Grove, IL: InterVarsity Press, 1985.

Honeycutt, Roy L. Jr. "The Child within the Old Testament Community." *Children and Conversion*, edited by Clifford Ingle. Nashville, TN: Broadman Press, 1970.

Hohmann, Pete. *Kids Making a Difference*, 2004.

Hohmann, Pete. *The Great Commissionary Kids*. Springfield, MO: Boys and Girls Missionary Crusade, 1997.

Hughes, Dewi. *The God of the Poor*. UK: M Publishing, 1998.

Ilnisky, Esther. *Let the Children Pray*. Ventura, CA: Regal, 2000.

Ingle, Clifford, ed. *Children and Conversion*. Nashville, TN: Broadman Press, 1970.

Jebb, Eglantyne. "Save the Children." http://www.saveth-echildren.ca/en/who-we-are/international-alliance/377

Kirk, Andrew. *What Is Mission?* Darton, UK: Longman & Todd Ltd., 1999.

Kostelnik. "Guiding Children's Social Department." In *Child Abuse and Neglect: A Self-Instructional Text for Head Start* Personnel. Washington, D.C.: U.S Government Printing Office, 1977.

Kraft, Charles. *Anthropology for Christian* Witness. New York: Orbis Books, 1996.

Kraybill, Donald. *The Upside Down Kingdom*. Scottsdale, PA: Herald Press, 1978.

Kumara, Sujitha Siri. *The Ethics of Conversion in the Sri Lankan Context*. Paper presented in the course "Child, Church and Mission," Penang, Malaysia: Malaysia Baptist Theological Seminary, June 2003.

Latourette, Kenneth Scott. *A History of Christianity (Vol. II): Reformation to the Present — A.D.* 1975. San Francisco, CA: Harper Collins, 1975.

Lewis, Jonathan, ed. *World Mission: An Analysis of the World Christian* Movement. Pasadena, CA: William Carey Library, 1987.

"Liturgia y Derechos Humanos del Movimiento Ecumenico por los Derechos Humanos." Latin American Council of Churches, 1984.

London, H.B. and N. Wiseman. *It Takes a Church Within a Village.* Nashville, TN: Thomas Nelson, 1996.

Mangalwadi, Vishal and Ruth. *William Carey: A Tribute by an Indian* Woman. New Delhi, India: Nividit Good Books, 1993.

McDonald, Patrick. *Reaching Children in Need.* Eastbourne, UK: Kingsway Publications, 2000.

Michael, Shiferaw. *Covenant on Ministering to Children.* Unpublished, 2002.

Michael, Shiferaw. "Rate Your Church on Children Friendliness." Unpublished, 2002.

Michael, Shiferaw. "Advocacy: Its Relations With and Support for Our Core Program." Compassion International Discussion Paper (March 2002): 4.

Miles, Glenn, and Josephine-Joy Wright, eds., *Celebrating Children.* Carlisle, Cumbria: Paternoster Press, 2003.

Miller, Darrow. *Discipling Nations: The Power of Truth to Transform Cultures.* Seattle, WA: YWAM Publishers, 1998.

Miller, Darrow. "The Development Ethic: Hope for a Culture of Poverty." *Christian Relief and Development*, edited by Edgar Elliston. Dallas, TX: Word Publishing, 1989.

Miller, Donald. "Child Development." Unpublished and undated paper (Compassion International). Moffitt, Bob. *If Jesus Were Mayor*. Phoenix, AZ: Harvest India, 2004.

Myers, Bryant. *Exploring World* Mission. Federal Way, WA: World Vision International, 2003).

Olasky, Marvin. *Renewing American Compassion*. New York: The Free Press, 1996.

Olasky, Marvin. *The Tragedy of American Compassion*. Washington, D.C.: Regnery Gateway, 1992.

Oxford Statement on Children at Risk, 1997. Produced by Oxford Centre for Mission Studies and Viva Network. Pate, Larry. "The Changing Balance in Global Mission" in *Worldwide Perspectives*, edited by Meg

Postman, Neil. *Amusing Ourselves to Death: Public Discourse in the Age of Show Business*. New York: Viking Penguin, 1985.

Rin Ro, Bong. "The Perspective of Church History from New Testament Times to 1960." *In Word and Deed: Evangelism and Social Responsibility*, edited by Bruce J. Nicholls. Carlisle, Cumbria: Paternoster Press, 1985.

Samuel, Vinay. "Some Theological Perspectives on Children at Risk." *Transformation* 14, no. 2 (April/June 1997).

Sider, Ronald. *Rich Christians in an Age of Hunger* (Dallas TX: Word Publishing, 1990).

Stafford, Wess. Compassion Asia Area Conference. Chiang Rai, Thailand, August 2003.

Stark, Rodney. *The Rise of Christianity*. San Francisco, CA: Harper Collins, 1997.

Stephenson, Paul. "The 'Rights' of the Child and the Christian Response." *Celebrating Children*, edited by Glenn Miles and Josephine-Joy Wright. Carlisle, UK: Paternoster Press, 2003.

UNICEF. "Convention on the Fights of the Child: Promoting and protecting rights for children." http://www.unicef.org/crc/index_30168.html.

UNICEF. "State of the World's Children, 2005." http://www.unicef.org/sowc/.

UNICEF. "World Declaration on the Survival, Protection and Development of Children." *World Summit for Children*, 1990.

United Nations. "Millennium Development Goals." http://www.developmentgoals.org/About_the_goals.htm.

United Nations. "A World Fit for Children." http://www.unicef.org/specialsession/wffc/. Valdez, Edna, ed., *Protecting Children: A Biblical Perspective on Child Rights*. Federal Way, WA: World Vision, 2002.

Viva Network. "About Viva." http://www.viva.org/about-viva.aspx

Wamberg, Steve. *Youth and Faith Development.* Prepared as a Continuing Education Training Module for Compassion International, January 2004.

Wattenburg, Ben. *Fewer.* Chicago, IL: Ivan R. Dee, 2004.

White, Keith. "An Integrated Biblical and Theoretical Typology of Children's Needs." *Celebrating Children.* Carlisle, UK: Paternoster Press, 2003.

White, Keith. *Creation Regained.* Grand Rapids, MI: Eerdmans Publishing, 1986.

Wolters, Albert. "Small Matters." *Third Way Journal* (February 2002).

Wolters, Albert. "A Little Child Shall Lead Them." Paper presented at the Cutting Edge Conference, De Bron, Holland, 2001.

Winter, Ralph. *Two Structures of God's Redemptive Mission.* U.S. Center for World Missions Series No. 01 –995, 1995.

Zuck, Roy. *Precious in His Sight.* Grand Rapids, MI: Baker Book House, 1996.

INDEX

abortion, 81, 219
Abraham (patriarch), 136–137
  as advocate, 253
  Mission and, 207–208
abundant life, 89–91
accountability, age of, 154, 159
activism, 254
Acts of the Apostles, 112
Adeyemo, Tokumboh, 120
adults, God's expectations of, 40–43
advocacy, 247–289
  biblical examples, 252–254
  in Compassion International,
    259–263
  contributing to, 263–264
  defined, 248, 251
  development and, 257–259
  by local churches, 188
  nonconfrontational, 254–257
Africa, 117, 209–210
Amos (prophet), 46
animism, 87–89, 93, 95–96
Asia, 209, 274–275
  See also specific locales
awareness-raising, 71

Bangkok, 117
baptism, parents' support of, 234
Barna, George, 166–167
the beatitudes, 124–125
Beeftu, Alemu, 139

Bible
  advocacy in, 252–254
  centrality of children in, 22
  on children, 21–43
  as foundation of rights, 275–276
  higher criticism of, 116
  holism and, 53–57
  study materials, 184, 186
  translation, 209, 212–213
  See also specific books; New
    Testament; Old Testament
Bocaue, Philippines, 133–134
"born again", 39–40
bubble generation, 11–13
Buddhism, 87, 222
Budijanto, Bambang, 112, 125–126,
  241
Bush, Luis, 212–213

caregivers, 41–42, 287
  See also parents
Carey, William, 209
caste system, 93
Catholic Church, 14, 128
Cebu, Philippines, 94–95
Chambers, Robert, 76
charismatic churches, 116, 123
Checklist for Spiritual Training,
  167–168
child abuse, 189–200
  biblical accounts of, 26

CRC on, 273–274
prevention, 193, 196–197
recognition, 192, 194–195
response to allegations of,
    197–200
sexual exploitation, 97, 190–191
See also exploitation
child development *See*
    development
child-friendly churches, 169–188
    basic needs in, 171–174
    checklist for, 180–181
    covenant on, 179, 182–188
    facilities of, 176–177
    programming for, 174–176
    staff of, 177–179
child in the midst, 16, 28, 32, 38,
    169–170, 253, 291–294
Child Theology Movement, 169, 288
children
    active/passive role in
        development, 63–64
    adults' expectations of, 240–242
    emotional needs of, 171–172
    evangelism by, 242–243
    faith development in, 151–168
    God's heart for, 153, 288
    One Child Policy and, 81
    parents influenced through,
        140–143
    as particular responsibility of
        the Church, 99, 131–145
    as people group, 219
    as priority for God, 6
    receptivity of, 166–168, 223
    as resource for Mission,
        224–225, 238–245
    rights of *See* United Nations
        Convention on the Rights
        of the Child
    as stakeholders, 124–127

strategic importance, 237
strategic importance in
    missions, 223–226
transcendence of, 15–20
unborn, 24–25, 81, 219
understanding of God by, 28–30,
    157–161
See also child abuse; child-
    friendly churches
China, 81, 210
Christian, Jayakumar, 83
Christianity, global spread, 214–215
Christobal, Roberto, 133–134
the Church
    as instrument of redemption,
        110–115, 123–124
    missions at heart of, 205–208
    particular responsibility for
        children, 99, 131–145
    removing curses, 144–145
    structures of, 127–129
churches
    God's intention for children in,
        153–156
    mainline, 116–117, 123
    See also child-friendly churches;
        the Church
Colossians, 63, 92, 98, 109–110,
    123–124
Committee on the Rights of the
    Child, 273–274
communism, 82, 211
communities, nurturing children,
    42–43
Compassion International
    advocacy in, 259–263
    on children's malleability, 14–15
    launch, 213
    missiology and, 225
    profile, 296
    as sodality, 128

sponsored children, 57, 133–134, 163

congresses on world evangelization, 123, 236, 242

conscience, age and, 158

conscientization, 71

conventions, international, 267

conversion
contested need for, 153–156
material inducements to, 230–231, 234–235
vs. proselytism, 229–230

Copsey, Katherine, 17–19, 159–160

core of the core, 212–213

1 Corinthians, 189

2 Corinthians, 205

corruption, 82

cosmos, 105, 109–110

covenant
Lausanne Covenant, 122
on ministering to children, 179, 182–188
in Old Testament, 154–156, 207–208

CRC *See* United Nations Convention on the Rights of the Child

creation, 106–110

Crossman, Meg, 123, 208

culture, evangelism and, 227–228, 235

curses, 144–145

Daddy, Are We There Yet?, 157–158, 243

Damon, William, 241–242

Daniel (prophet), 222

David (king), 157–158

DAWN Ministries, 216

Declaration of the Rights of the Child, 266

dependence, vs. self-reliance, 66–67

Deuteronomy, 27, 29, 34, 41–42, 46–48, 151, 252

development, 53–74
advocacy and, 257–259
bounded, 58–60
Christian specifically, 60–62
facilitating, 70–73
holism and, 53–57, 73–74
as ministry, 123–124
self-reliance through, 65–70
vs. welfare, etc., 62–64
See also faith development in children; growth

dignity, 93–95, 114

discipline, physical, 273–274

Do Hard Things, 241

Dobson, James, 167–168

dominion, 95–96

Ecclesia, 112, 126
See also Church

Ecclesiastes, 168

economic systems, 8, 81–82

education
covenant on, 184, 186, 187
wisdom and, 133–134

Eli (high priest), 31–32

Elijah (prophet), 131, 137, 140–143

Elisha (prophet), 32–33

emotional abuse, 195
See also child abuse

entanglements, web of, 76–77

Ephesians (letter), 110–111, 269–270

equality, 93–95, 114

equipping, as advocacy, 257

Eschelman, Paul, 236–237

Esther Network, 242

Europe, 114, 116, 226

evangelicals, 116–120, 214

evangelism
  by children, 242–243
  children's maturity and, 228–229
  culture and, 227–228, 235
  social action and, 114–117,
      119–121
Exodus, 29, 31, 54, 252–253
expectations
  adults', of children, 240–242
  God's, of adults, 40–43
exploitation
  biblical accounts of, 26
  in evangelistic tactics, 228–229,
      232–234
  poverty and, 82
  Satan and, 91–92, 98
  sexual, 97, 190–191

faith development in children,
      151–168
  conversion and, 153–156,
      166–167
  developmental capacity and,
      157–161
  4/14 Window, 166–168
  stages in, 162–165
fallenness, 84–85, 107–110
families
  active/passive role in
      development, 63–64
  extended, 81
  pressures upon, 10–11
  See also fathers; mothers
fatalism, 77, 83, 88, 96–98
Father, God as, 28, 30, 34, 36
fathers
  in biblical accounts, 39, 72
  duties of, 40–42, 49, 144–145
  duties toward, 48
  God's covenant including family,
      154–156

  imperfect, 34
  paternalism and, 64
  prayers of, 240
  as spiritual head of family,
      155–156
  See also families
favor with God and man, 132–134
fertility, 80–81
Fewer, 80–81
Foth, Sylvia, 157–158, 243–244
4/14 Window, 166–168, 222–223,
      236–237
Francis of Assisi, 232
freedom
  of thought, conscience, and
      religion, 271–273
  through God's truth, 93, 97–99
Fuller, Harold, 217

Galatians, 168
gathered church, 127–129
Genesis
  creation and the fall, 84, 94–95,
      106–107
  Hagar and Ishmael, 27, 106–107,
      136–138
  and missions, 207–208, 226, 253
genocide, 57
Ghana, 122
Global Congress on World
      Evangelization (GCOWE), 242
Global Mapping International, 216
globalization, 8, 11–14, 215–217
gnosticism, 106
God
  children's damaged image of,
      160
  covenant with Abraham,
      154–156, 207–208
  as Father, 28, 34
  favor with, 134

giver of meaning, 96
hearing children's cry, 23,
136–140
intending people's wholeness,
89–91, 98–99
intention for children in
churches, 153–156
kingdom of, 35, 37–40, 126
love for children, 27–28
love for the poor, 45–49, 51,
113–114
and mother/child relationship,
34
regard for children's
understanding, 28–30
as source of all good things, 66
in theism, 87–88
using children as messengers or
instruments, 23, 239–240,
293
Gothard, Bill, 133
Great Commandment, 117, 122–124
Great Commission, 122–124, 218,
224
Great Omission, 118
growth
of faith, 161–165
holistic, 3, 55–56, 61, 132–135
See also development; faith
development in children
Guatemala, 212–213

Hagar (mother of Ishmael),
136–139
Harris, Alex, 241
Harris, Brett, 241
Hayes, Tom, 11–13
heaven, kingdom of *See* kingdom
of God
Hendricks, William, 156
Herod (king), 27

higher criticism, 116
Hinduism, 87, 93, 222
Hohmann, Pete, 239, 245
holism
overview, 53–57
See also wholeness
"hollow and deceptive
philosophies", 91–97
Holy Spirit, 125, 168, 214, 255
Honeycutt, Roy, 155–156
Hougn (Cambodian girl), 97
humility, 16, 23, 126, 286

Ilnisky, Esther, 242
the incarnation, 37
India, 209–211
indigenous people, Bibles for,
212–213
individualism, 65–66
interfaith evangelism, 227–235
International Save the Children
Union, 266
Internet, 11–14
Isaiah (prophet)
on care for the poor, 51
God's redemptive purpose,
123–124
God's righteous anger, 35
Messianic themes, 35–37, 39
mother/child relationship, 34
on the outcast, 125
shalom, 54
vision casting, 256
Ishmael, 136–139
Islam, 221–222
Israel, 46–47, 154–156, 208

Jairus' daughter, 36
James (apostle), 49, 52–53
Jebb, Eglantyne, 266
Jeremiah (prophet), 26, 49–50, 54

Jesuits, 14, 128
Jesus
    as advocate, 253–254
    the beatitudes, 124–125
    on corrupting children, 21–22
    on final judgment, 51–52
    firstborn over all creation,
        109–110
    giving abundant life, 89–91
    holistic growth of, 3, 55–56, 61,
        132–135
    incarnation as child, 37, 39
    incidents with children, 36
    on kingdom of God, 37–40,
        126–127
    as model of good development,
        71–73
    and the outcast, 125–126
    parables, 161
    on parental love, 42
    as preacher and healer, 122
    regard for children's
        understanding, 30
    and the rich young ruler, 50
    as teacher, 71–72
    transcendence and, 16–18
    on truth setting people free, 93,
        98
    welcoming children, 28, 41,
        126–127, 291
Jews, God's covenant with,
    154–156, 207–208
Job, 25–26
Joel, 26, 54
John (apostle), 52
John (gospel)
    and Church's care of children,
        105, 108–109
    on life in Christ, 39–40, 48
    and missions, 254

and spiritual understanding of
        poverty, 75, 90–91, 93, 98
1 John (letter), 52
Joshua (Ghanaian child), 122
Joshua (prophet), 29–30
Jump Point, 11–13

karma, 97
kingdom of God
    children's special place in, 35,
        37–40, 126
    Jesus on, 37–40, 126–127
    secular utopianism and, 116
1 Kings, 131, 140–143
2 Kings, 25, 32
Kirk, Andrew, 206
Korea, 211–212, 214
Kraft, Charles, 85
Kraybill, Donald, 38

Lamentations, 27, 252, 255
Latourette, Kenneth Scott, 210–211
Lausanne Congresses on World
    Evangelization, 123, 236
Lausanne Covenant, 122
Law (of Moses), 29–30, 252
laws
    on proselytism, 229
    against sexual abuse, 191–192,
        198
Lazarus (beggar), 50–51
League of Nations, 266
Leviticus, 29
liberation theology, 82
Living the Faith Community, 119
love
    adults' call to, 41
    for God and neighbor, 168
    revolutionary effect on ancient
        Rome, 113–114

Luke (gospel)
  on child as sign, 37, 39
  and Church's care of children,
    123–125, 132, 144
  and ministry of child
    development, 3, 50–51,
    55–56, 61
  and missions, 227, 253
  on parental love, 42

mainline churches, 116–117, 123
Malachi, 42, 144
Malaysia Baptist Theological
    Seminary, 299–301
Manila Manifesto, 123
Mark (gospel), 39, 55, 161, 168, 291
Marxism *See* communism
Matthew (gospel)
  on children's relationship with
    God, 22, 28, 37, 39, 41
  and Church's care of children,
    125
  and ministry of child
    development, 51–52, 55, 72
  and missions, 207, 218, 253
maturity, and evangelism to
    children, 228–229
McDonald, Patrick, 6, 287
McGavran, Donald, 117
MDG, 276–279, 282
meaninglessness, 96–97
media, 11–14
Menn, Esther, 32–33
mercy, 114
The Message, 56
Millennium Development Goals
    (MDG), 276–279, 282
Miller, Darrow, 85–88
Miriam (Moses' sister), 31
missiology, 218–223

Mission, 202–203, 206–208
  children as resource for,
    224–225, 238–245
  See also missions
Mission Aviation Foundation, 128,
    213
missions, 202–245
  children's strategic importance
    in, 223–226
  at heart of Church, 205–208
  holism in, 209
  missiological concepts, 15,
    218–223
  modern history of, 208–215
  national origins of, 209, 215–217
  practical issues in, 227–245
modalities, 127–129
modeling, 72–73
Moffitt, Bob, 116, 135
Moody, Dwight L., 118
Moses (prophet), 31, 252–253
mothers
  in biblical accounts, 31, 42, 131,
    136–139, 140–143
  duties of, 40
  duties toward, 48, 138
  as imperfect, 34, 97
  as nurturing, 24, 34, 94, 157–159
  See also families
Mukamwiza Jeannette, 57
Myers, Bryant, 76–77, 231–232
mystery, of redemption, 110–111

Naaman's serving girl, 32–33
Nam Soo Kim, 211–212
nature, 95–96
neglect, 25–26, 195
  See also child abuse
Nehemiah (prophet), 29–30
networking, 257, 283–289

New Age religions, 87, 218
New Testament
    great commandments, 55
    themes regarding children,
        36–40
    See also specific books
Nicodemus, 39
non-Christians, 99, 221–222,
    233–234
    See also missions
non-Western missions, 215–217

OC International, 216
Old Testament
    covenant in, 154–156
    last word in, 144
    shalom in, 54–55
    themes regarding children,
        34–36
    See also specific books
One Child Policy, 81
oppression, 49–50, 124–127
overpopulation, 79–81
owned faith, 164–165
Oxford Centre for Mission Studies,
    15

pagan gods, 113
parents
    consent of, 228, 234
    duties to children, 40–42
    encouraging owned faith, 165
    influenced through children,
        140–143
    non-Christian, 233–234
    rights, 270–276
Pate, Larry, 216–217
paternalism, 64
Patricia (girl evangelist), 242–243
patronism, 64, 235
Pattaya (Thailand), 236

Paul (apostle)
    on church as God's household,
        42–43
    on redemption, 109–111
    on rights and responsibilities,
        269–270
    on truth and lies, 91
pauperism, 83
pedophiles, 190, 191
Penang Child Theology
    Consultation, 169
pentecostalism, 123
people groups, 218–220
personhood, in Christian
    perspective, 53–54
Peter (apostle)
    on goodness then knowledge,
        133
    and servant girl, 240
Peterson, Eugene, 56
Philippians, 56
Philippines, 94–95, 133–134,
    242–243
physical abuse, 194, 274
    See also child abuse
physical discipline, 273–274
population trends, 79–81
postmodernism, 9–10
poverty, 75–99
    vs. abundant life, 89–91
    causes of, 79–83
    freedom through God's truth,
        97–99
    "hollow and deceptive
        philosophies" and, 91–97
    spiritual root of, 83–85, 98–99
    stakeholders and, 124–127
    10/40 Window, 222
    theoretical understandings,
        76–79
    welfare programs and, 63

worldview and, 85–89
prayer, 57, 168, 173, 180, 240, 242, 255
Precious in His Sight, 151–152
prophets *See specific names*
proselytism, 229–230
prosperity *See* wealth
prosperity gospel, 90
Proverbs
    on advocacy, 251, 293
    on poverty and material wealth, 45, 47–49, 51
    on training children, 14, 28, 34, 40–41
Psalms
    and children's relationship with God, 5, 24–25, 34–35, 47
    and faith development in children, 158, 161, 168
    and worldview, 90, 94–95
punishment, 273–274

Rachel (wife of Jacob), 226
Ramos, Juan, 163
Reaching Children at Risk, 289
receptivity, of children, 166–168, 223
reconciliation, 107–110
redemption, 107–115, 123–124
reincarnation, 96–97
relationship building, 72
research, 256–257
residential schools, 128–129, 213
resources
    for child-friendly churches, 184–185, 187
    children as, 224–225, 238–245
    dominion and, 95–96
    God revealing, 139
    linking, 73
reverence, 168

revivals, 214
the rich *See* wealth
rights, 270–276
    See also United Nations Convention on the Rights of the Child (CRC)
Romans (letter), 85, 283
Rome, ancient, 113–114
Rwanda, 57

St. Francis of Assisi, 232
salvation, 35–36, 109–110
Samaritan woman, 72
1 Samuel, 31–32
Samuel (prophet), 31–32
Samuel, Vinay, 15, 17, 159
Santa Mesa, Philippines, 242–243
Satan
    children's cries silencing, 35
    as liar, 91–92, 98
    source of curses, 144–145
10/40 Window, 222
Say Yes for Children, 279
schools, 128–129, 210–213
secularism, 63, 87–89, 93, 95–96, 116
self-control, 168
self-reliance, 65–70
Selome (child convert), 224
servant girls, 32–33, 240
service missions, 213
sexual abuse, 97, 190–191, 194, 197–198
    See also child abuse
shalom, 54–55
sin, poverty and, 84
social action, evangelism and, 114–117, 119–121
social gospel, 116, 118–119
socialism, 66
sodalities, 127–129

Somalia, CRC and, 266
spanking, 273–274
speaking out, 256
sponsorship, 57, 133–134, 163
Stafford, Wess, 14–15, 20, 31–32
stakeholders, 124–127
Stark, Rodney, 113–114
the State, parents and, 270–276
State of the World's Children
        (SOWC), 7, 267
stature, 132–134
Stephenson, Paul, 269–270
structures
    of the Church, 127–129
    of evil, 99
    poverty and, 82–83
suffering, 91–92, 98, 235
Sun Yat-Sen, 211

Taylor, Hudson, 210
teaching
    by Jesus, 71–72
    obedience, 168
    parents' consent, 228
    as parents' duty, 40–41
    See also schools
Ten Commandments, 48
10/40 Window, 214, 220–222
Thailand, 211–212, 236
theism, 87–89, 98–99
2 Thessalonians, 161
Timothy (church leader), 30
Timothy (letter), 42–43
Too Small to Ignore, 20
Total Fertility Rate, 80–81
Townsend, Cameron, 212–213
training
    as advocacy, 257
    churches' responsibilities for,
        184–185, 187
    networking and, 286

as parents' duty, 40–41
transcendence, 15–19, 159
transformation, 58
    See also development
*Transforming Children into
        Spiritual Champions*,
        166–167
tree metaphor, 161–162
tribal groups, 213
trust, 157–158, 164
truth, 87, 92–93, 97–99
Two-Thirds World, missions from,
        216–217

*Understanding God's Heart for
        Children*, 153, 288
UNICEF, on family, 271
United Nations Convention on the
        Rights of the Child (CRC),
        265–276
    Christians' concerns about,
        269–276
    nonratification, 266, 269
    origins and overview, 266–267
    pervasiveness, 248–249, 276, 282
    provisions of, 267–268
    on sexual exploitation, 191
United States of America
    CRC and, 266
    faith decisions in, 166–167
    welfare programs, 63
Uppsala Assembly, 116–117
The Upside Down Kingdom, 38

victim posture, 83
vision casting, 256
Viva Network, 6, 153, 287–289,
        297–298

Wamberg, Steve, 160–161, 165
war on poverty, 63

wars, 8, 57
Wattenberg, Ben, 80–81
wealth, 9–11, 48–53, 88–89
web of entanglements, 76–77
welfare, 62–63
Westerhoff, John H., III, 116,
    161–165
westernization, 63, 65, 93
"What Is a Child?", 17–19
What Is Mission?, 206
wheel of poverty, 78
White, Keith
    on biblical themes regarding
        children, 34–40
    on children's emotional needs,
        171
    on consequences of overlooking
        children, 23–24
    on spirituality as integral, 56
    on transcendence of children,
        16
wholeness
    of creation, 106–107
    embodied in genocide survivor,
        56–57
    God's intent for, 89–91, 98–99
    in Manila Manifesto, 123

poverty and, 78–79
windows
    4/14 Window, 166–168, 222–223,
        236–237
    10/40 Window, 214, 220–222
Winter, Ralph, 127–128
wisdom, 132–134
Wolters, Albert, 106–108
Wong, John, 54–55
World Council of Churches (WCC),
    116
World Evangelical Alliance (WEA),
    116
A World Fit for Children (WFFC),
    279–282
World Vision, 213
worldviews, 85–99
Worldwide Perspectives
    (Crossman), 208
Wycliffe Bible Translators, 212–213

Yen, James, 63–64

Zarephath, widow of, 140–143
Zechariah (prophet), 169
Zuck, Roy, 151–152